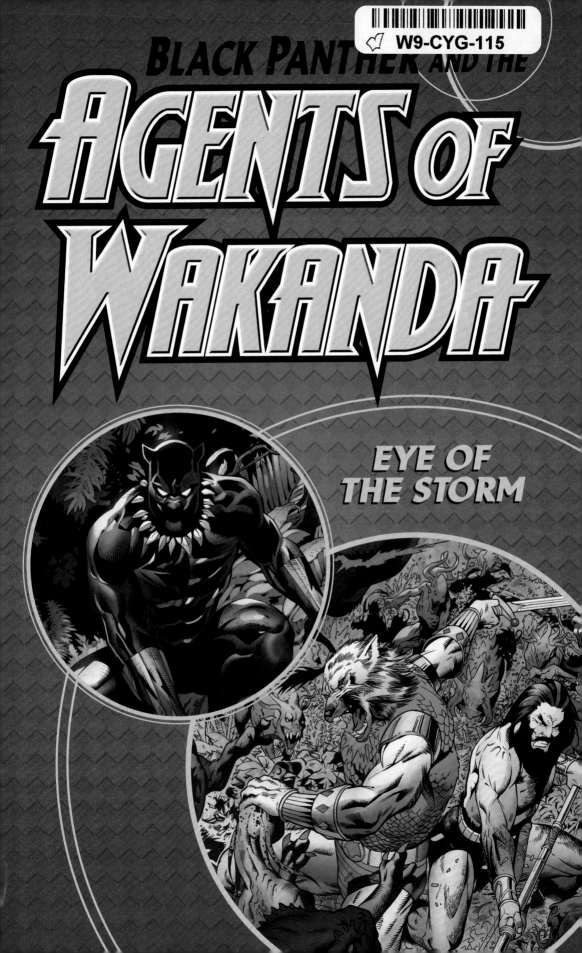

BLACK PANTHER AND THE

AGENTS OF WAKANDA

EYE OF THE STORM

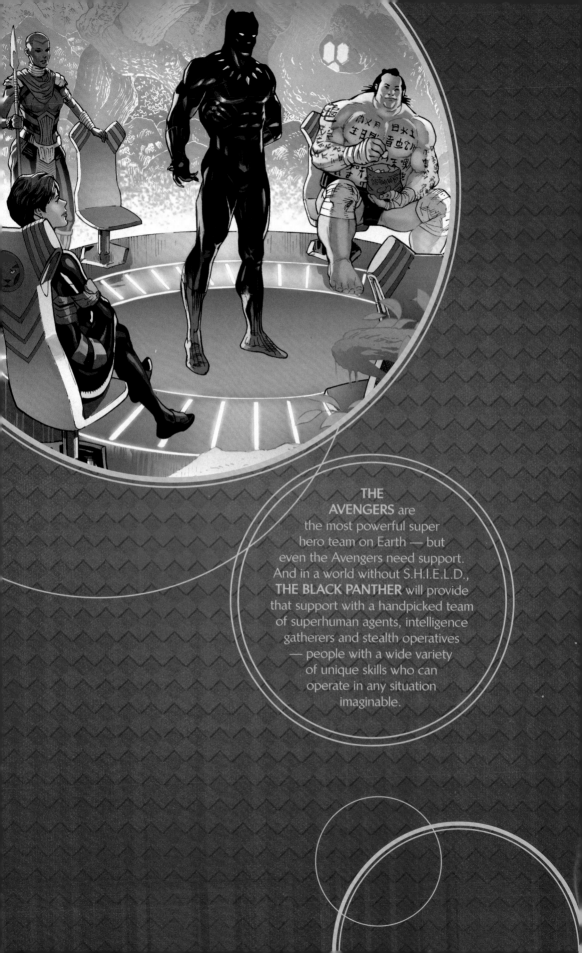

THE
AVENGERS are
the most powerful super
hero team on Earth — but
even the Avengers need support.
And in a world without S.H.I.E.L.D.,
THE BLACK PANTHER will provide
that support with a handpicked team
of superhuman agents, intelligence
gatherers and stealth operatives
— people with a wide variety
of unique skills who can
operate in any situation
imaginable.

BLACK PANTHER AND THE
AGENTS OF WAKANDA
EYE OF THE STORM

Jim Zub
WRITER

Lan Medina (#1-4) & Scot Eaton (#5-6)
PENCILERS

Lan Medina (#1), Craig Yeung (#2-4) & Sean Parsons (#5-6)
INKERS

Marcio Menyz with
Federico Blee (#3) & Erick Arciniega (#4-5)
COLOR ARTISTS

VC's Joe Sabino
LETTERER

Jorge ▮▮▮▮▮▮▮▮ ▮▮▮▮▮▮ (#5-6)

Sara ▮▮▮▮▮
ASSO▮▮▮▮

SPECIAL THANKS TO
Jason Aaron & Mike del Mundo

BLACK PANTHER CREATED BY
Stan Lee & Jack Kirby

COLLECTION EDITOR Jennifer Grünwald
ASSISTANT MANAGING EDITOR Maia Loy
ASSISTANT MANAGING EDITOR Lisa Montalbano
EDITOR, SPECIAL PROJECTS Mark D. Beazley

VP PRODUCTION & SPECIAL PROJECTS Jeff Youngquist
BOOK DESIGNER Adam Del Re
SVP PRINT, SALES & MARKETING David Gabriel
EDITOR IN CHIEF C.B. Cebulski

BLACK PANTHER AND THE AGENTS OF WAKANDA VOL. 1: ▮▮▮
2020. ISBN 978-1-302-92008-1. Published by MARVEL WOR▮▮▮
similarity between any of the names, characters, persons, an▮▮▮
Printed in Canada. KEVIN FEIGE, Chief Creative Officer; DAN▮▮▮
Associate Publisher & SVP of Talent Affairs; Publishing & Pa▮▮▮
Technology; ALEX MORALES, Director of Publishing Operation▮▮▮
or on Marvel.com, please contact Vit DeBellis, Custom Solutio▮▮▮
and 2/25/2020 by SOLISCO PRINTERS, SCOTT, QC, CANAD▮▮▮

▮▮▮ND THE AGENTS OF WAKANDA (2019) #1-6. First printing
▮▮▮ f the Americas, New York, NY 10104. © 2020 MARVEL No
▮▮▮ any such similarity which may exist is purely coincidental.
▮▮▮ ctor; TOM BREVOORT, SVP of Publishing; DAVID BOGART,
▮▮▮ cial Projects; DAN CARR, Executive Director of Publishing
▮▮▮ s. For information regarding advertising in Marvel Comics
▮▮▮ e call 888-511-5480. Manufactured between 1/24/2020

10 9 8 7 6 5 4 3 2 1

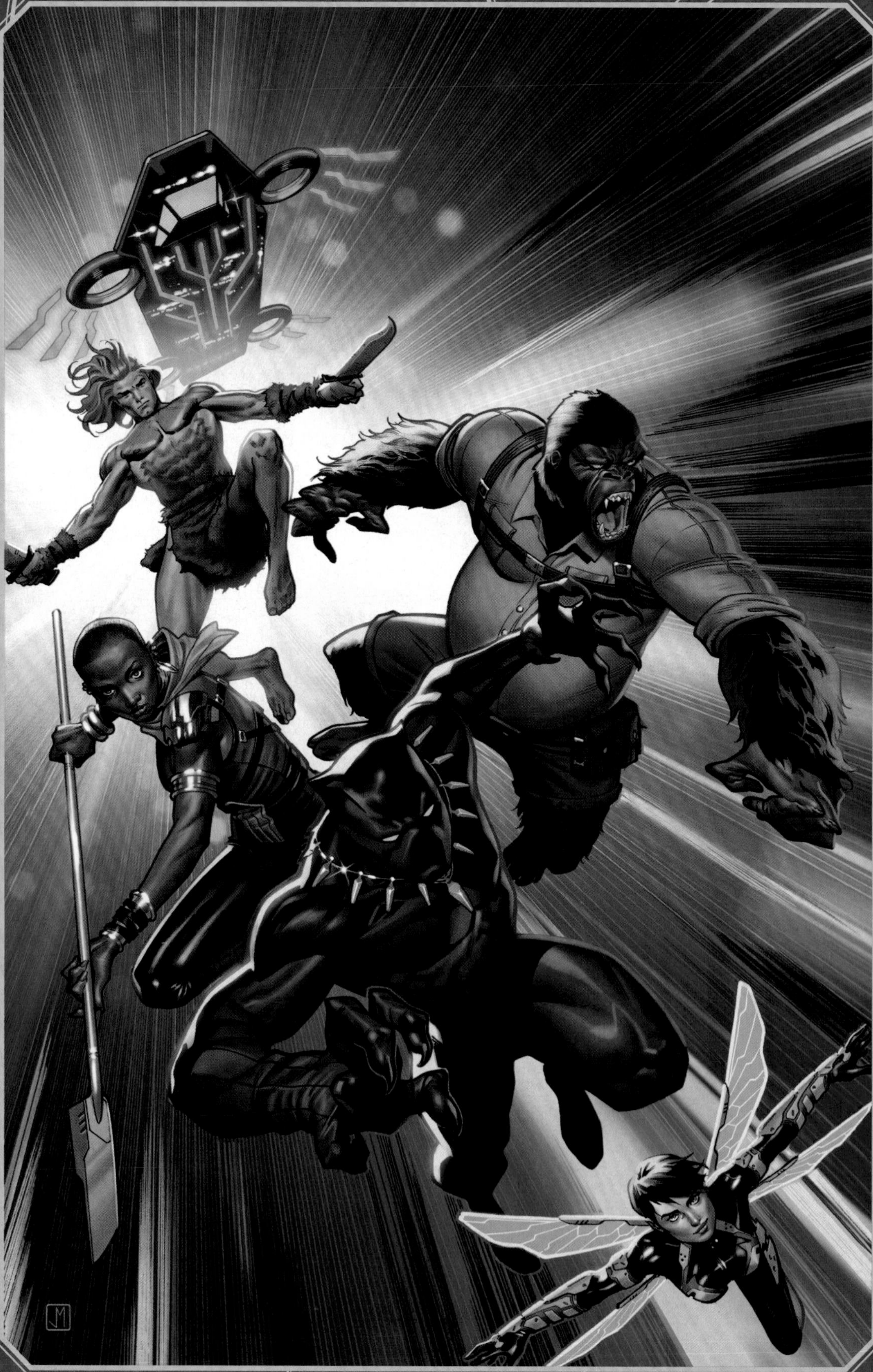

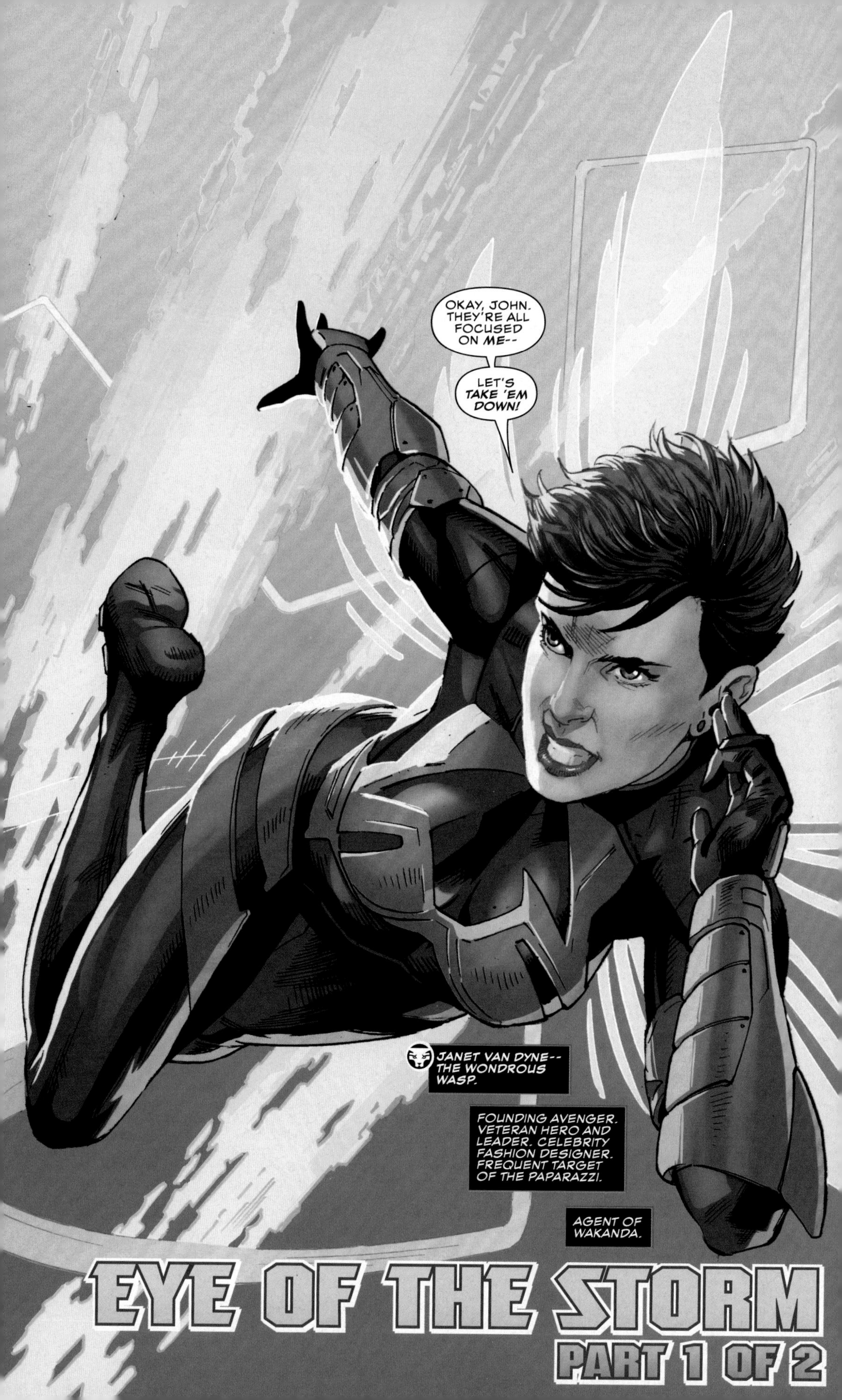

OKAY, JOHN. THEY'RE ALL FOCUSED ON ME--
LET'S TAKE 'EM DOWN!
JANET VAN DYNE-- THE WONDROUS WASP.
FOUNDING AVENGER. VETERAN HERO AND LEADER. CELEBRITY FASHION DESIGNER. FREQUENT TARGET OF THE PAPARAZZI.
AGENT OF WAKANDA.
EYE OF THE STORM
PART 1 OF 2

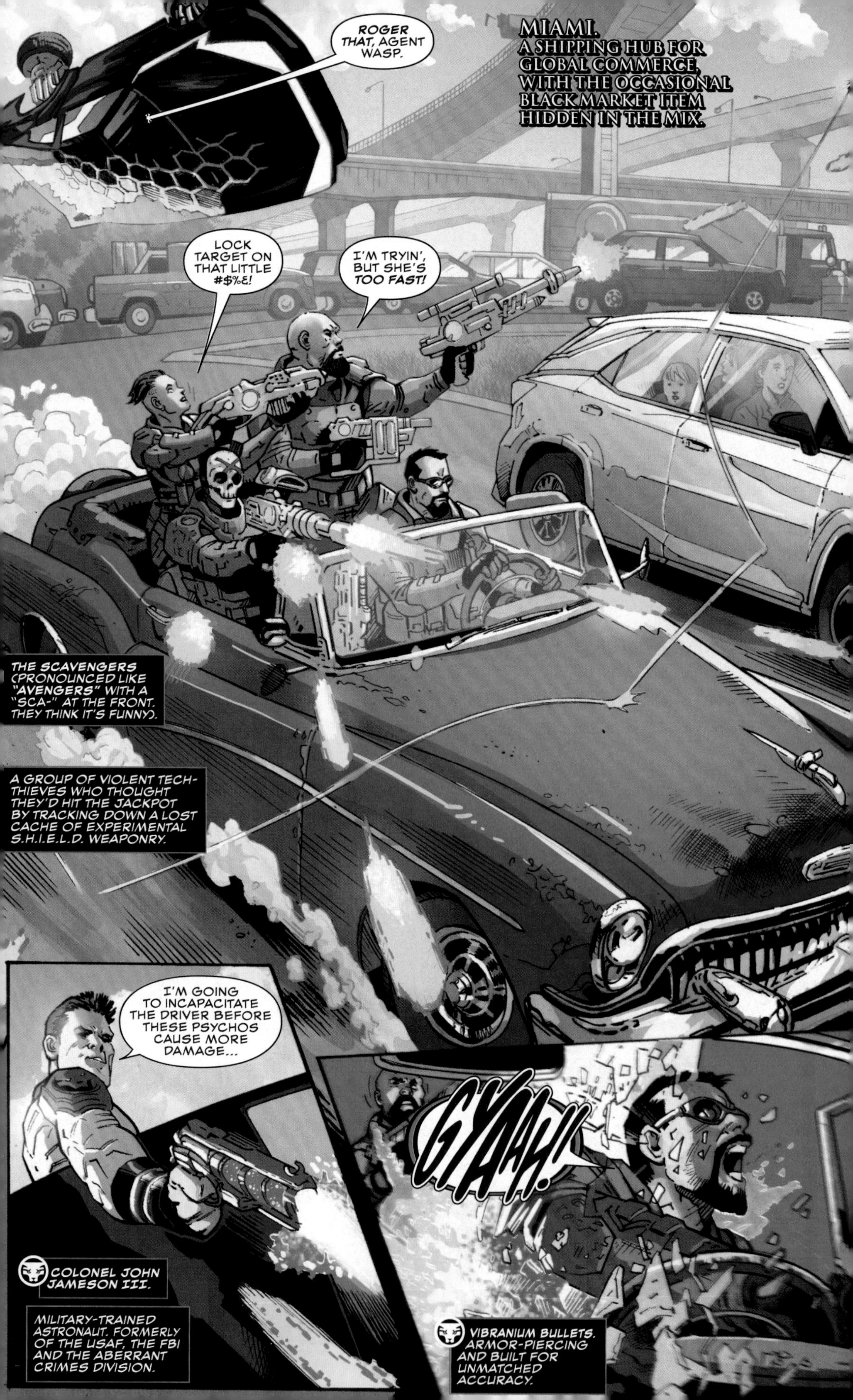
MIAMI. A SHIPPING HUB FOR GLOBAL COMMERCE, WITH THE OCCASIONAL BLACK MARKET ITEM HIDDEN IN THE MIX.
ROGER THAT, AGENT WASP.
LOCK TARGET ON THAT LITTLE #$%&!
I'M TRYIN', BUT SHE'S TOO FAST!
THE SCAVENGERS (PRONOUNCED LIKE "AVENGERS" WITH A "SCA-" AT THE FRONT. THEY THINK IT'S FUNNY).
A GROUP OF VIOLENT TECH-THIEVES WHO THOUGHT THEY'D HIT THE JACKPOT BY TRACKING DOWN A LOST CACHE OF EXPERIMENTAL S.H.I.E.L.D. WEAPONRY.
I'M GOING TO INCAPACITATE THE DRIVER BEFORE THESE PSYCHOS CAUSE MORE DAMAGE...
COLONEL JOHN JAMESON III.
MILITARY-TRAINED ASTRONAUT. FORMERLY OF THE USAF, THE FBI AND THE ABERRANT CRIMES DIVISION.
GYAAH!
VIBRANIUM BULLETS. ARMOR-PIERCING AND BUILT FOR UNMATCHED ACCURACY.

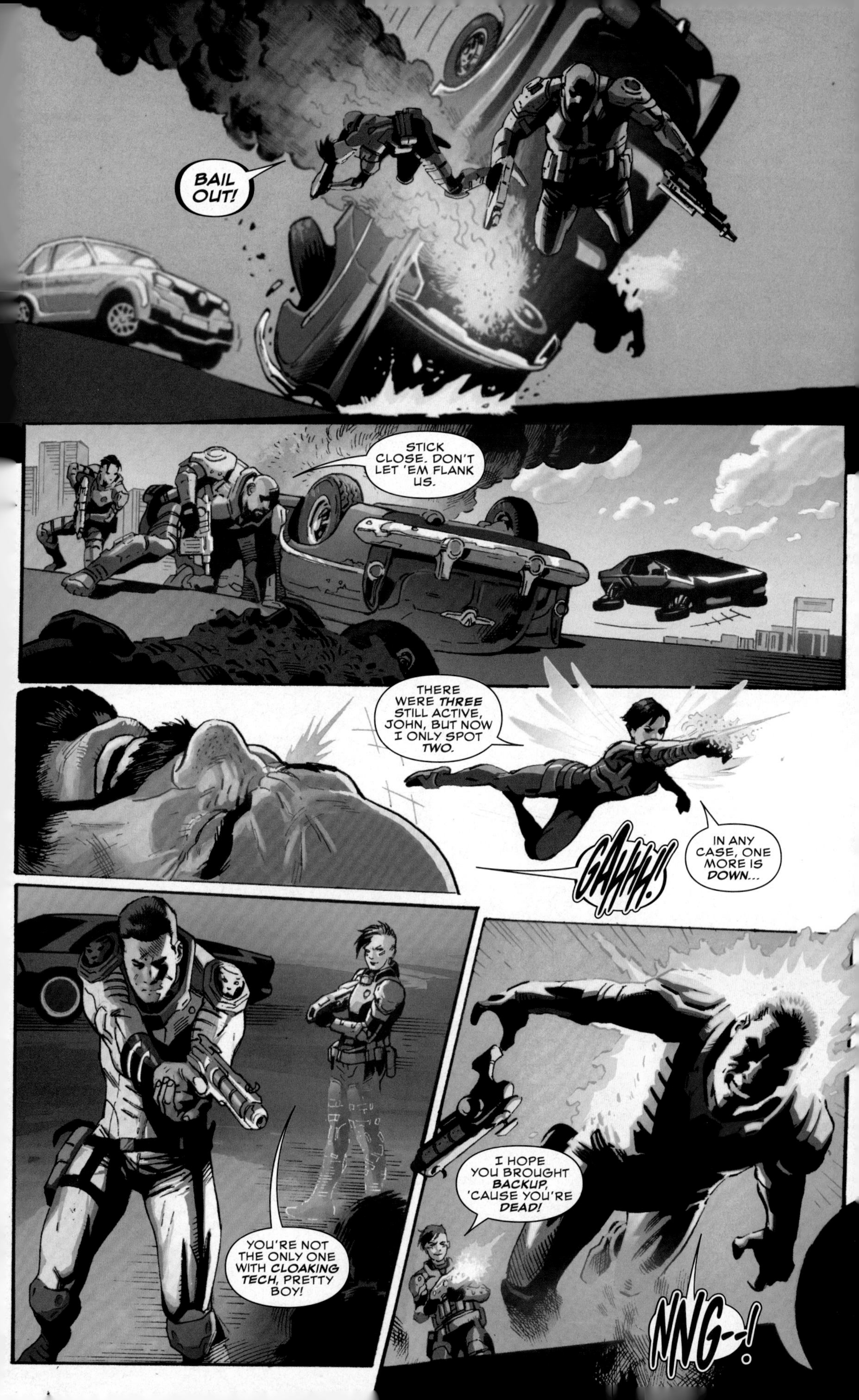
BAIL OUT!
STICK CLOSE. DON'T LET 'EM FLANK US.
THERE WERE THREE STILL ACTIVE, JOHN, BUT NOW I ONLY SPOT TWO.
GAHHH!
IN ANY CASE, ONE MORE IS DOWN...
YOU'RE NOT THE ONLY ONE WITH CLOAKING TECH, PRETTY BOY!
I HOPE YOU BROUGHT BACKUP, 'CAUSE YOU'RE DEAD!
NNG--!

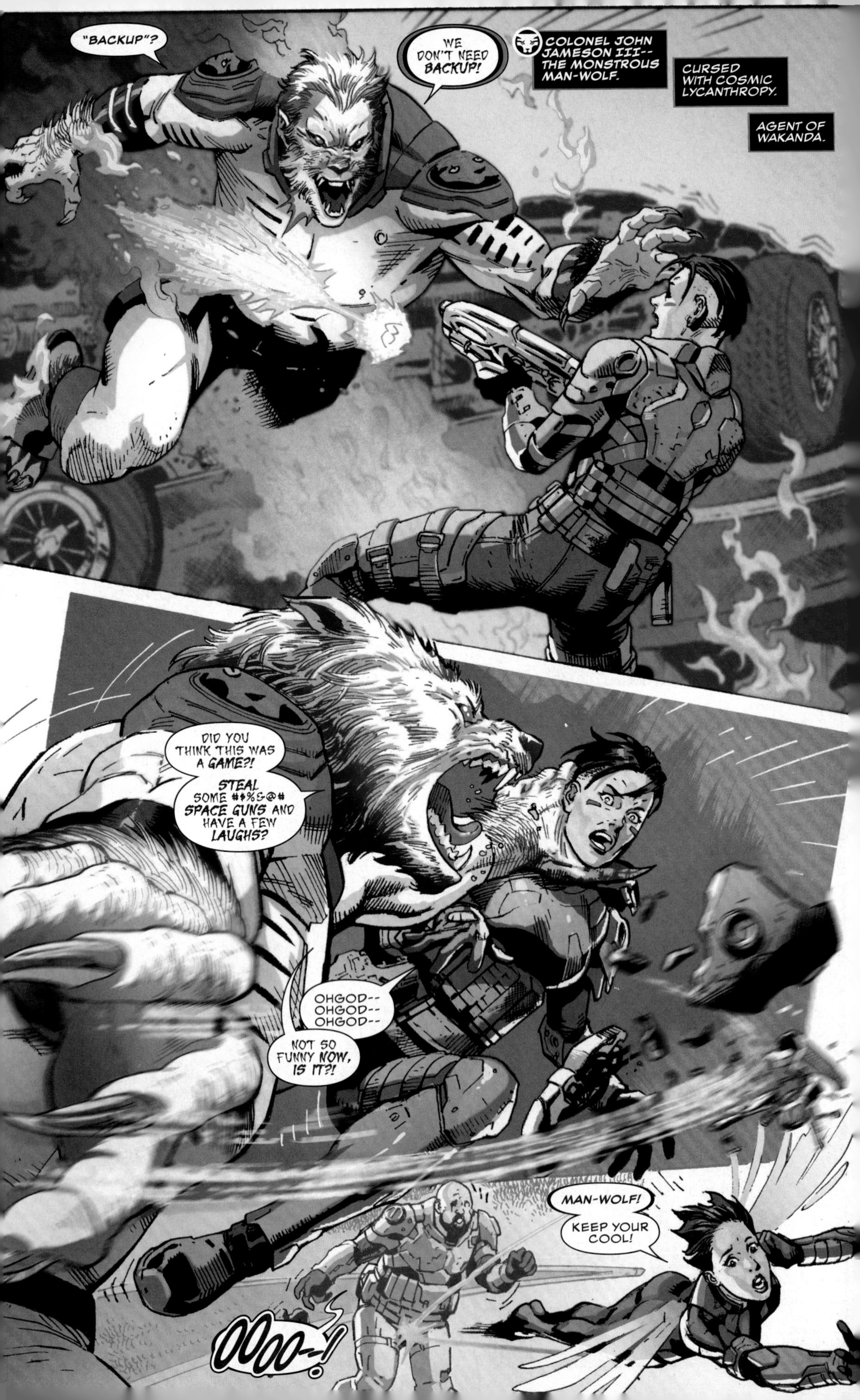
"BACKUP"?
WE DON'T NEED BACKUP!
COLONEL JOHN JAMESON III-- THE MONSTROUS MAN-WOLF.
CURSED WITH COSMIC LYCANTHROPY.
AGENT OF WAKANDA.
DID YOU THINK THIS WAS A GAME?!
STEAL SOME #$%&@# SPACE GUNS AND HAVE A FEW LAUGHS?
OHGOD-- OHGOD-- OHGOD--
NOT SO FUNNY NOW, IS IT?!
MAN-WOLF!
KEEP YOUR COOL!
OOOO--!

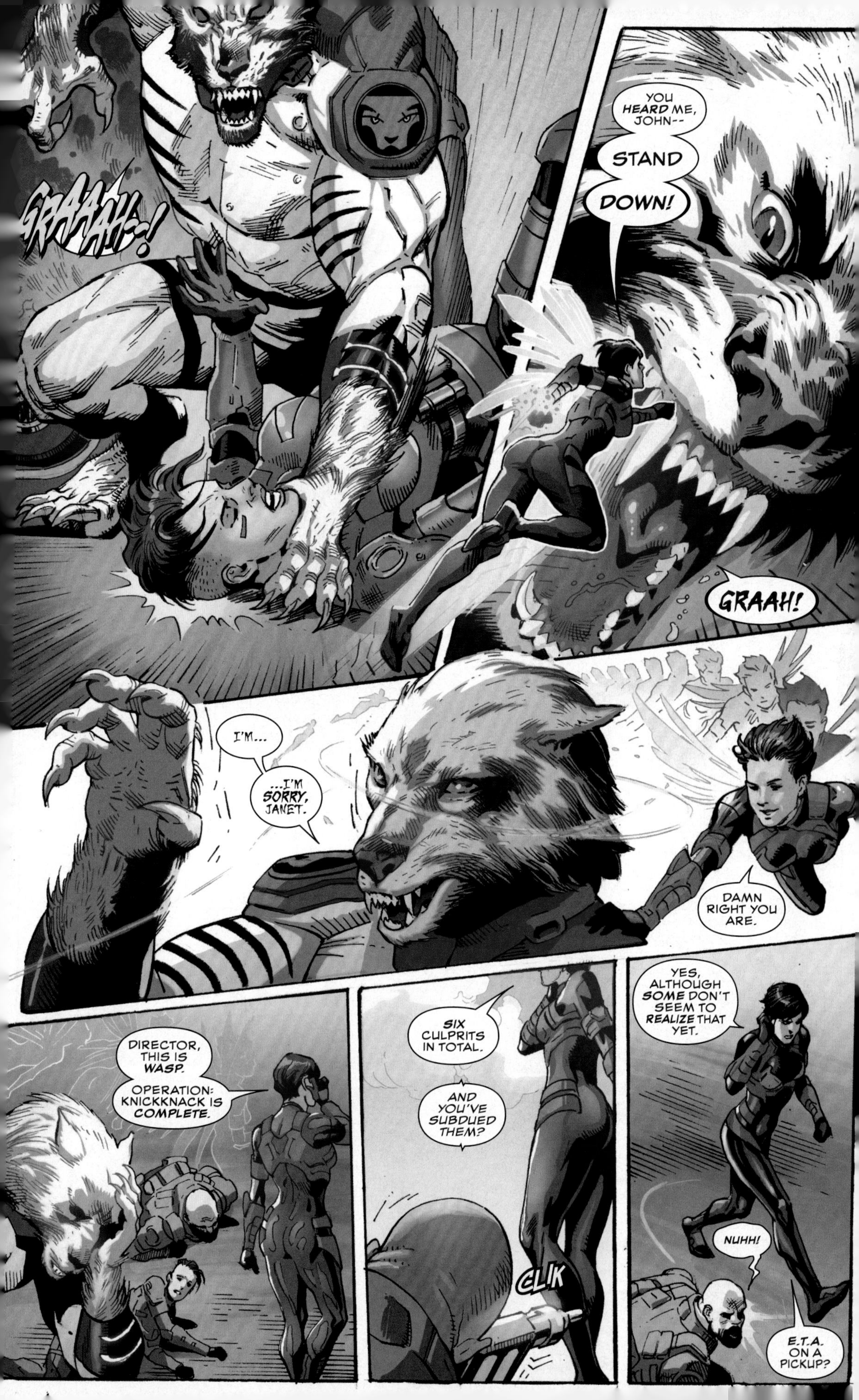
GRAAAAH--!
YOU HEARD ME, JOHN--
STAND
DOWN!
GRAAH!
I'M...
...I'M SORRY, JANET.
DAMN RIGHT YOU ARE.
DIRECTOR, THIS IS WASP.
OPERATION: KNICKKNACK IS COMPLETE.
SIX CULPRITS IN TOTAL.
AND YOU'VE SUBDUED THEM?
CLIK
YES, ALTHOUGH SOME DON'T SEEM TO REALIZE THAT YET.
NUHH!
E.T.A. ON A PICKUP?

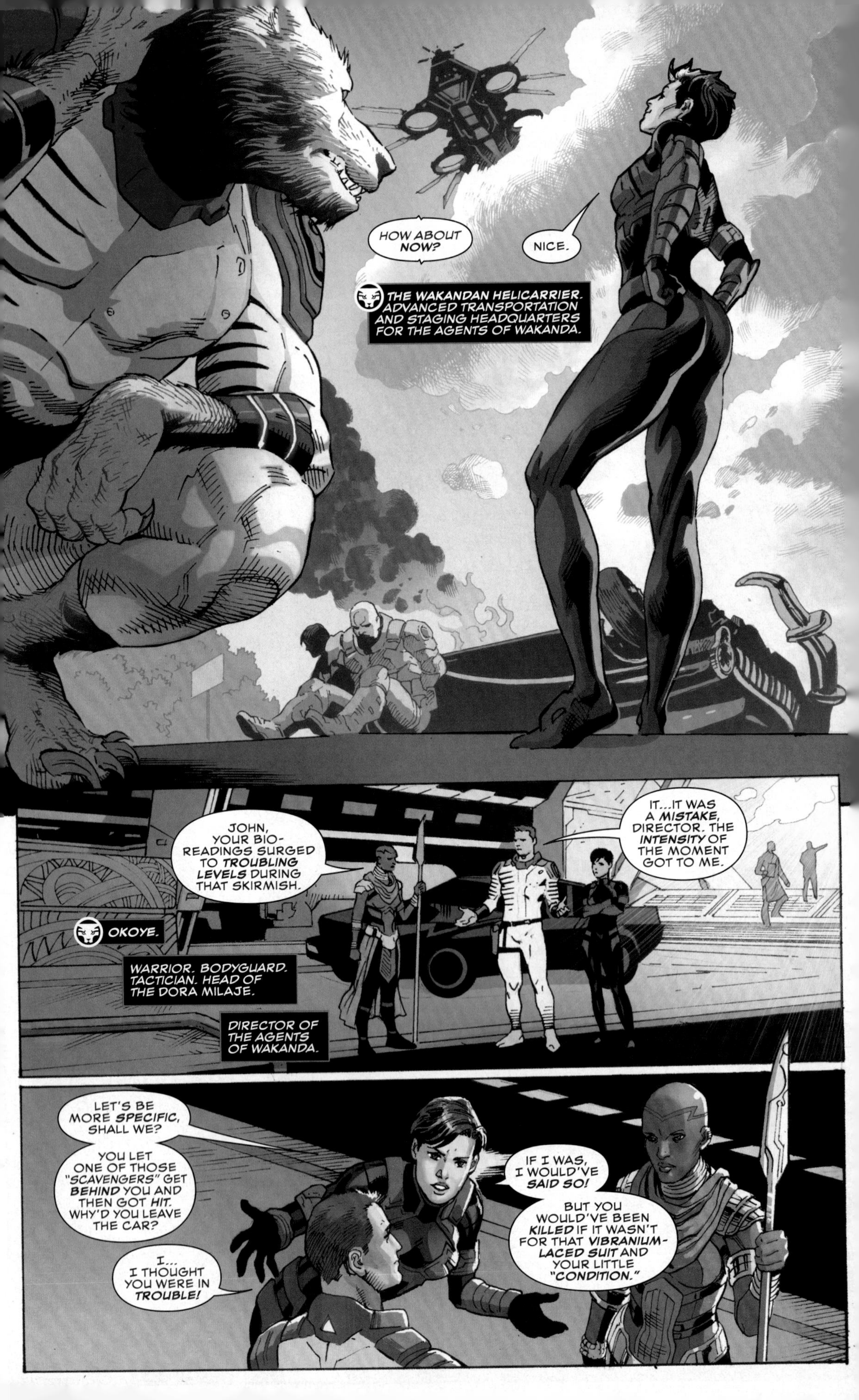
HOW ABOUT NOW?
NICE.
THE WAKANDAN HELICARRIER. ADVANCED TRANSPORTATION AND STAGING HEADQUARTERS FOR THE AGENTS OF WAKANDA.
JOHN, YOUR BIO-READINGS SURGED TO TROUBLING LEVELS DURING THAT SKIRMISH.
OKOYE.
WARRIOR. BODYGUARD. TACTICIAN. HEAD OF THE DORA MILAJE.
DIRECTOR OF THE AGENTS OF WAKANDA.
IT...IT WAS A MISTAKE, DIRECTOR. THE INTENSITY OF THE MOMENT GOT TO ME.
LET'S BE MORE SPECIFIC, SHALL WE?
YOU LET ONE OF THOSE "SCAVENGERS" GET BEHIND YOU AND THEN GOT HIT. WHY'D YOU LEAVE THE CAR?
I... I THOUGHT YOU WERE IN TROUBLE!
IF I WAS, I WOULD'VE SAID SO!
BUT YOU WOULD'VE BEEN KILLED IF IT WASN'T FOR THAT VIBRANIUM-LACED SUIT AND YOUR LITTLE "CONDITION."

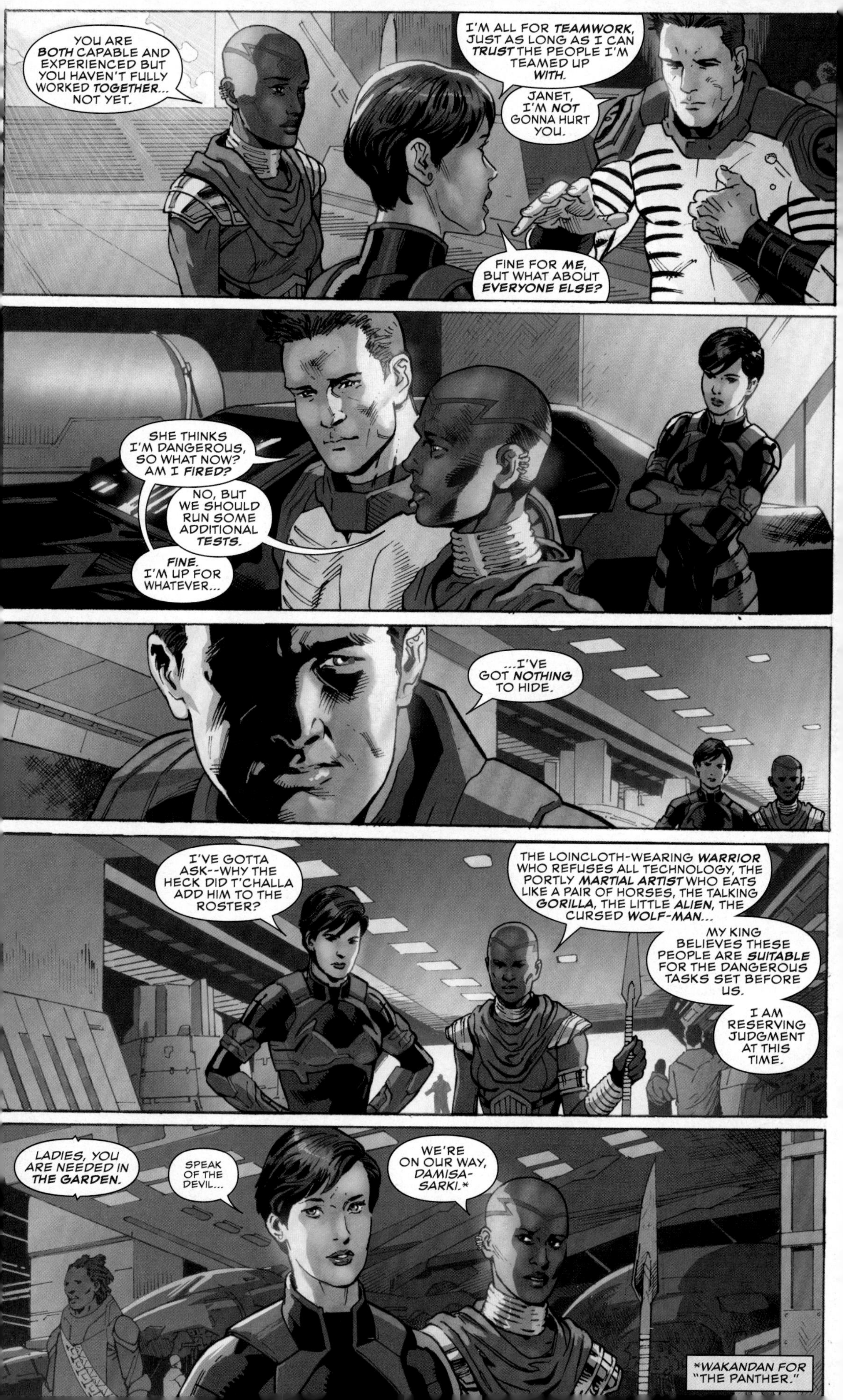
YOU ARE BOTH CAPABLE AND EXPERIENCED BUT YOU HAVEN'T FULLY WORKED TOGETHER... NOT YET.
I'M ALL FOR TEAMWORK, JUST AS LONG AS I CAN TRUST THE PEOPLE I'M TEAMED UP WITH.
JANET, I'M NOT GONNA HURT YOU.
FINE FOR ME, BUT WHAT ABOUT EVERYONE ELSE?
SHE THINKS I'M DANGEROUS, SO WHAT NOW? AM I FIRED?
NO, BUT WE SHOULD RUN SOME ADDITIONAL TESTS.
FINE. I'M UP FOR WHATEVER...
...I'VE GOT NOTHING TO HIDE.
I'VE GOTTA ASK--WHY THE HECK DID T'CHALLA ADD HIM TO THE ROSTER?
THE LOINCLOTH-WEARING WARRIOR WHO REFUSES ALL TECHNOLOGY, THE PORTLY MARTIAL ARTIST WHO EATS LIKE A PAIR OF HORSES, THE TALKING GORILLA, THE LITTLE ALIEN, THE CURSED WOLF-MAN...
MY KING BELIEVES THESE PEOPLE ARE SUITABLE FOR THE DANGEROUS TASKS SET BEFORE US.
I AM RESERVING JUDGMENT AT THIS TIME.
LADIES, YOU ARE NEEDED IN THE GARDEN.
SPEAK OF THE DEVIL...
WE'RE ON OUR WAY, DAMISA-SARKI.*
*WAKANDAN FOR "THE PANTHER."

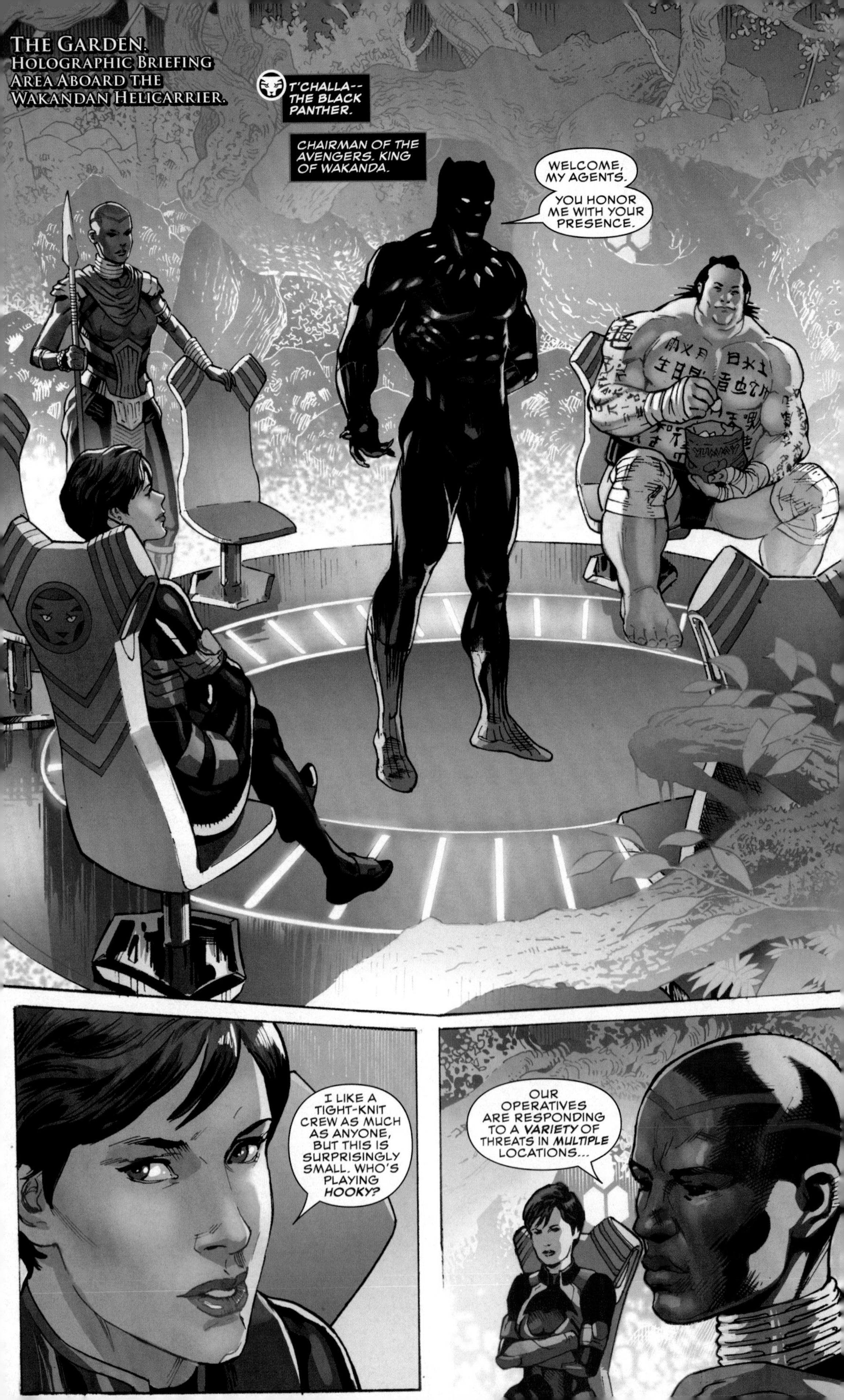

THE GARDEN. HOLOGRAPHIC BRIEFING AREA ABOARD THE WAKANDAN HELICARRIER.
T'CHALLA-- THE BLACK PANTHER.
CHAIRMAN OF THE AVENGERS. KING OF WAKANDA.
WELCOME, MY AGENTS.
YOU HONOR ME WITH YOUR PRESENCE.
I LIKE A TIGHT-KNIT CREW AS MUCH AS ANYONE, BUT THIS IS SURPRISINGLY SMALL. WHO'S PLAYING *HOOKY*?
OUR OPERATIVES ARE RESPONDING TO A *VARIETY* OF THREATS IN *MULTIPLE* LOCATIONS...

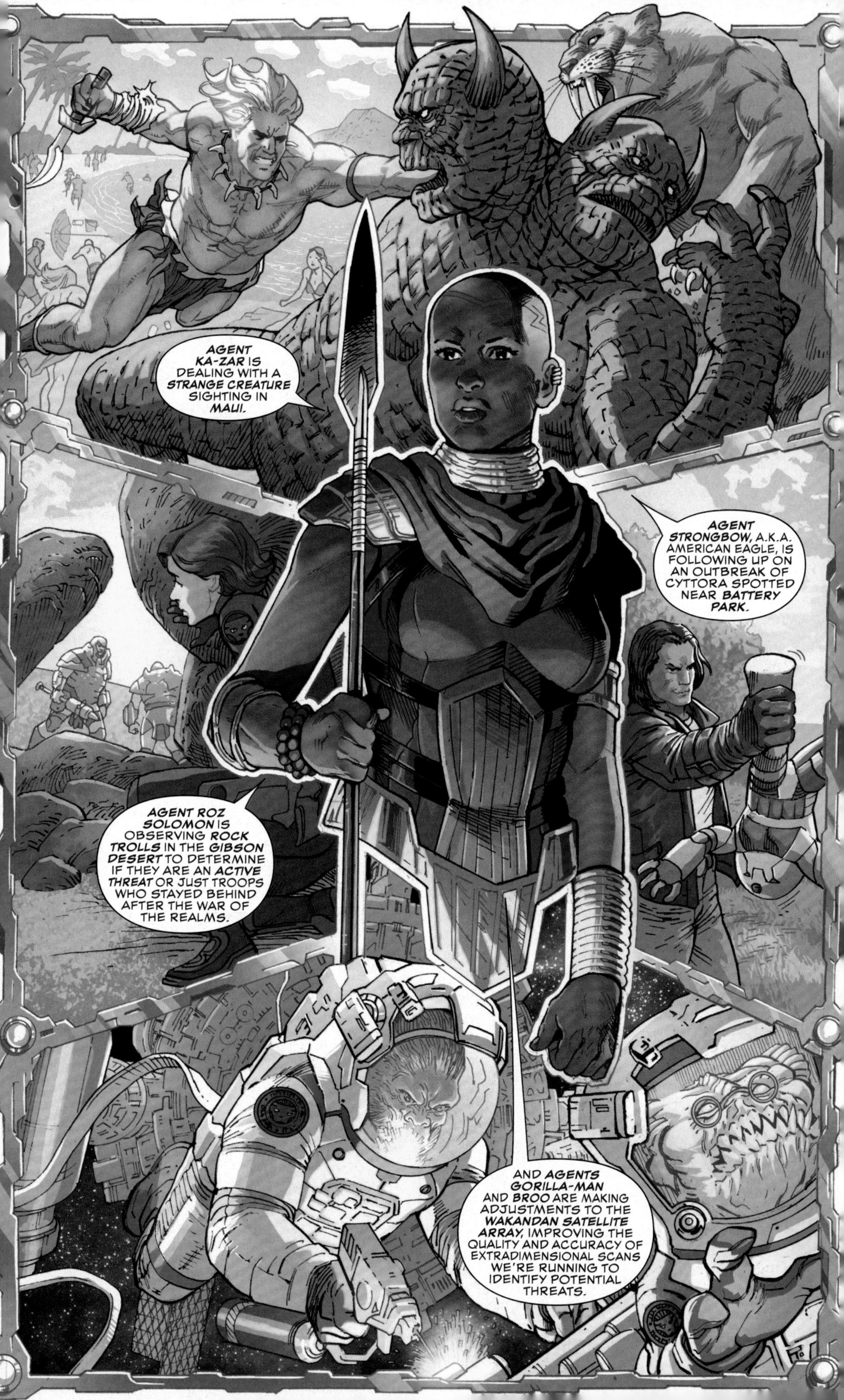
AGENT KA-ZAR IS DEALING WITH A STRANGE CREATURE SIGHTING IN MAUI.
AGENT STRONGBOW, A.K.A. AMERICAN EAGLE, IS FOLLOWING UP ON AN OUTBREAK OF CYTTORA SPOTTED NEAR BATTERY PARK.
AGENT ROZ SOLOMON IS OBSERVING ROCK TROLLS IN THE GIBSON DESERT TO DETERMINE IF THEY ARE AN ACTIVE THREAT OR JUST TROOPS WHO STAYED BEHIND AFTER THE WAR OF THE REALMS.
AND AGENTS GORILLA-MAN AND BROO ARE MAKING ADJUSTMENTS TO THE WAKANDAN SATELLITE ARRAY, IMPROVING THE QUALITY AND ACCURACY OF EXTRADIMENSIONAL SCANS WE'RE RUNNING TO IDENTIFY POTENTIAL THREATS.

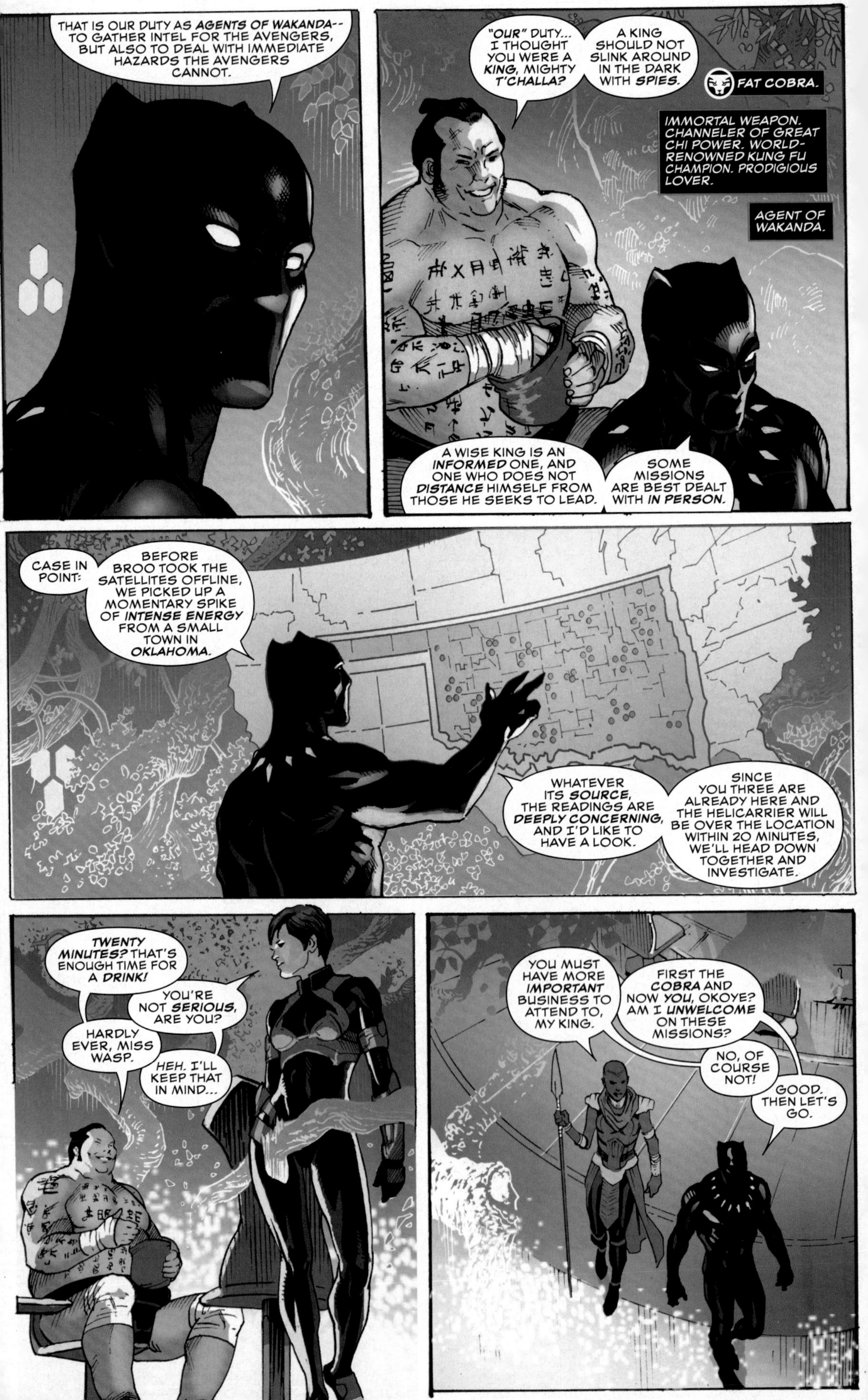

THAT IS OUR DUTY AS AGENTS OF WAKANDA--TO GATHER INTEL FOR THE AVENGERS, BUT ALSO TO DEAL WITH IMMEDIATE HAZARDS THE AVENGERS CANNOT.
"OUR" DUTY... I THOUGHT YOU WERE A KING, MIGHTY T'CHALLA?
A KING SHOULD NOT SLINK AROUND IN THE DARK WITH SPIES.
FAT COBRA.
IMMORTAL WEAPON. CHANNELER OF GREAT CHI POWER. WORLD-RENOWNED KUNG FU CHAMPION. PRODIGIOUS LOVER.
AGENT OF WAKANDA.
A WISE KING IS AN INFORMED ONE, AND ONE WHO DOES NOT DISTANCE HIMSELF FROM THOSE HE SEEKS TO LEAD.
SOME MISSIONS ARE BEST DEALT WITH IN PERSON.
CASE IN POINT:
BEFORE BROO TOOK THE SATELLITES OFFLINE, WE PICKED UP A MOMENTARY SPIKE OF INTENSE ENERGY FROM A SMALL TOWN IN OKLAHOMA.
WHATEVER ITS SOURCE, THE READINGS ARE DEEPLY CONCERNING, AND I'D LIKE TO HAVE A LOOK.
SINCE YOU THREE ARE ALREADY HERE AND THE HELICARRIER WILL BE OVER THE LOCATION WITHIN 20 MINUTES, WE'LL HEAD DOWN TOGETHER AND INVESTIGATE.
TWENTY MINUTES? THAT'S ENOUGH TIME FOR A DRINK!
YOU'RE NOT SERIOUS, ARE YOU?
HARDLY EVER, MISS WASP.
HEH. I'LL KEEP THAT IN MIND...
YOU MUST HAVE MORE IMPORTANT BUSINESS TO ATTEND TO, MY KING.
FIRST THE COBRA AND NOW YOU, OKOYE? AM I UNWELCOME ON THESE MISSIONS?
NO, OF COURSE NOT!
GOOD. THEN LET'S GO.

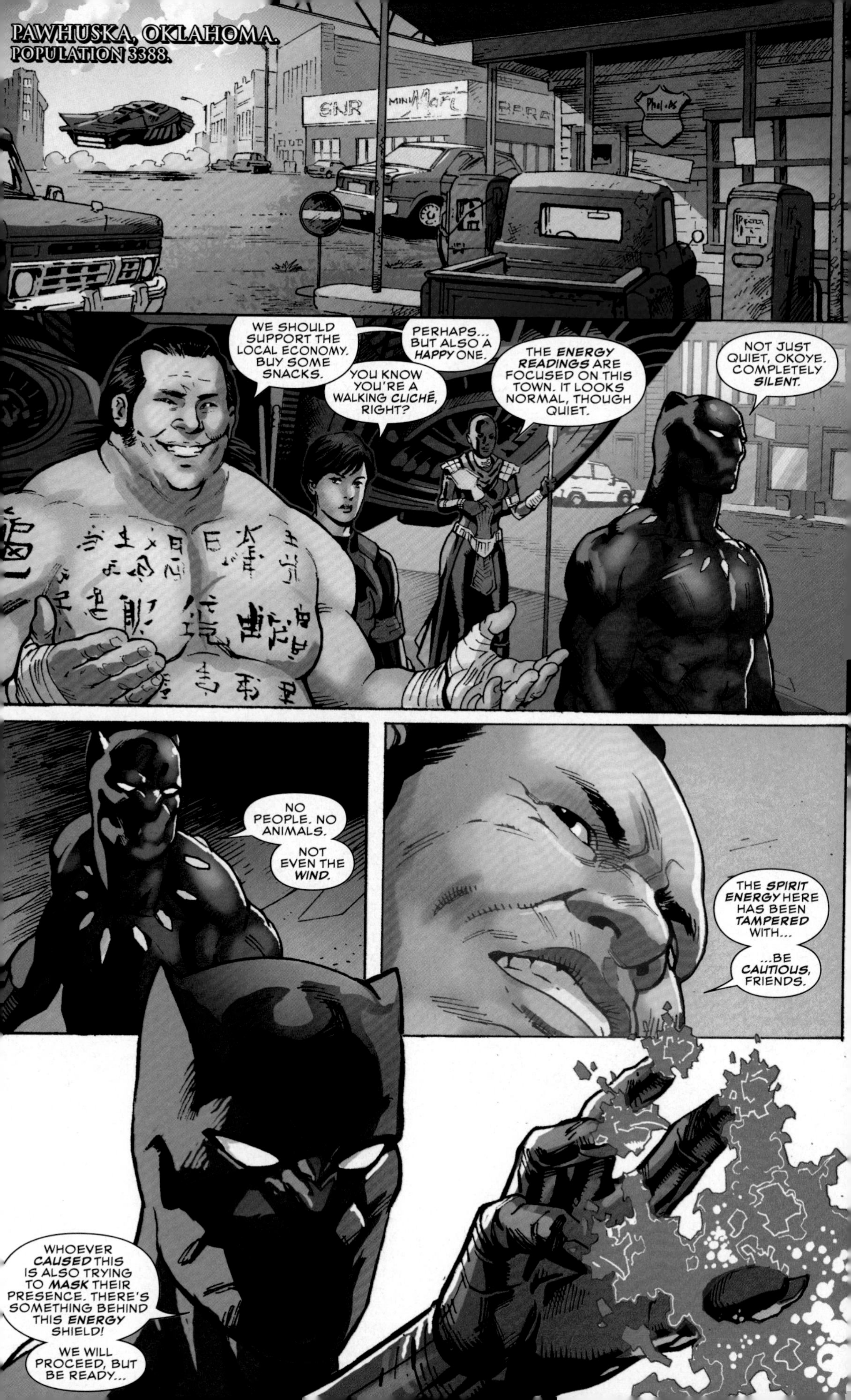
PAWHUSKA, OKLAHOMA.
POPULATION 3388.
WE SHOULD SUPPORT THE LOCAL ECONOMY. BUY SOME SNACKS.
PERHAPS... BUT ALSO A HAPPY ONE.
YOU KNOW YOU'RE A WALKING CLICHÉ, RIGHT?
THE ENERGY READINGS ARE FOCUSED ON THIS TOWN. IT LOOKS NORMAL, THOUGH QUIET.
NOT JUST QUIET, OKOYE. COMPLETELY SILENT.
NO PEOPLE. NO ANIMALS.
NOT EVEN THE WIND.
THE SPIRIT ENERGY HERE HAS BEEN TAMPERED WITH...
...BE CAUTIOUS, FRIENDS.
WHOEVER CAUSED THIS IS ALSO TRYING TO MASK THEIR PRESENCE. THERE'S SOMETHING BEHIND THIS ENERGY SHIELD!
WE WILL PROCEED, BUT BE READY...

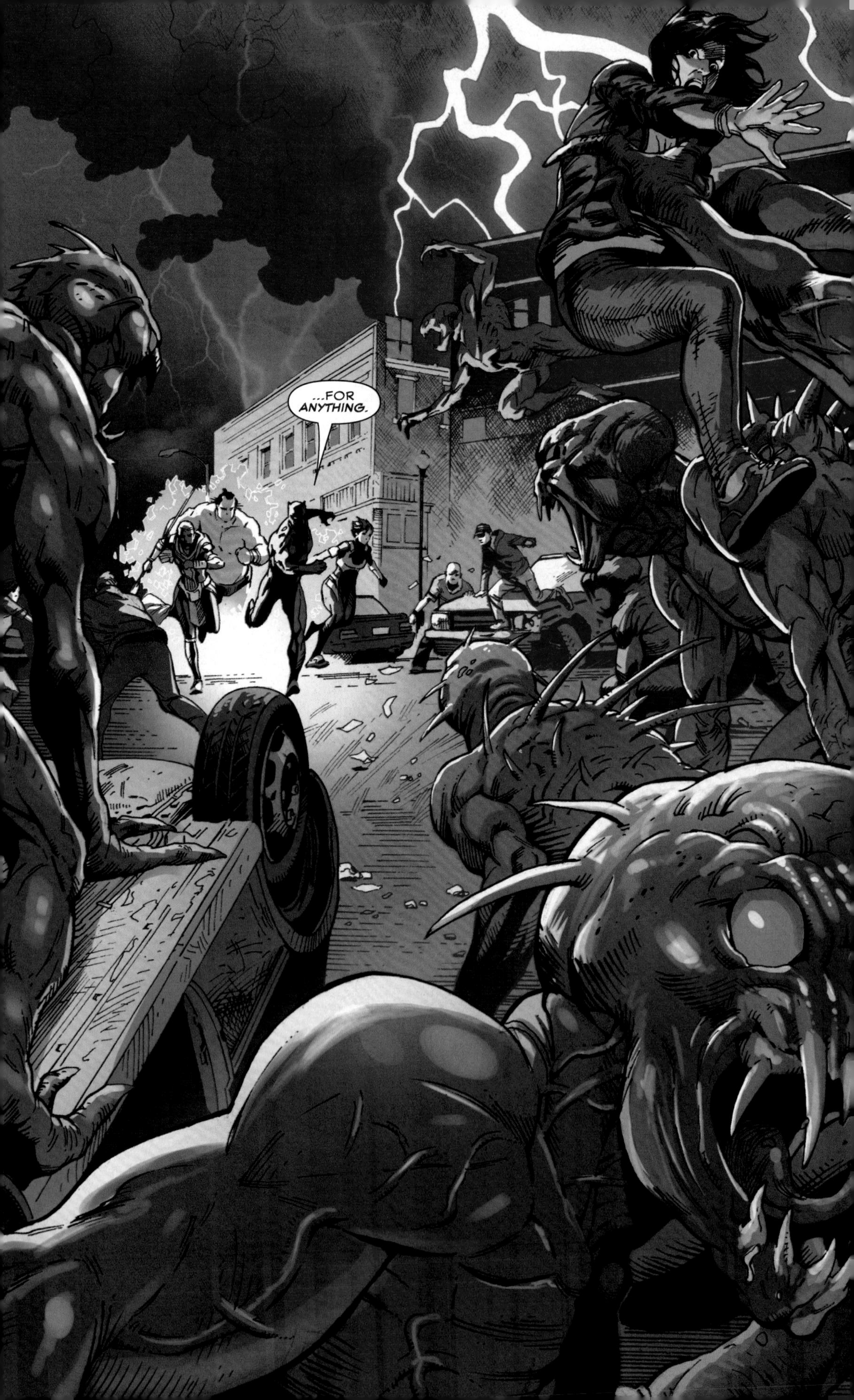
...FOR ANYTHING.

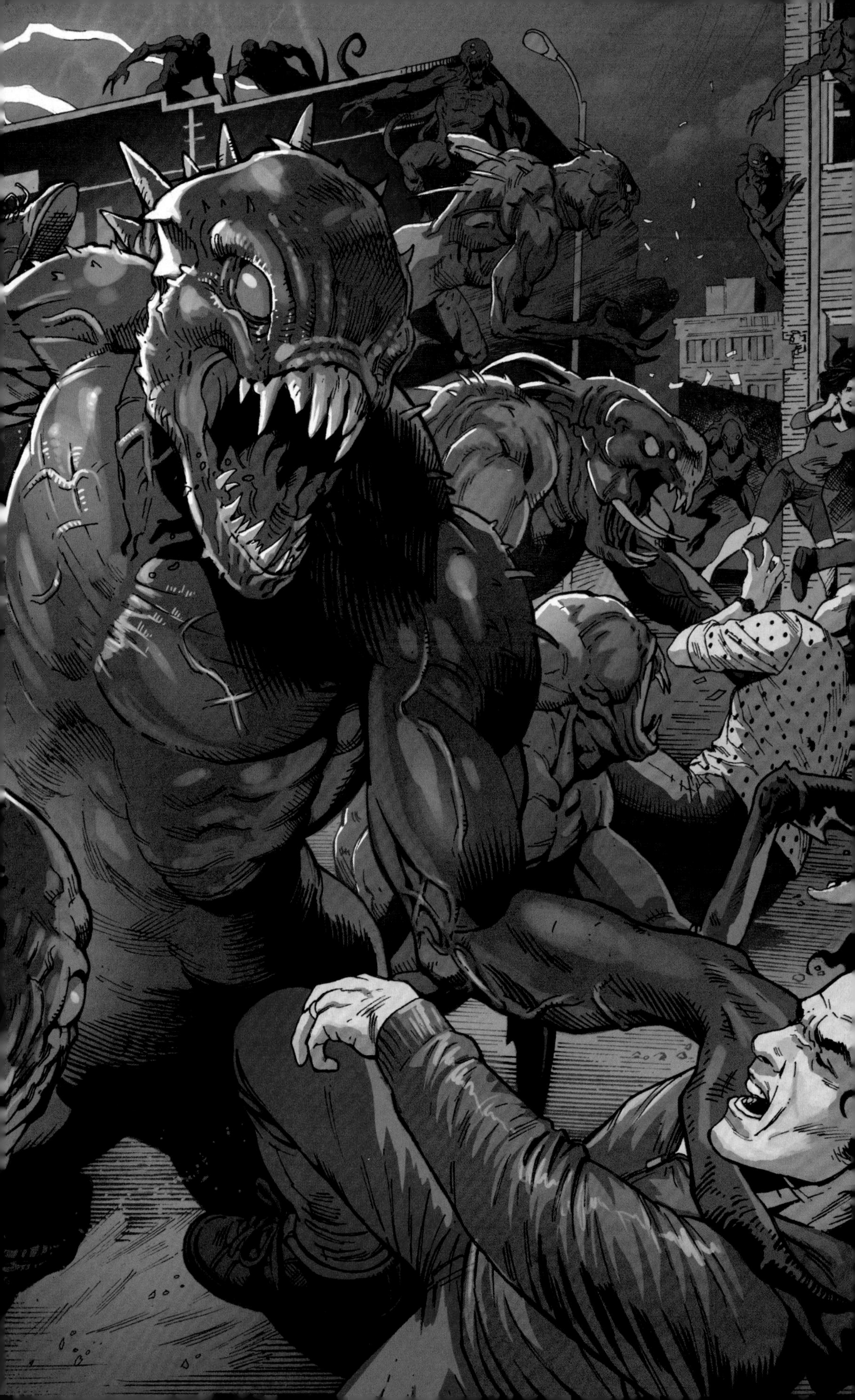

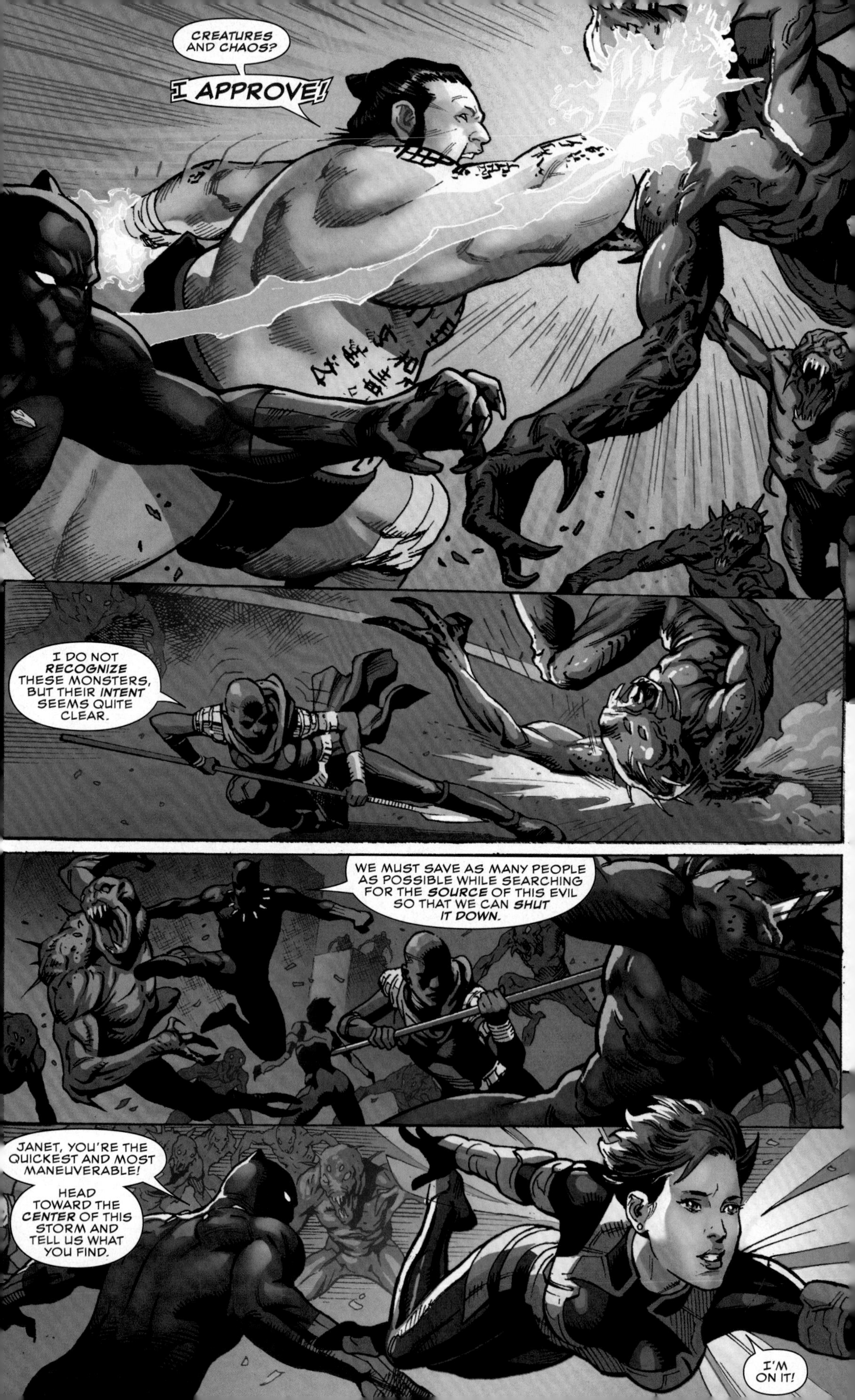
CREATURES AND CHAOS?
I APPROVE!
I DO NOT RECOGNIZE THESE MONSTERS, BUT THEIR INTENT SEEMS QUITE CLEAR.
WE MUST SAVE AS MANY PEOPLE AS POSSIBLE WHILE SEARCHING FOR THE SOURCE OF THIS EVIL SO THAT WE CAN SHUT IT DOWN.
JANET, YOU'RE THE QUICKEST AND MOST MANEUVERABLE!
HEAD TOWARD THE CENTER OF THIS STORM AND TELL US WHAT YOU FIND.
I'M ON IT!

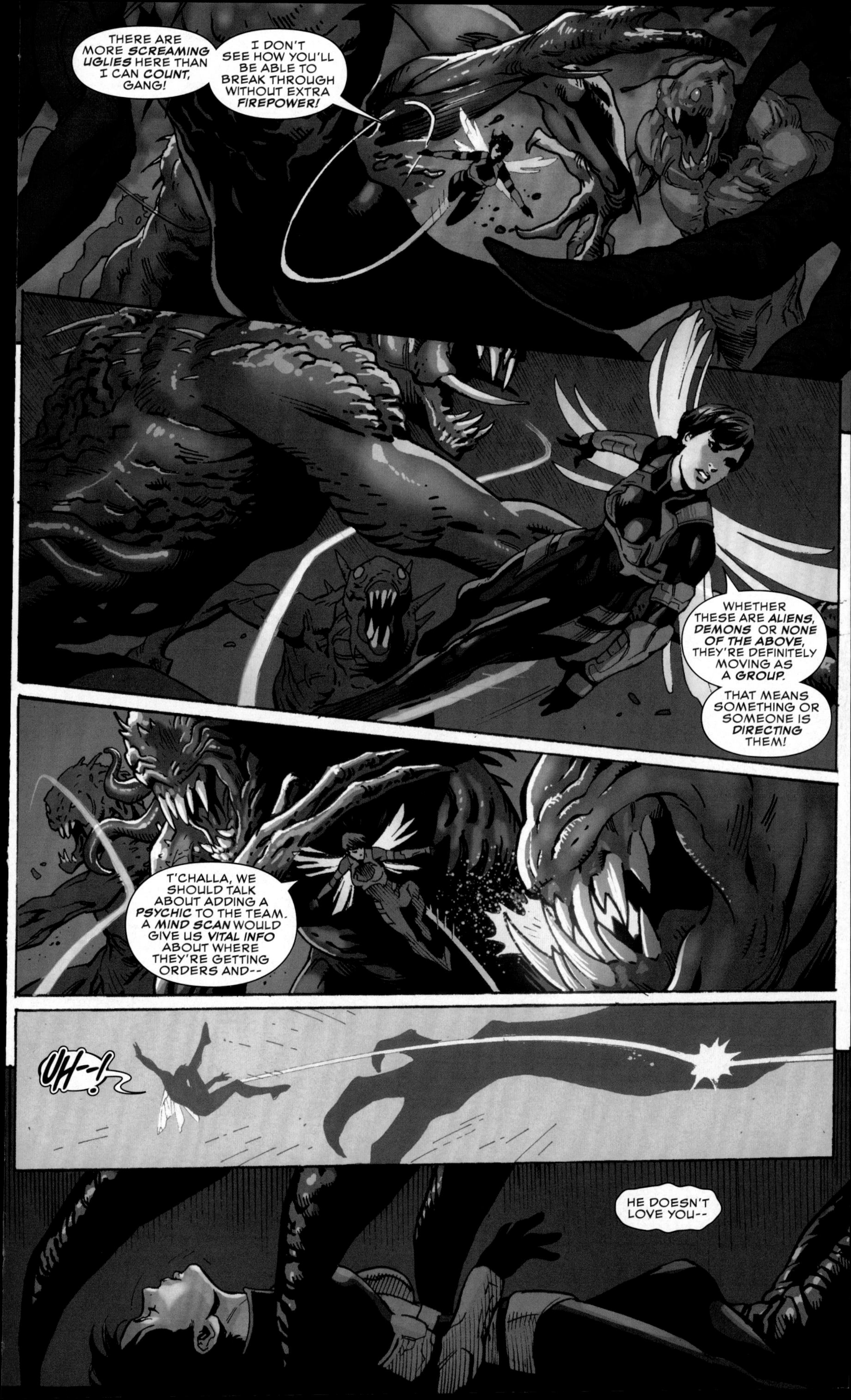
THERE ARE MORE SCREAMING UGLIES HERE THAN I CAN COUNT, GANG!
I DON'T SEE HOW YOU'LL BE ABLE TO BREAK THROUGH WITHOUT EXTRA FIREPOWER!
WHETHER THESE ARE ALIENS, DEMONS OR NONE OF THE ABOVE, THEY'RE DEFINITELY MOVING AS A GROUP.
THAT MEANS SOMETHING OR SOMEONE IS DIRECTING THEM!
T'CHALLA, WE SHOULD TALK ABOUT ADDING A PSYCHIC TO THE TEAM. A MIND SCAN WOULD GIVE US VITAL INFO ABOUT WHERE THEY'RE GETTING ORDERS AND--
UH--!
HE DOESN'T LOVE YOU--

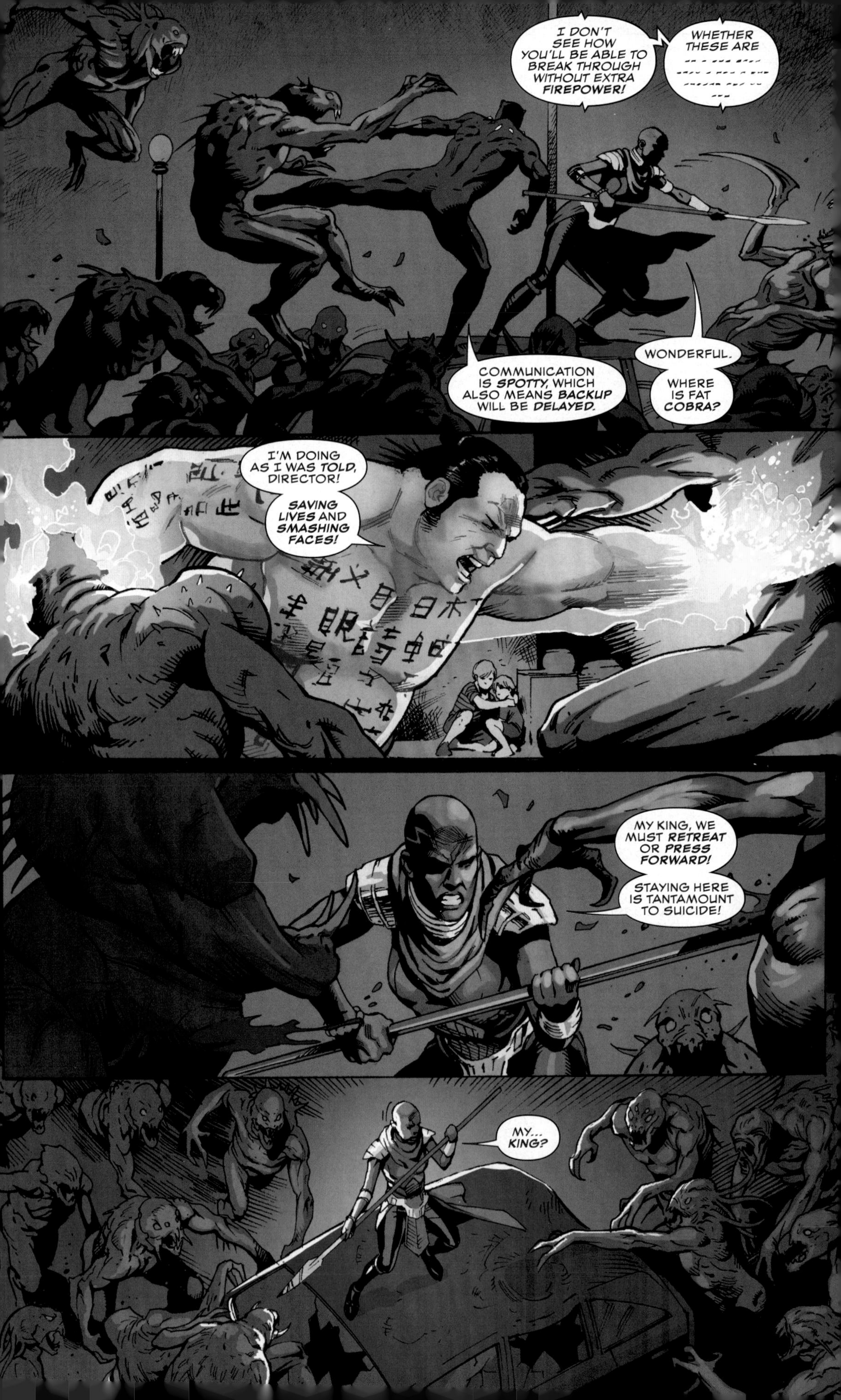
I DON'T SEE HOW YOU'LL BE ABLE TO BREAK THROUGH WITHOUT EXTRA FIREPOWER!
WHETHER THESE ARE
COMMUNICATION IS SPOTTY, WHICH ALSO MEANS BACKUP WILL BE DELAYED.
WONDERFUL.
WHERE IS FAT COBRA?
I'M DOING AS I WAS TOLD, DIRECTOR!
SAVING LIVES AND SMASHING FACES!
MY KING, WE MUST RETREAT OR PRESS FORWARD!
STAYING HERE IS TANTAMOUNT TO SUICIDE!
MY... KING?

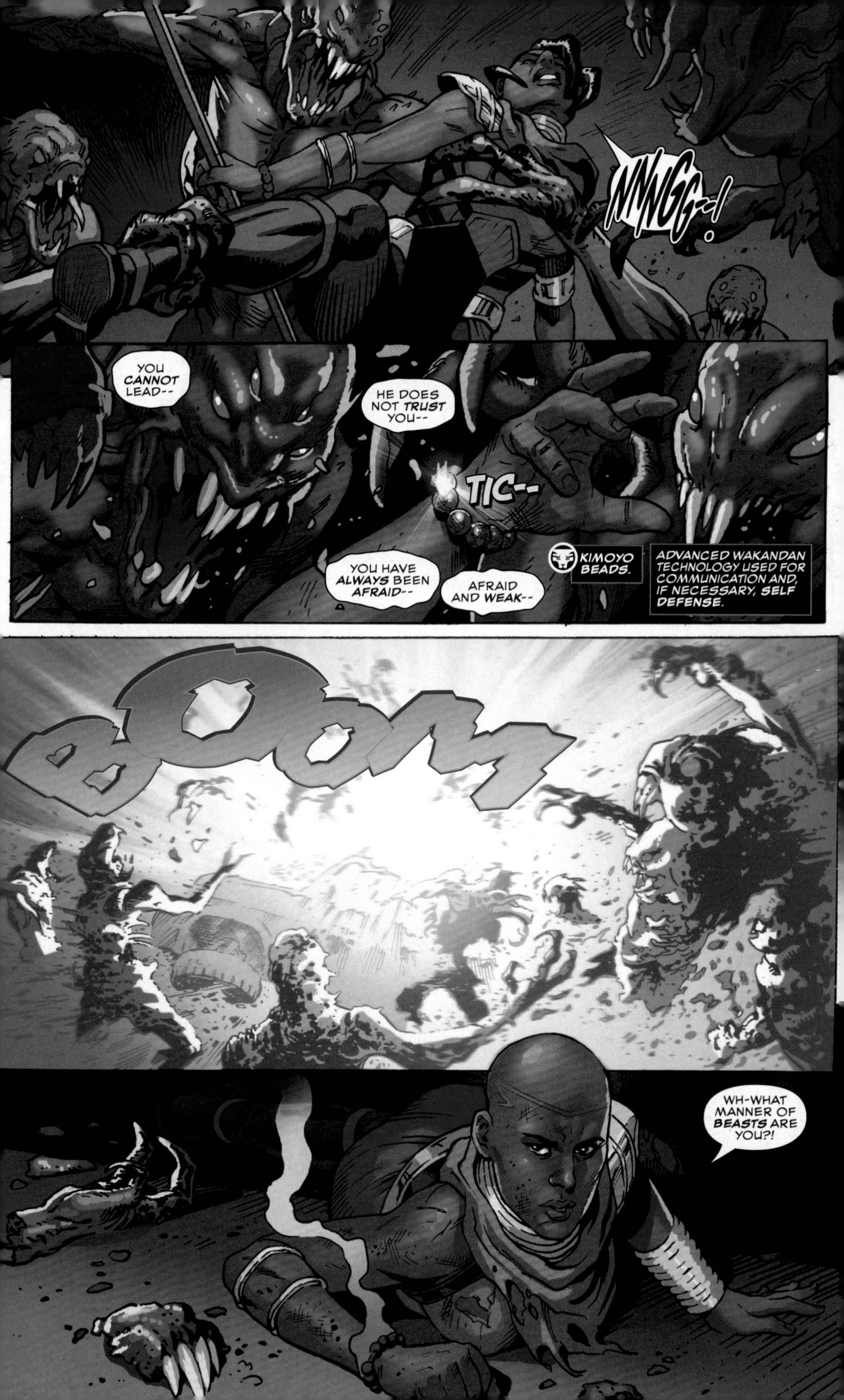
NNNGG--!
YOU CANNOT LEAD--
HE DOES NOT TRUST YOU--
TIC--
YOU HAVE ALWAYS BEEN AFRAID--
AFRAID AND WEAK--
KIMOYO BEADS.
ADVANCED WAKANDAN TECHNOLOGY USED FOR COMMUNICATION AND, IF NECESSARY, SELF DEFENSE.
BOOM
WH-WHAT MANNER OF BEASTS ARE YOU?!

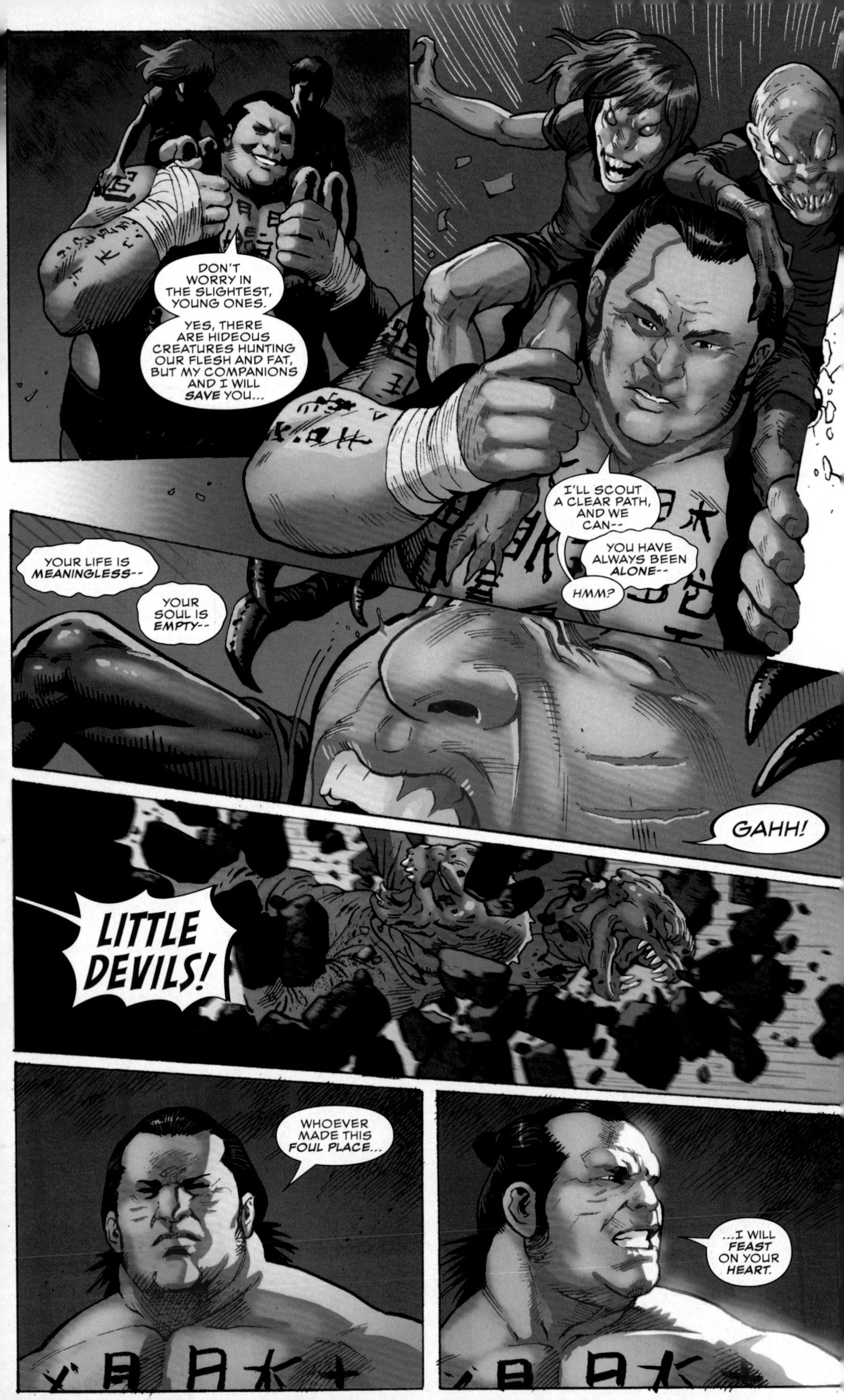
DON'T WORRY IN THE SLIGHTEST, YOUNG ONES.
YES, THERE ARE HIDEOUS CREATURES HUNTING OUR FLESH AND FAT, BUT MY COMPANIONS AND I WILL SAVE YOU...
I'LL SCOUT A CLEAR PATH, AND WE CAN--
YOU HAVE ALWAYS BEEN ALONE--
HMM?
YOUR LIFE IS MEANINGLESS--
YOUR SOUL IS EMPTY--
GAHH!
LITTLE DEVILS!
WHOEVER MADE THIS FOUL PLACE...
...I WILL FEAST ON YOUR HEART.

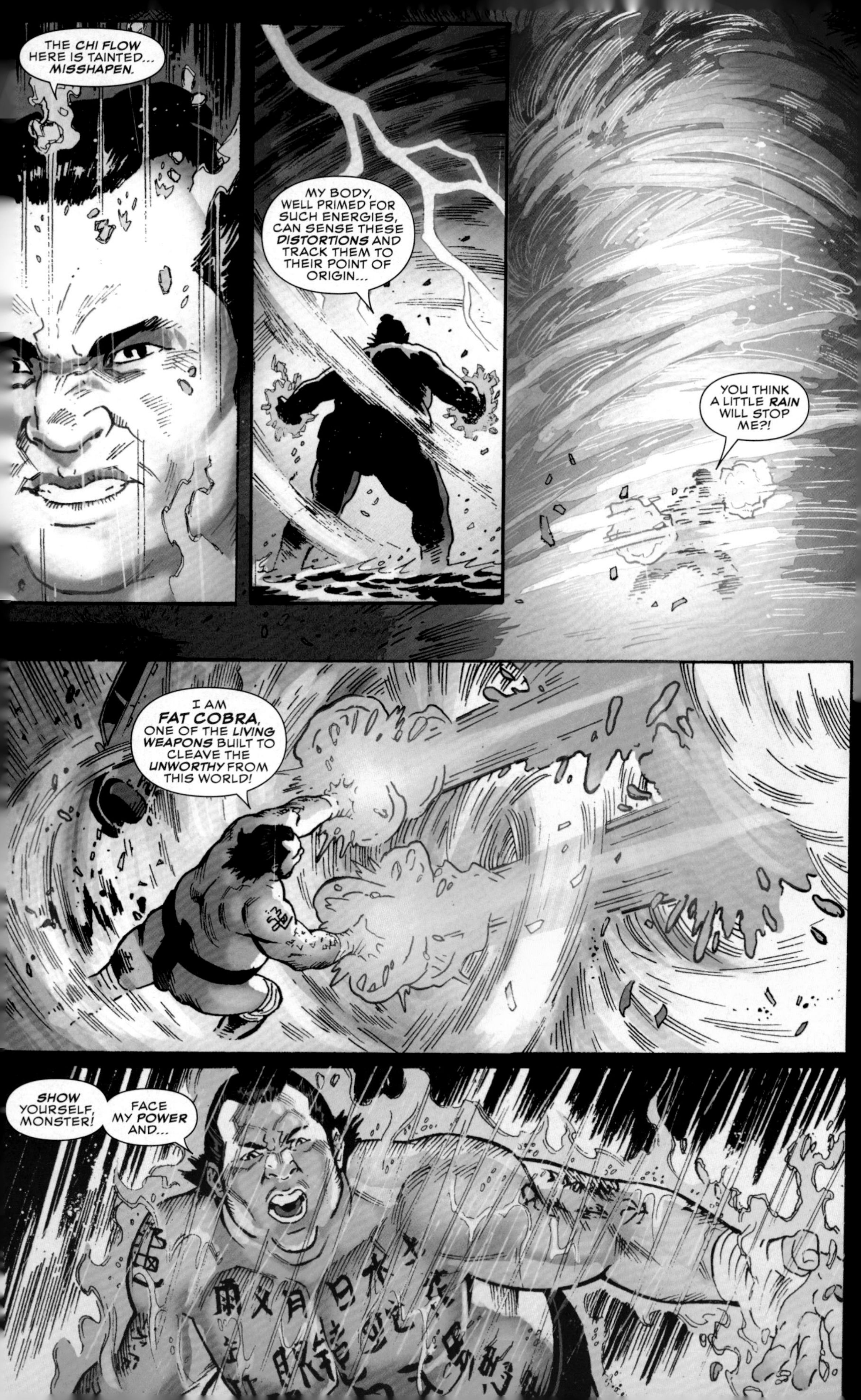
THE CHI FLOW HERE IS TAINTED... MISSHAPEN.
MY BODY, WELL PRIMED FOR SUCH ENERGIES, CAN SENSE THESE DISTORTIONS AND TRACK THEM TO THEIR POINT OF ORIGIN...
YOU THINK A LITTLE RAIN WILL STOP ME?!
I AM FAT COBRA, ONE OF THE LIVING WEAPONS BUILT TO CLEAVE THE UNWORTHY FROM THIS WORLD!
SHOW YOURSELF, MONSTER!
FACE MY POWER AND...

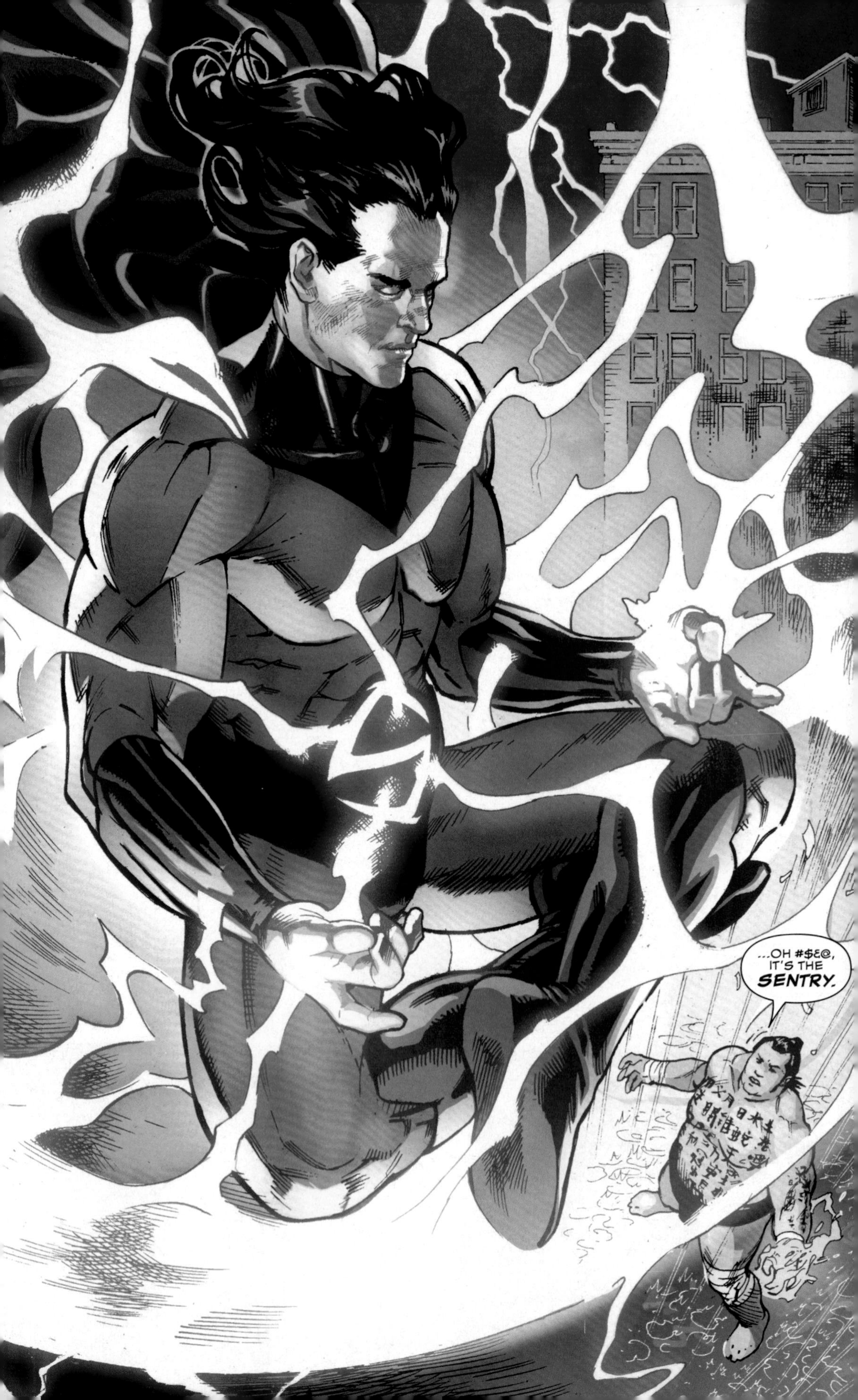
...OH #$&@, IT'S THE SENTRY.

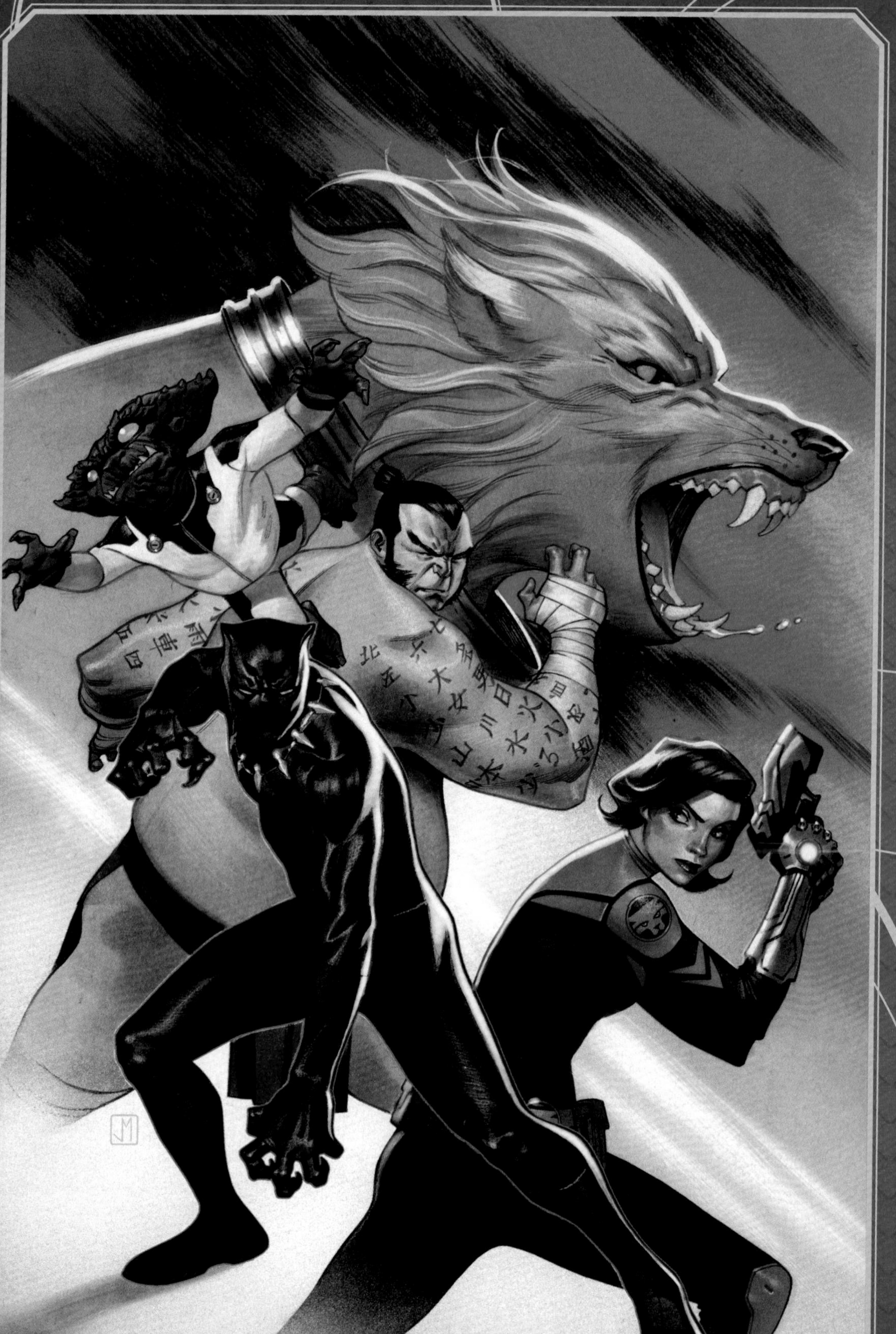

2

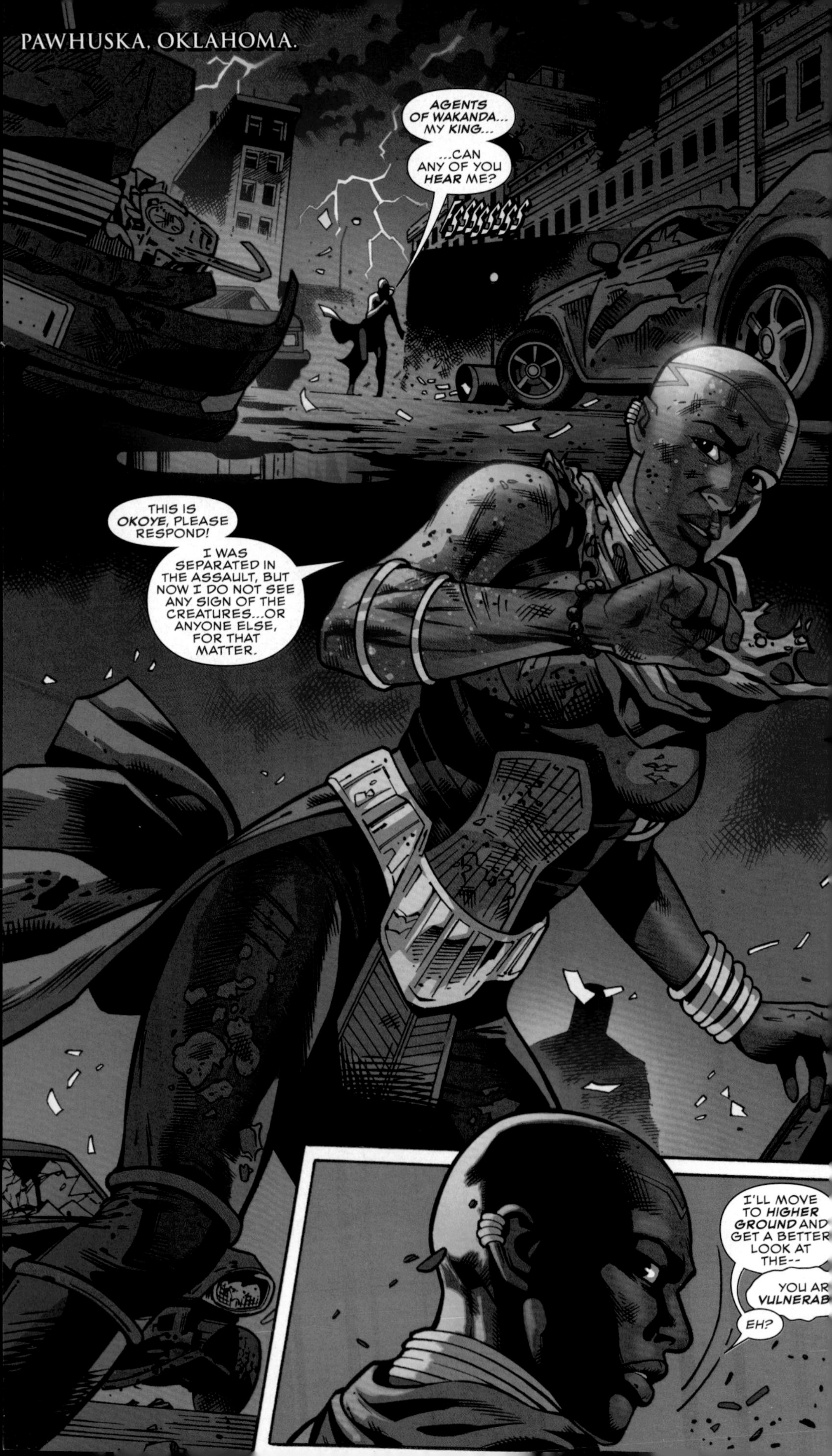
PAWHUSKA, OKLAHOMA.
AGENTS OF WAKANDA... MY KING...
...CAN ANY OF YOU HEAR ME?
FSSSSSSS
THIS IS OKOYE, PLEASE RESPOND!
I WAS SEPARATED IN THE ASSAULT, BUT NOW I DO NOT SEE ANY SIGN OF THE CREATURES...OR ANYONE ELSE, FOR THAT MATTER.
I'LL MOVE TO HIGHER GROUND AND GET A BETTER LOOK AT THE--
EH?

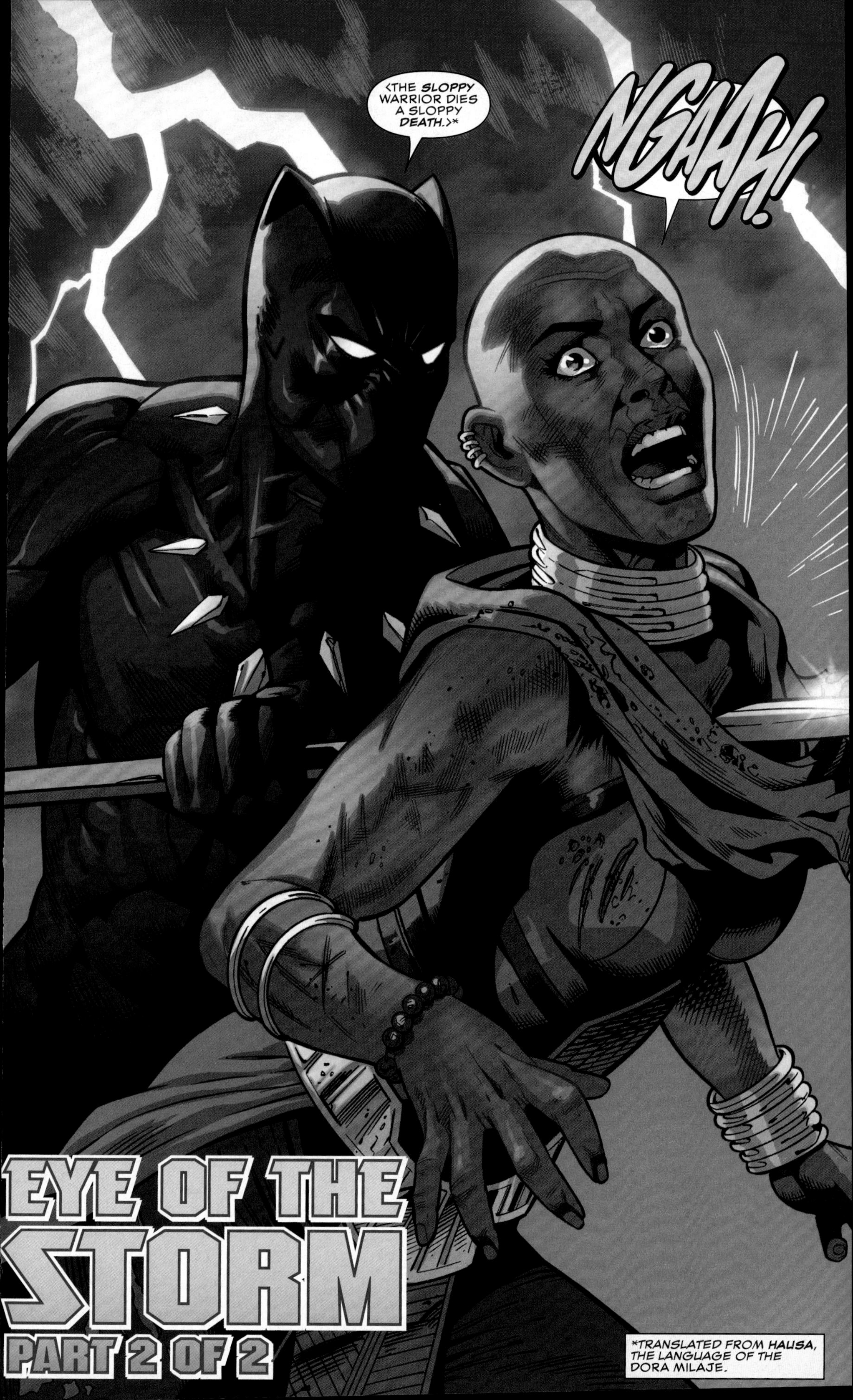

<THE SLOPPY WARRIOR DIES A SLOPPY DEATH.>*
NGAAAH!
EYE OF THE STORM
PART 2 OF 2
*TRANSLATED FROM HAUSA, THE LANGUAGE OF THE DORA MILAJE.

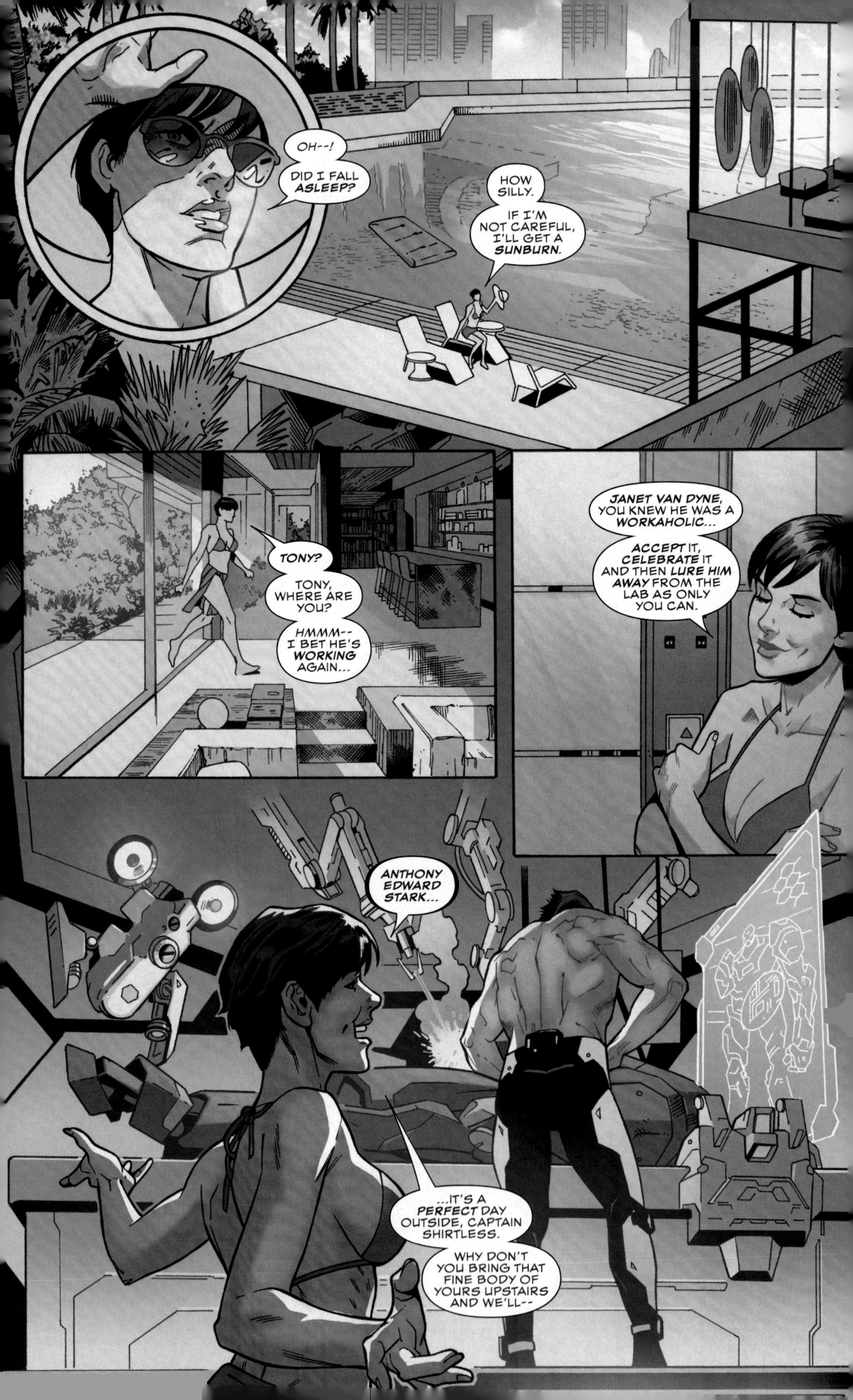
OH--!
DID I FALL ASLEEP?
HOW SILLY.
IF I'M NOT CAREFUL, I'LL GET A SUNBURN.
TONY?
TONY, WHERE ARE YOU?
HMMM-- I BET HE'S WORKING AGAIN...
JANET VAN DYNE, YOU KNEW HE WAS A WORKAHOLIC...
ACCEPT IT, CELEBRATE IT AND THEN LURE HIM AWAY FROM THE LAB AS ONLY YOU CAN.
ANTHONY EDWARD STARK...
...IT'S A PERFECT DAY OUTSIDE, CAPTAIN SHIRTLESS.
WHY DON'T YOU BRING THAT FINE BODY OF YOURS UPSTAIRS AND WE'LL--

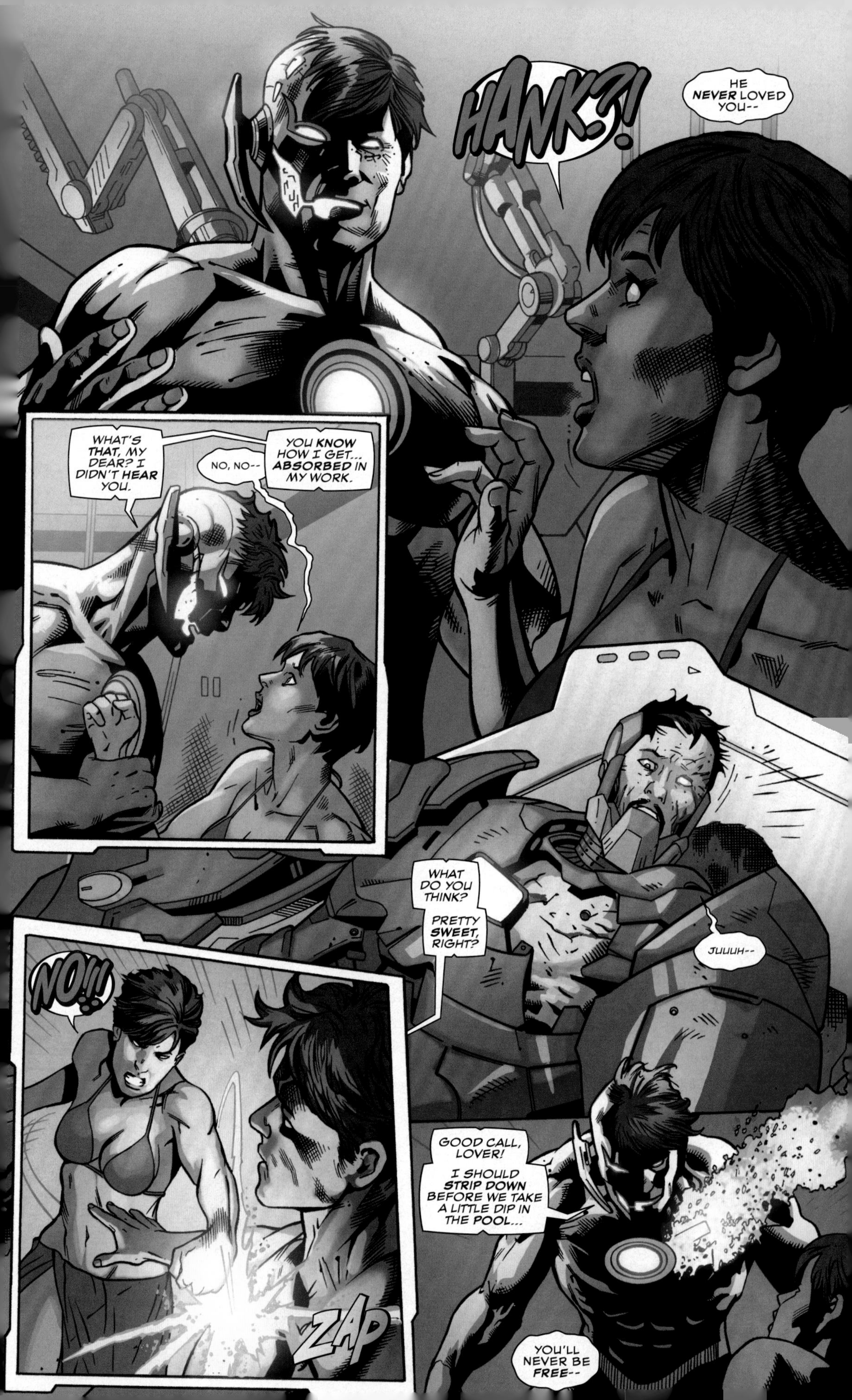

HANK?!
HE NEVER LOVED YOU--
WHAT'S THAT, MY DEAR? I DIDN'T HEAR YOU.
NO, NO--
YOU KNOW HOW I GET... ABSORBED IN MY WORK.
WHAT DO YOU THINK?
PRETTY SWEET, RIGHT?
JUUUH--
NO!!!
ZAP
GOOD CALL, LOVER!
I SHOULD STRIP DOWN BEFORE WE TAKE A LITTLE DIP IN THE POOL...
YOU'LL NEVER BE FREE--

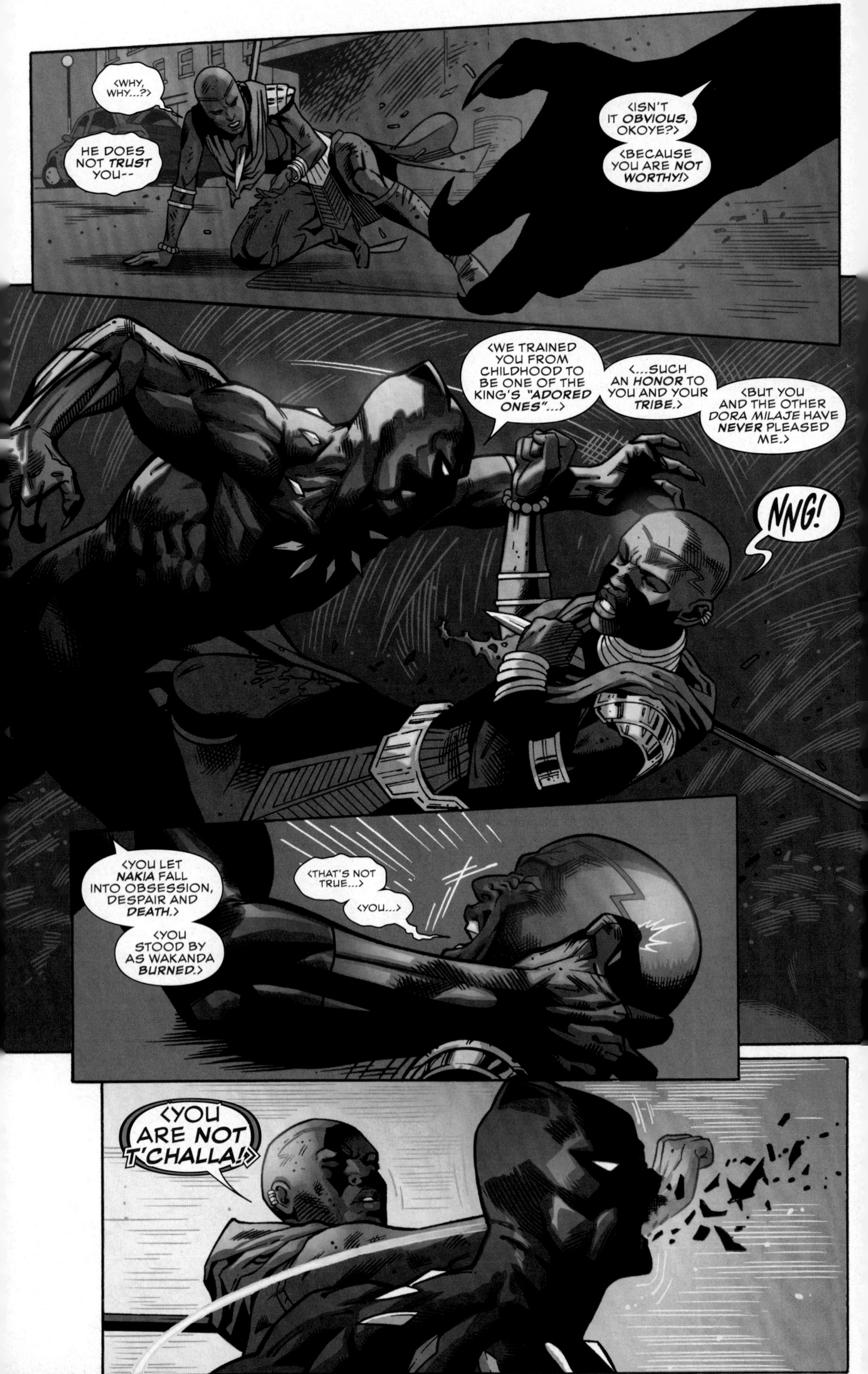
<WHY, WHY...?>
HE DOES NOT TRUST YOU--
<ISN'T IT OBVIOUS, OKOYE?>
<BECAUSE YOU ARE NOT WORTHY!>
<WE TRAINED YOU FROM CHILDHOOD TO BE ONE OF THE KING'S "ADORED ONES"...>
<...SUCH AN HONOR TO YOU AND YOUR TRIBE.>
<BUT YOU AND THE OTHER DORA MILAJE HAVE NEVER PLEASED ME.>
NNG!
<YOU LET NAKIA FALL INTO OBSESSION, DESPAIR AND DEATH.>
<YOU STOOD BY AS WAKANDA BURNED.>
<THAT'S NOT TRUE...>
<YOU...>
<YOU ARE NOT T'CHALLA!>

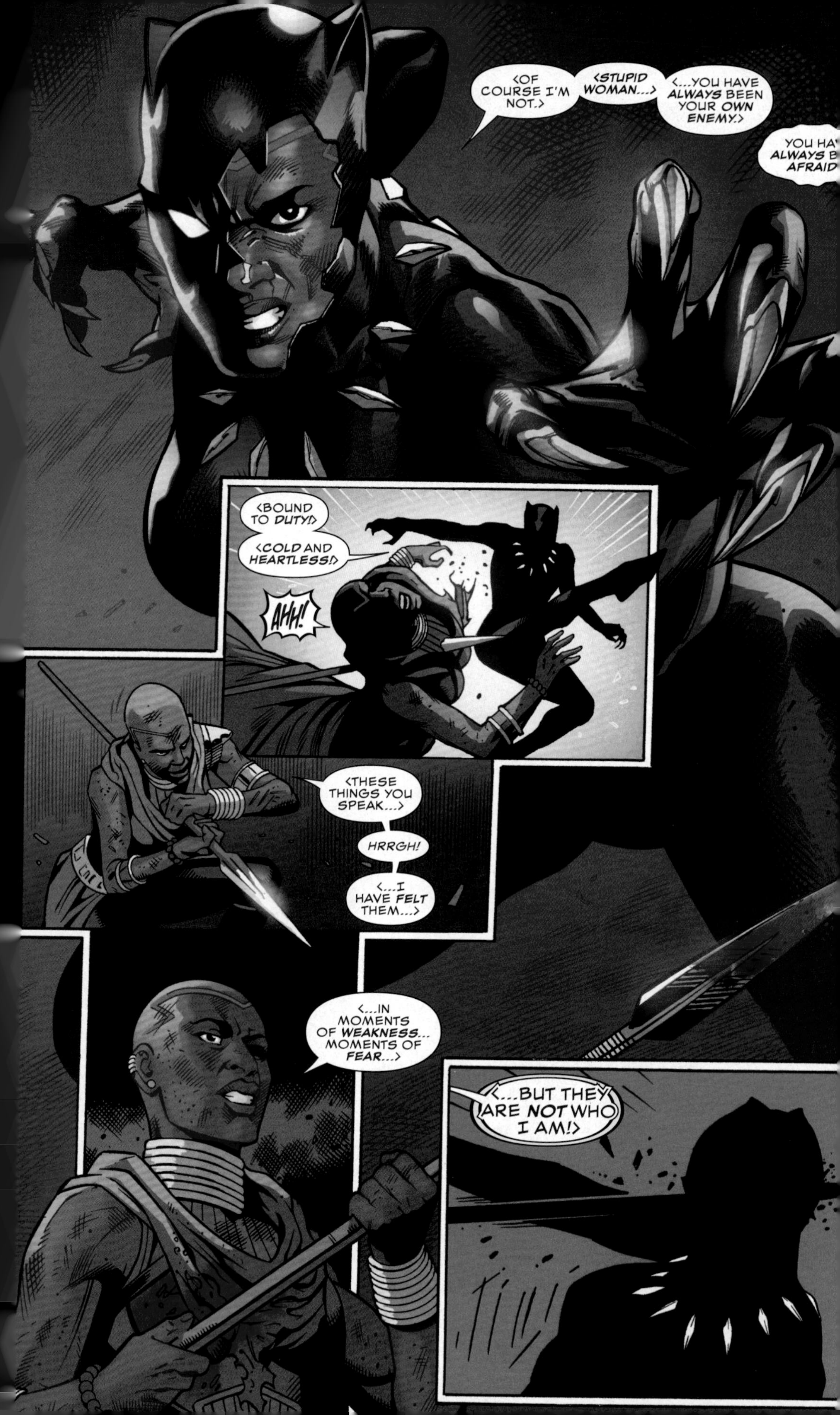
<OF COURSE I'M NOT.>
<STUPID WOMAN...>
<...YOU HAVE ALWAYS BEEN YOUR OWN ENEMY.>
YOU HA ALWAYS B AFRAID
<BOUND TO DUTY!>
<COLD AND HEARTLESS!>
AHH!
<THESE THINGS YOU SPEAK...>
HRRGH!
<...I HAVE FELT THEM...>
<...IN MOMENTS OF WEAKNESS... MOMENTS OF FEAR...>
<...BUT THEY ARE NOT WHO I AM!>

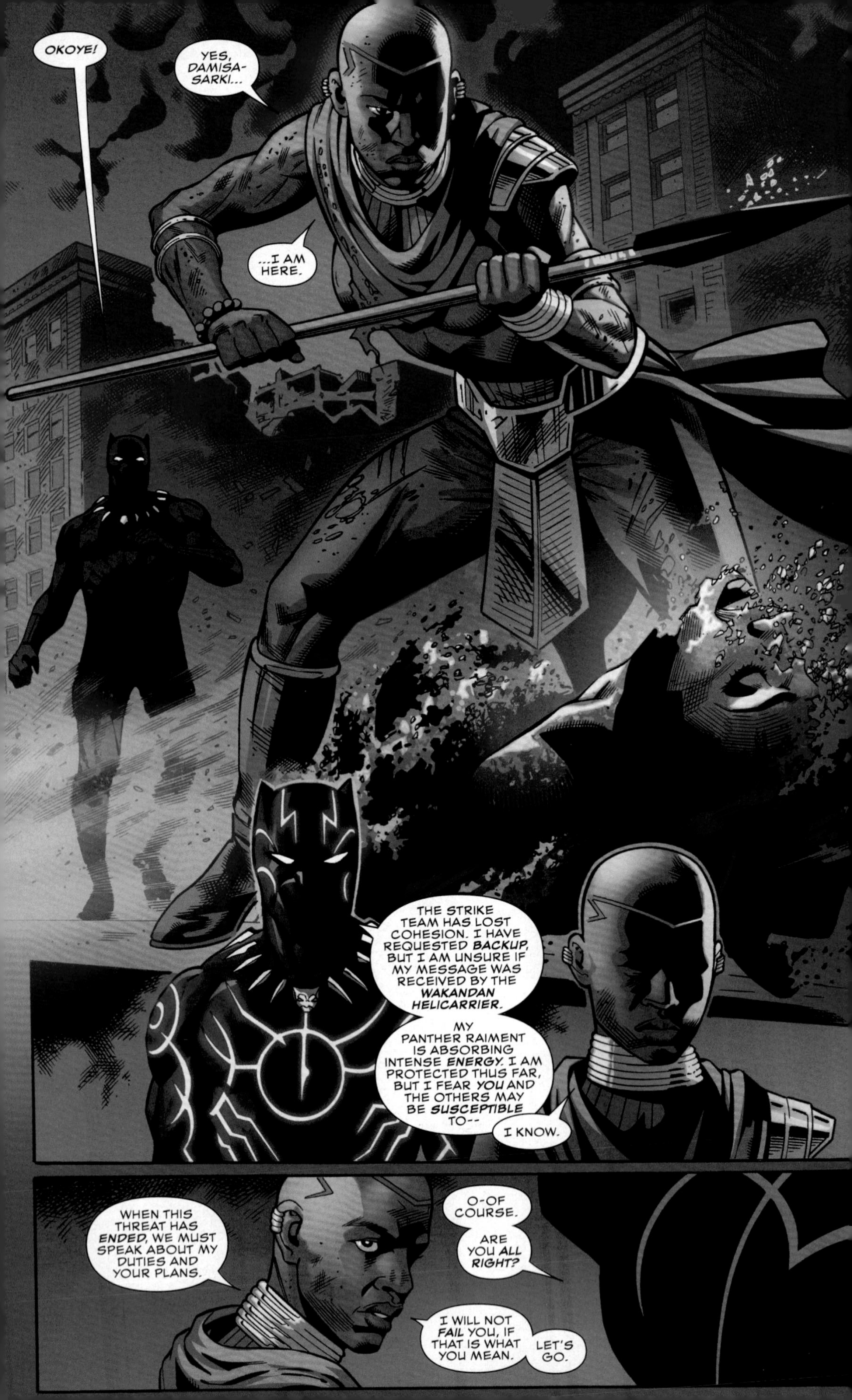
OKOYE!
YES, DAMISA-SARKI...
...I AM HERE.
THE STRIKE TEAM HAS LOST COHESION. I HAVE REQUESTED BACKUP, BUT I AM UNSURE IF MY MESSAGE WAS RECEIVED BY THE WAKANDAN HELICARRIER.
MY PANTHER RAIMENT IS ABSORBING INTENSE ENERGY. I AM PROTECTED THUS FAR, BUT I FEAR YOU AND THE OTHERS MAY BE SUSCEPTIBLE TO--
I KNOW.
WHEN THIS THREAT HAS ENDED, WE MUST SPEAK ABOUT MY DUTIES AND YOUR PLANS.
O-OF COURSE.
ARE YOU ALL RIGHT?
I WILL NOT FAIL YOU, IF THAT IS WHAT YOU MEAN.
LET'S GO.

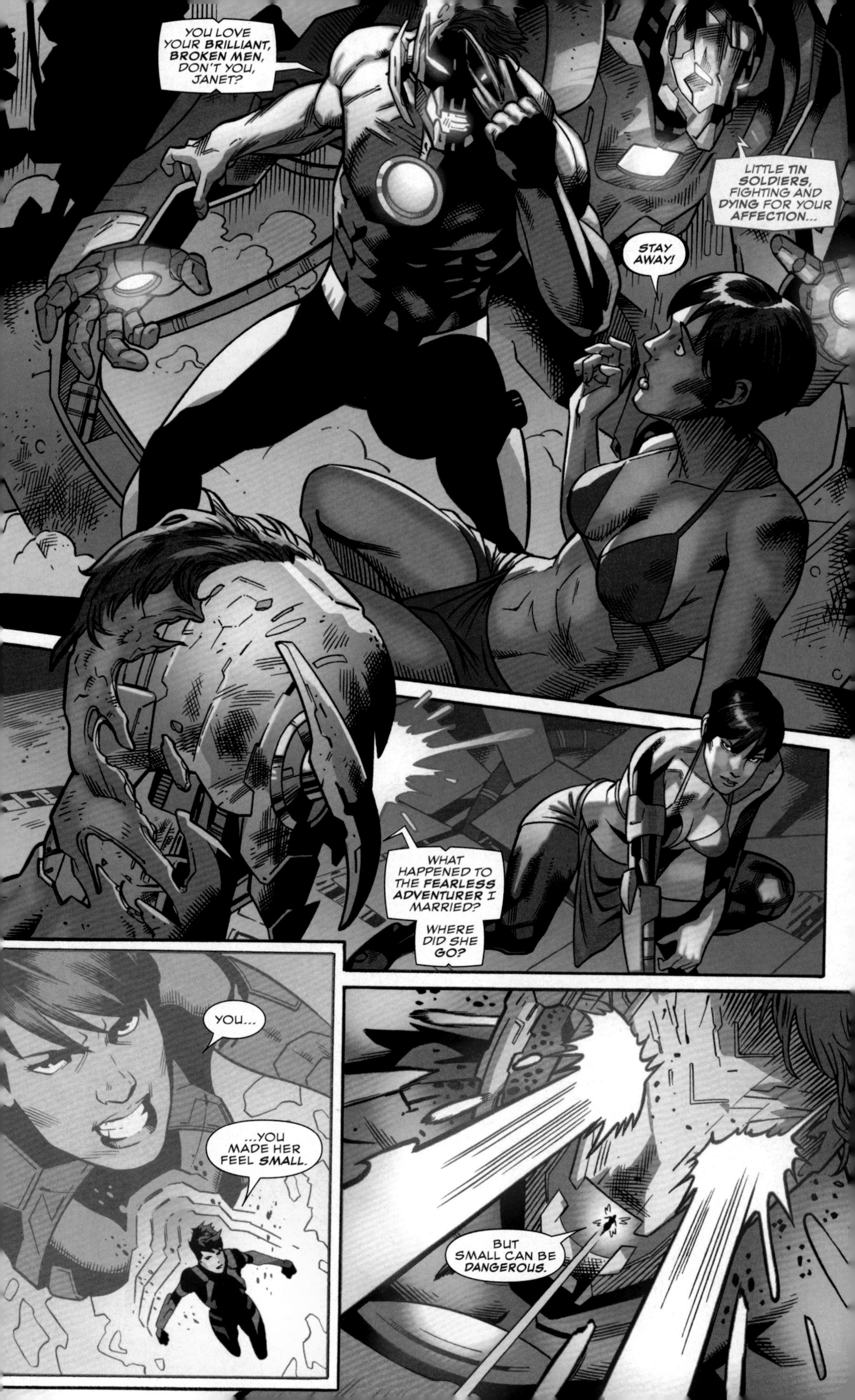
YOU LOVE YOUR BRILLIANT, BROKEN MEN, DON'T YOU, JANET?
LITTLE TIN SOLDIERS, FIGHTING AND DYING FOR YOUR AFFECTION...
STAY AWAY!
WHAT HAPPENED TO THE FEARLESS ADVENTURER I MARRIED?
WHERE DID SHE GO?
YOU...
...YOU MADE HER FEEL SMALL.
BUT SMALL CAN BE DANGEROUS.

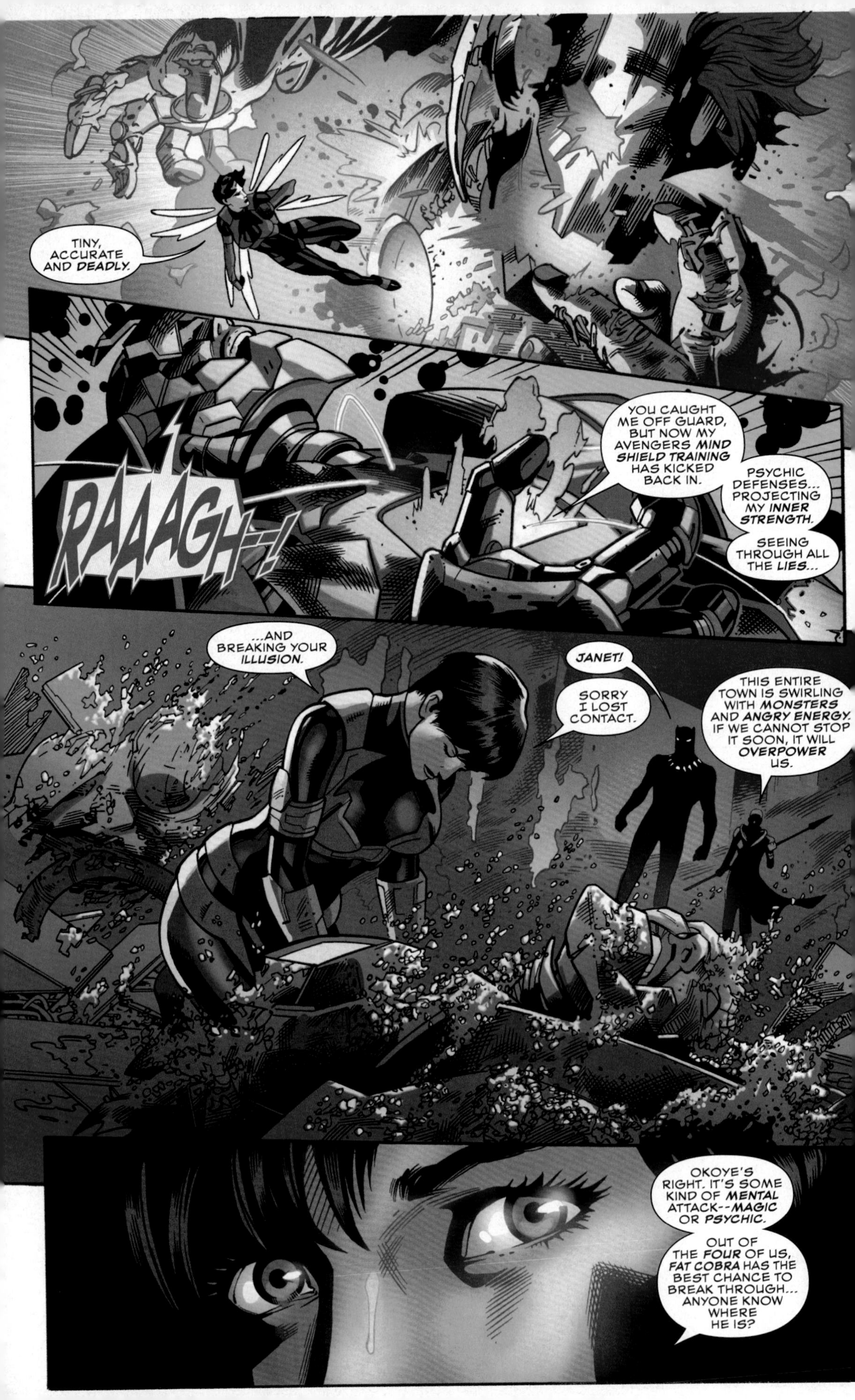
TINY, ACCURATE AND DEADLY.
RAAAGH--!
YOU CAUGHT ME OFF GUARD, BUT NOW MY AVENGERS MIND SHIELD TRAINING HAS KICKED BACK IN.
PSYCHIC DEFENSES... PROJECTING MY INNER STRENGTH.
SEEING THROUGH ALL THE LIES...
...AND BREAKING YOUR ILLUSION.
JANET!
SORRY I LOST CONTACT.
THIS ENTIRE TOWN IS SWIRLING WITH MONSTERS AND ANGRY ENERGY. IF WE CANNOT STOP IT SOON, IT WILL OVERPOWER US.
OKOYE'S RIGHT. IT'S SOME KIND OF MENTAL ATTACK--MAGIC OR PSYCHIC.
OUT OF THE FOUR OF US, FAT COBRA HAS THE BEST CHANCE TO BREAK THROUGH... ANYONE KNOW WHERE HE IS?

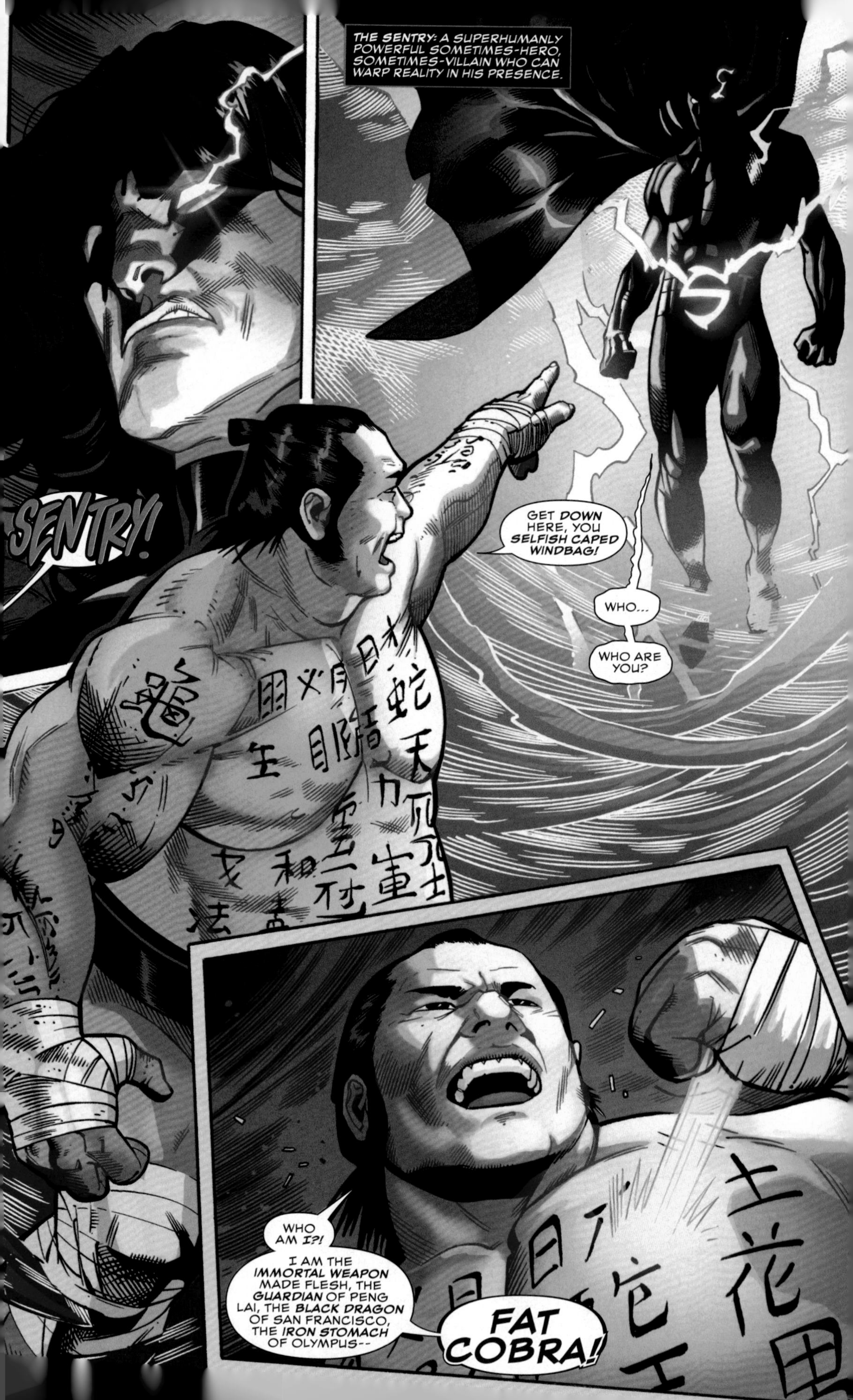
THE SENTRY: A SUPERHUMANLY POWERFUL SOMETIMES-HERO, SOMETIMES-VILLAIN WHO CAN WARP REALITY IN HIS PRESENCE.
SENTRY!
GET DOWN HERE, YOU SELFISH CAPED WINDBAG!
WHO...
WHO ARE YOU?
WHO AM I?!
I AM THE IMMORTAL WEAPON MADE FLESH, THE GUARDIAN OF PENG LAI, THE BLACK DRAGON OF SAN FRANCISCO, THE IRON STOMACH OF OLYMPUS--
FAT COBRA!

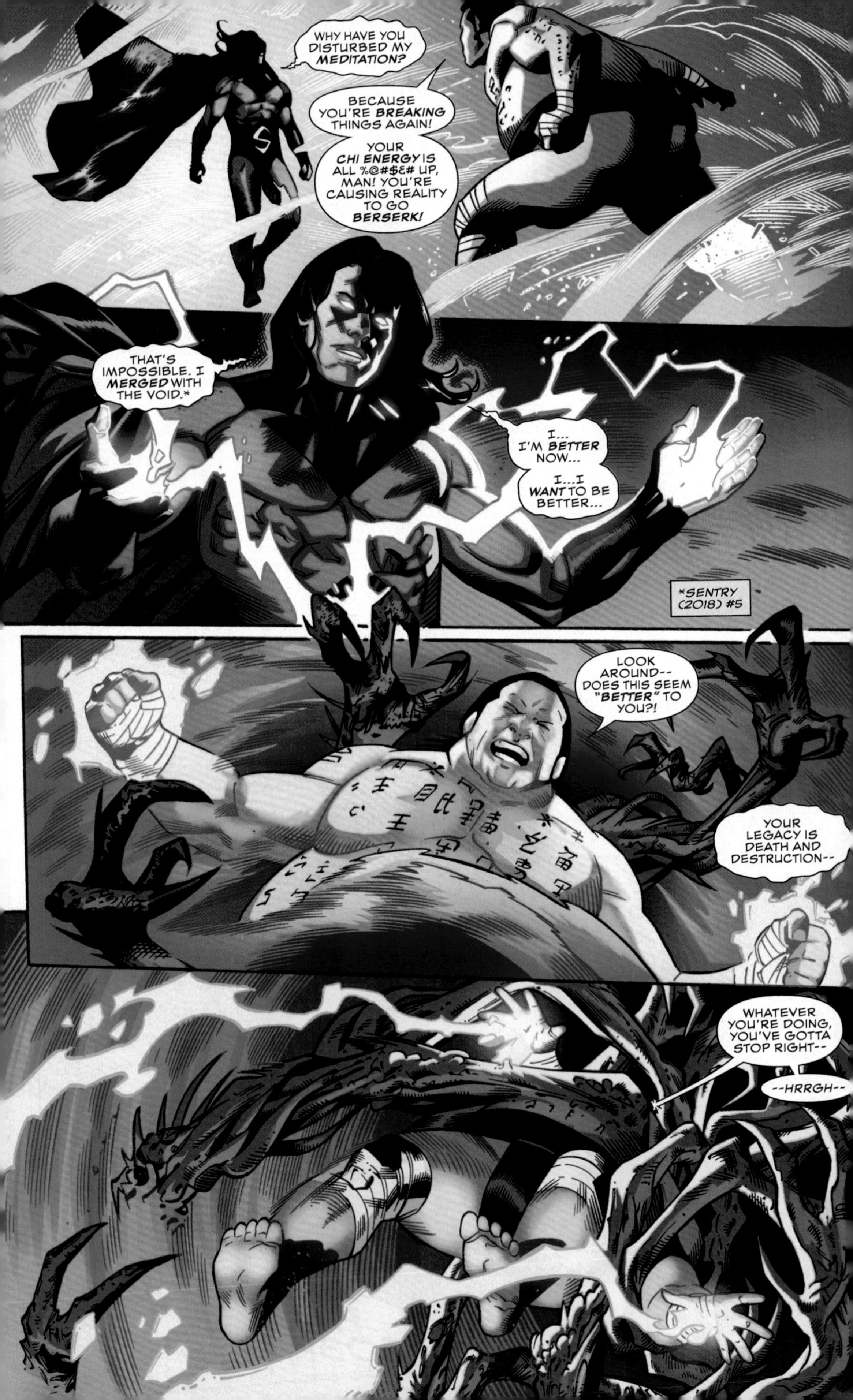
WHY HAVE YOU DISTURBED MY MEDITATION?
BECAUSE YOU'RE BREAKING THINGS AGAIN!
YOUR CHI ENERGY IS ALL %@#$&# UP, MAN! YOU'RE CAUSING REALITY TO GO BERSERK!
THAT'S IMPOSSIBLE. I MERGED WITH THE VOID.*
I... I'M BETTER NOW...
I...I WANT TO BE BETTER...
*SENTRY (2018) #5
LOOK AROUND--DOES THIS SEEM "BETTER" TO YOU?!
YOUR LEGACY IS DEATH AND DESTRUCTION--
WHATEVER YOU'RE DOING, YOU'VE GOTTA STOP RIGHT--
--HRRGH--

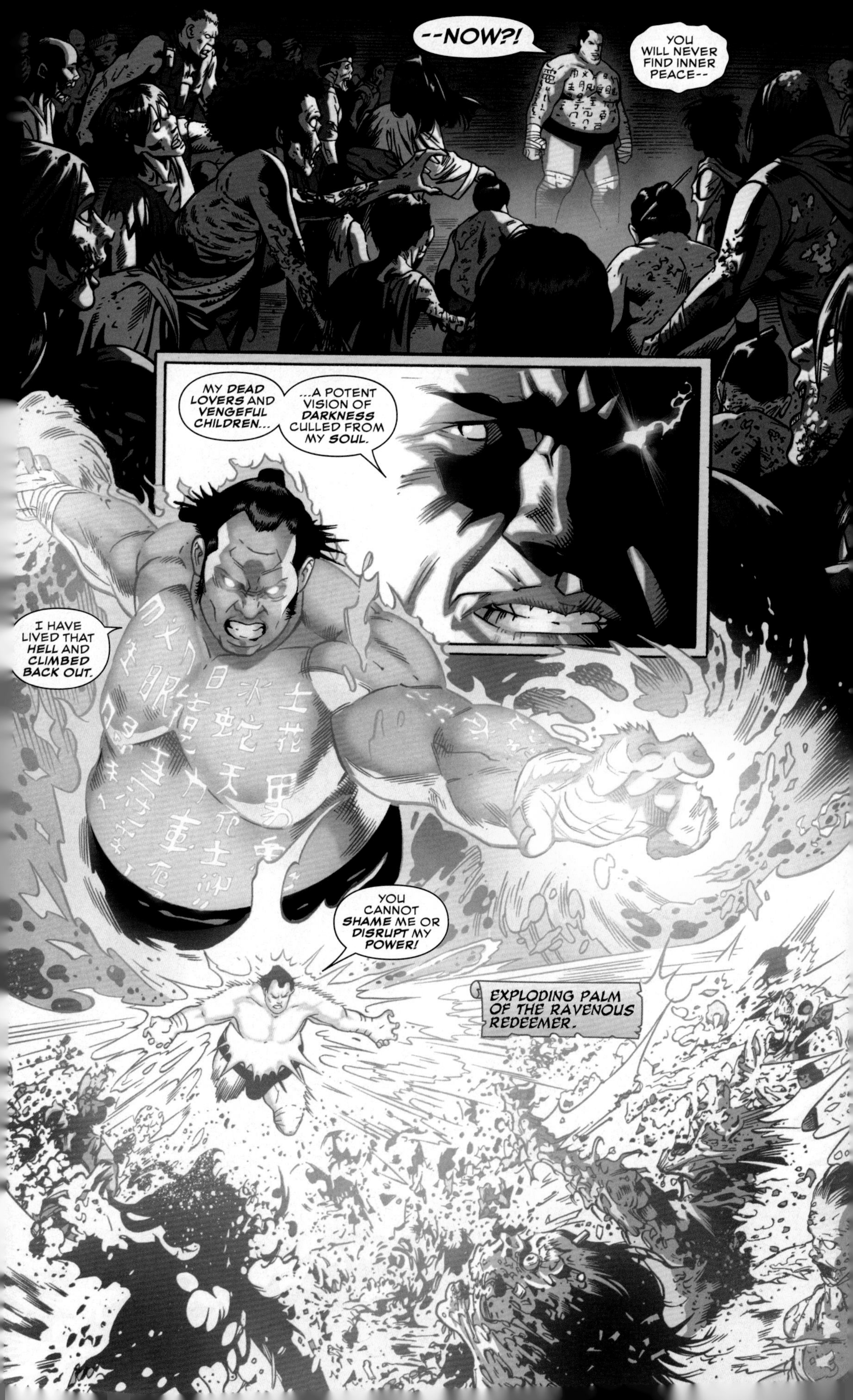
--NOW?!
YOU WILL NEVER FIND INNER PEACE--
MY DEAD LOVERS AND VENGEFUL CHILDREN...
...A POTENT VISION OF DARKNESS CULLED FROM MY SOUL.
I HAVE LIVED THAT HELL AND CLIMBED BACK OUT.
YOU CANNOT SHAME ME OR DISRUPT MY POWER!
EXPLODING PALM OF THE RAVENOUS REDEEMER.

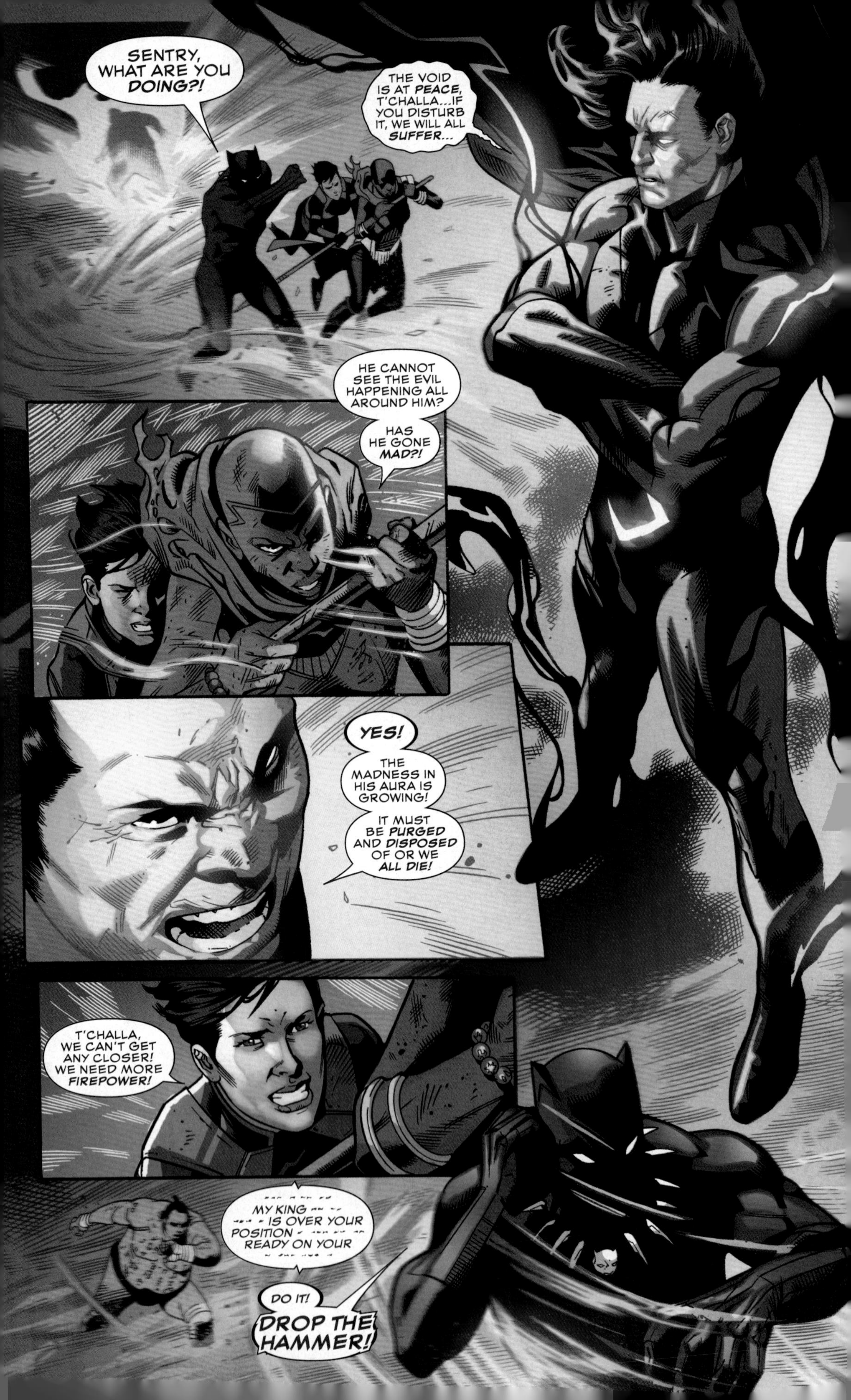
SENTRY, WHAT ARE YOU DOING?!
THE VOID IS AT PEACE, T'CHALLA...IF YOU DISTURB IT, WE WILL ALL SUFFER...
HE CANNOT SEE THE EVIL HAPPENING ALL AROUND HIM?
HAS HE GONE MAD?!
YES!
THE MADNESS IN HIS AURA IS GROWING!
IT MUST BE PURGED AND DISPOSED OF OR WE ALL DIE!
T'CHALLA, WE CAN'T GET ANY CLOSER! WE NEED MORE FIREPOWER!
MY KING
IS OVER YOUR
POSITION
READY ON YOUR
DO IT!
DROP THE HAMMER!

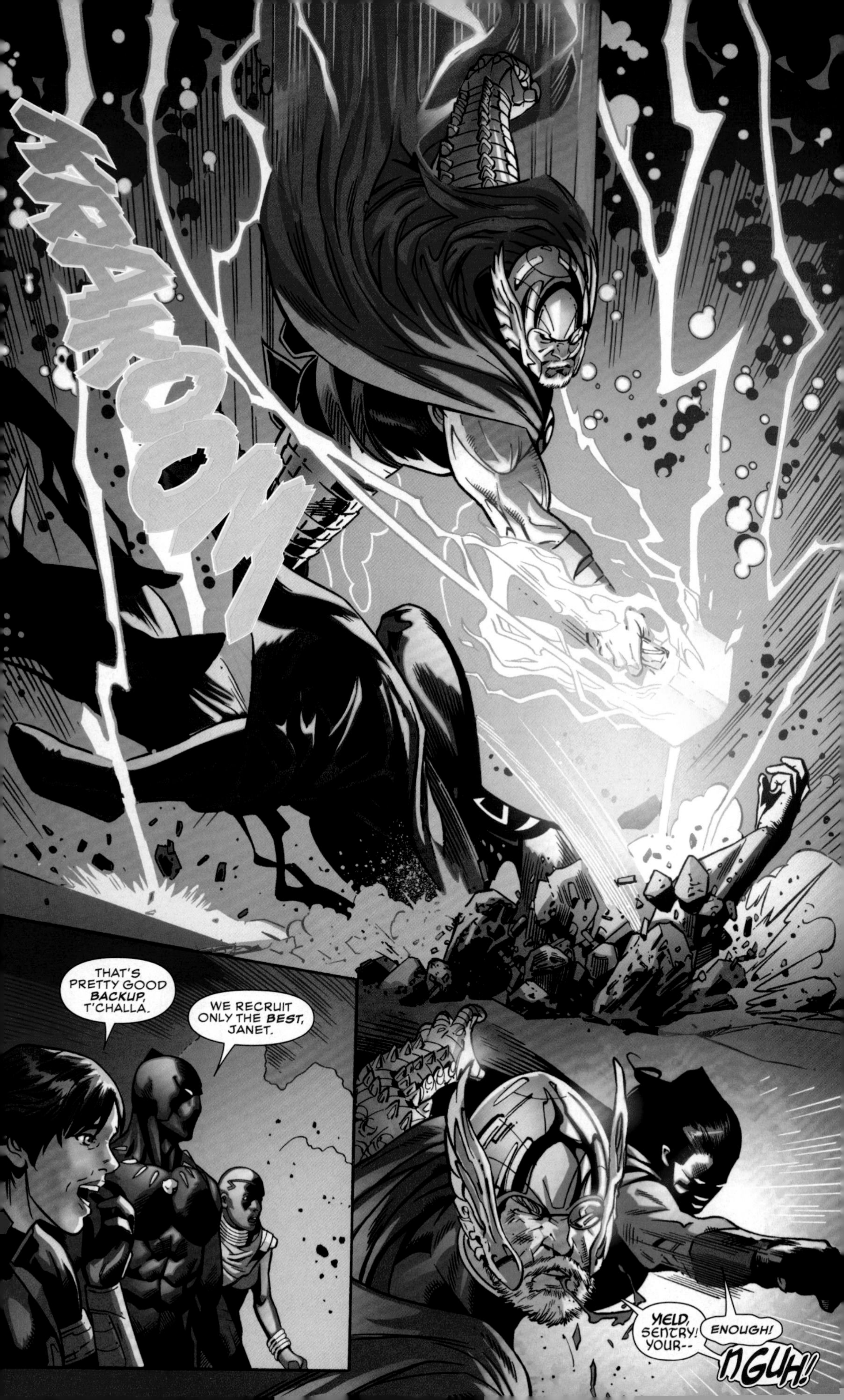
KRRAKOOM
THAT'S PRETTY GOOD BACKUP, T'CHALLA.
WE RECRUIT ONLY THE BEST, JANET.
YIELD, SENTRY! YOUR--
ENOUGH!
NGUH!

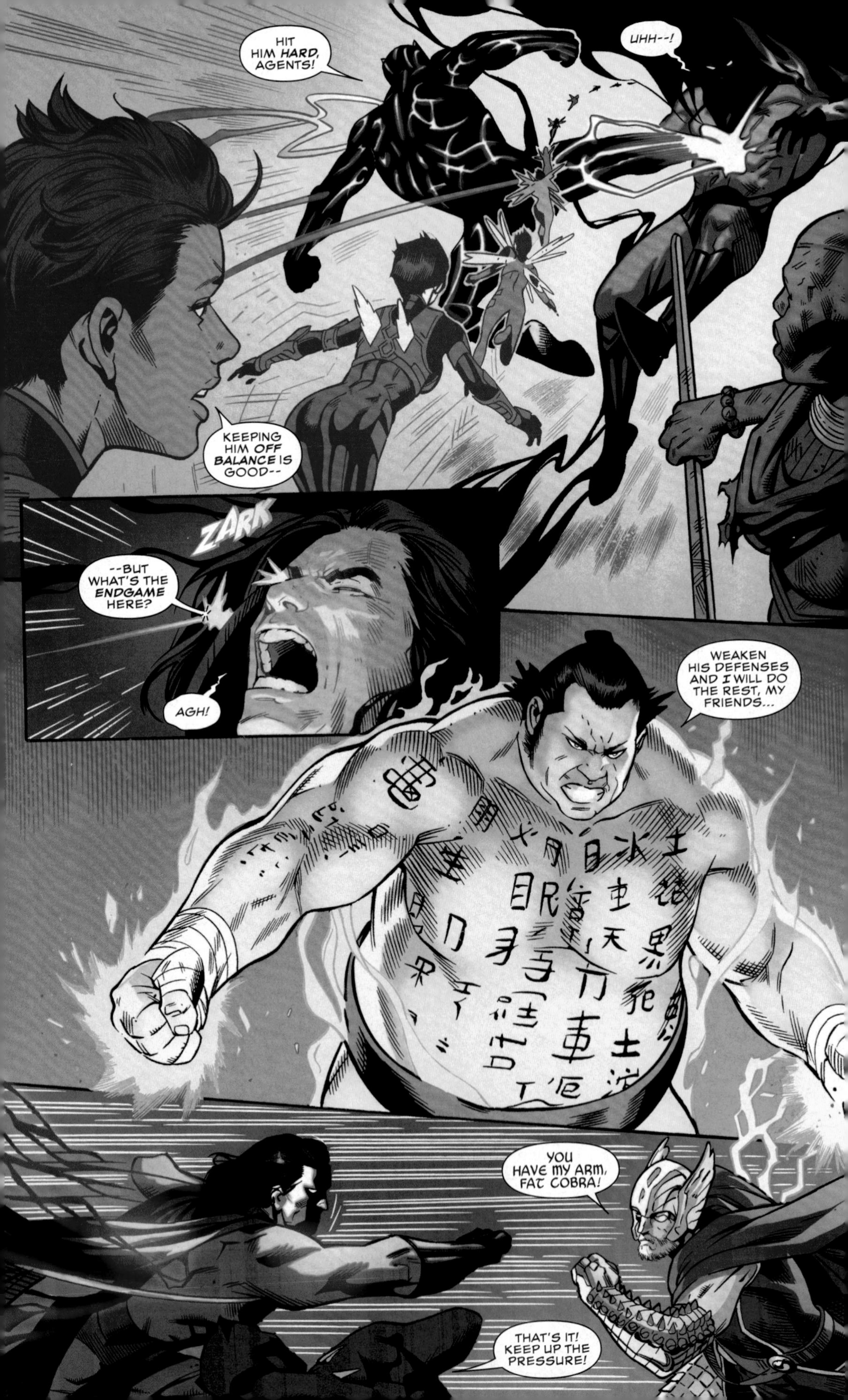
HIT HIM HARD, AGENTS!
UHH--!
KEEPING HIM OFF BALANCE IS GOOD--
ZARK
--BUT WHAT'S THE ENDGAME HERE?
AGH!
WEAKEN HIS DEFENSES AND I WILL DO THE REST, MY FRIENDS...
YOU HAVE MY ARM, FAT COBRA!
THAT'S IT! KEEP UP THE PRESSURE!

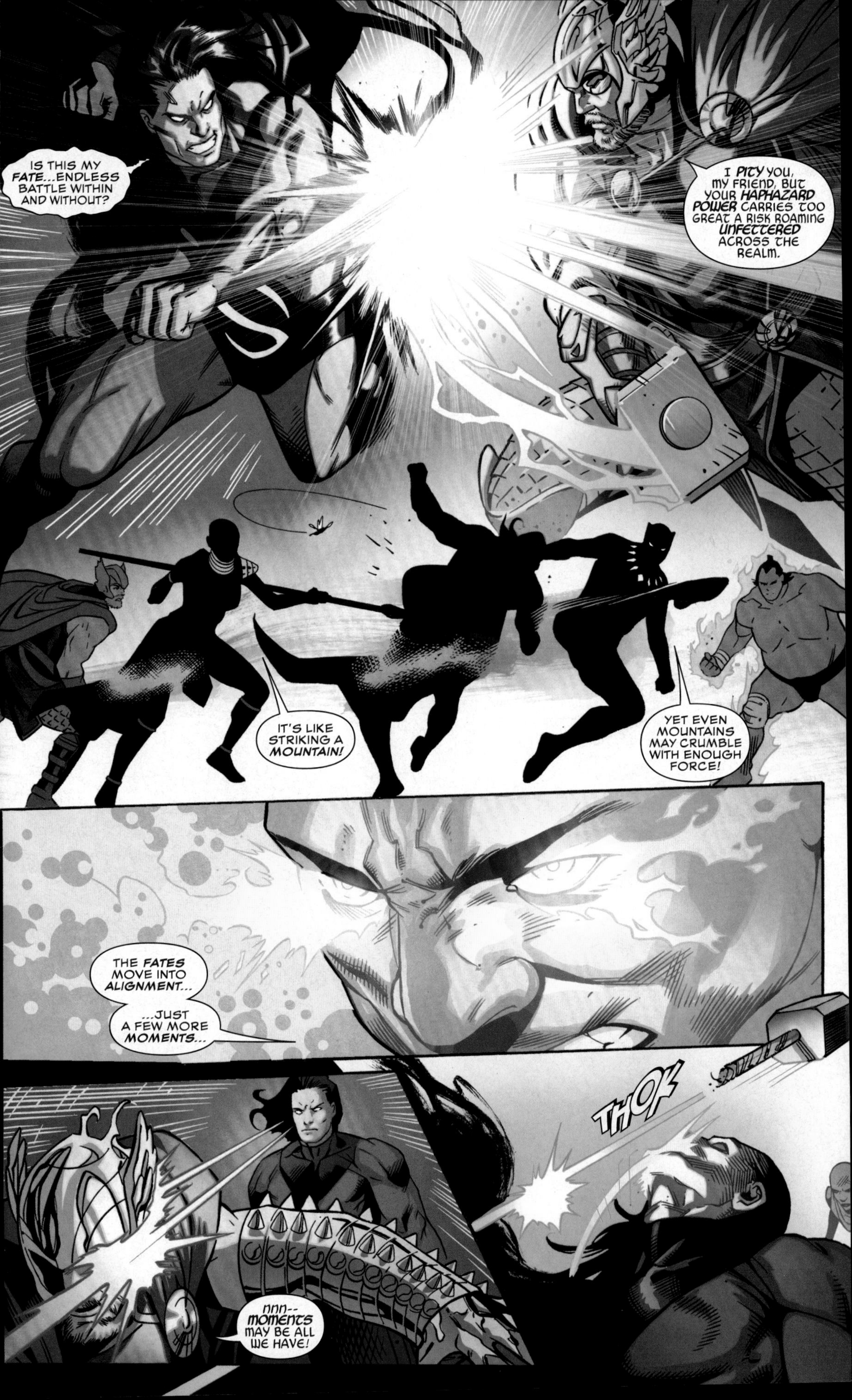
IS THIS MY FATE...ENDLESS BATTLE WITHIN AND WITHOUT?
I PITY YOU, MY FRIEND, BUT YOUR HAPHAZARD POWER CARRIES TOO GREAT A RISK ROAMING UNFETTERED ACROSS THE REALM.
IT'S LIKE STRIKING A MOUNTAIN!
YET EVEN MOUNTAINS MAY CRUMBLE WITH ENOUGH FORCE!
THE FATES MOVE INTO ALIGNMENT...
...JUST A FEW MORE MOMENTS...
THOK
NNN-- MOMENTS MAY BE ALL WE HAVE!

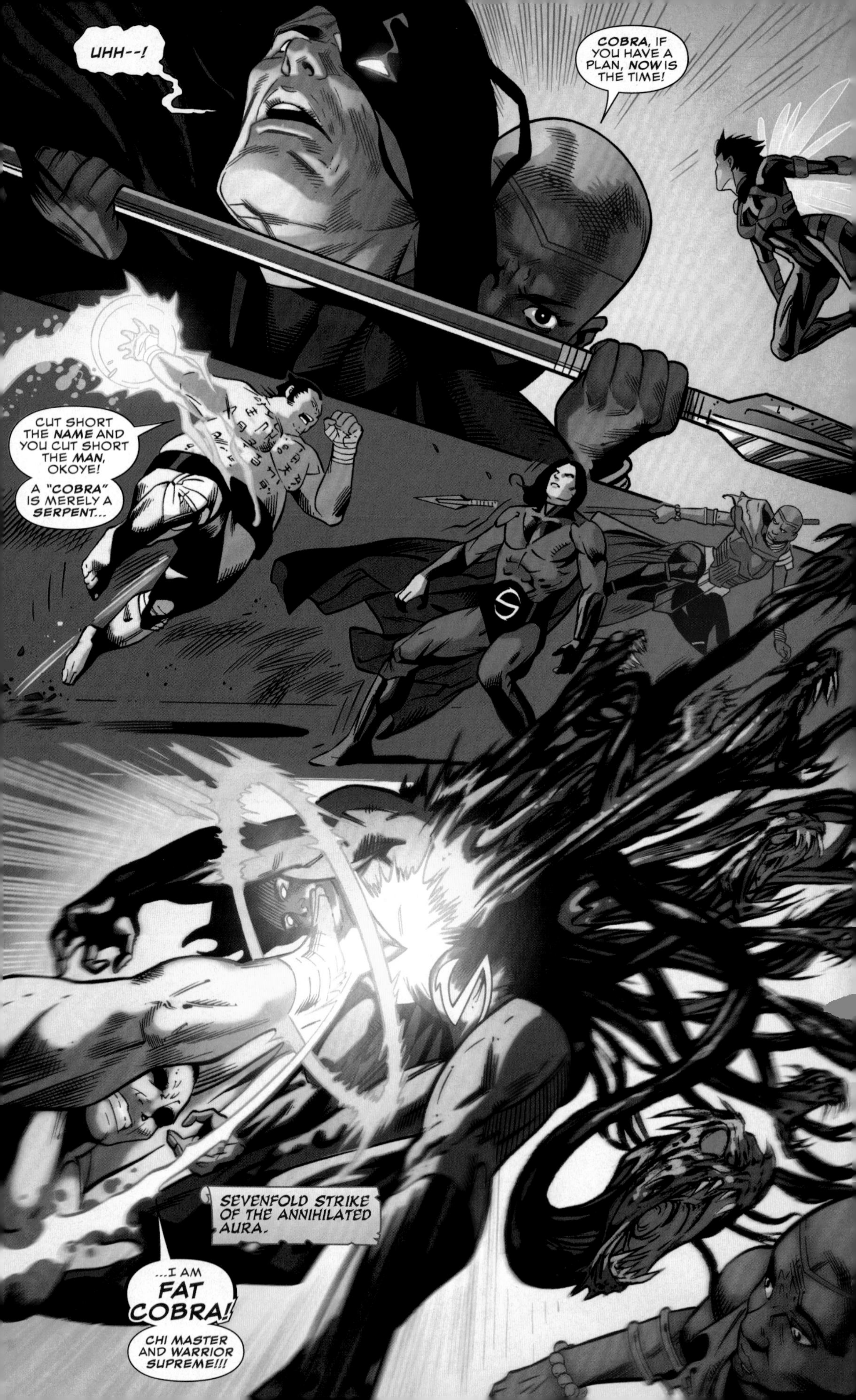
UHH--!
COBRA, IF YOU HAVE A PLAN, NOW IS THE TIME!
CUT SHORT THE NAME AND YOU CUT SHORT THE MAN, OKOYE!
A "COBRA" IS MERELY A SERPENT...
SEVENFOLD STRIKE OF THE ANNIHILATED AURA.
...I AM FAT COBRA!
CHI MASTER AND WARRIOR SUPREME!!!

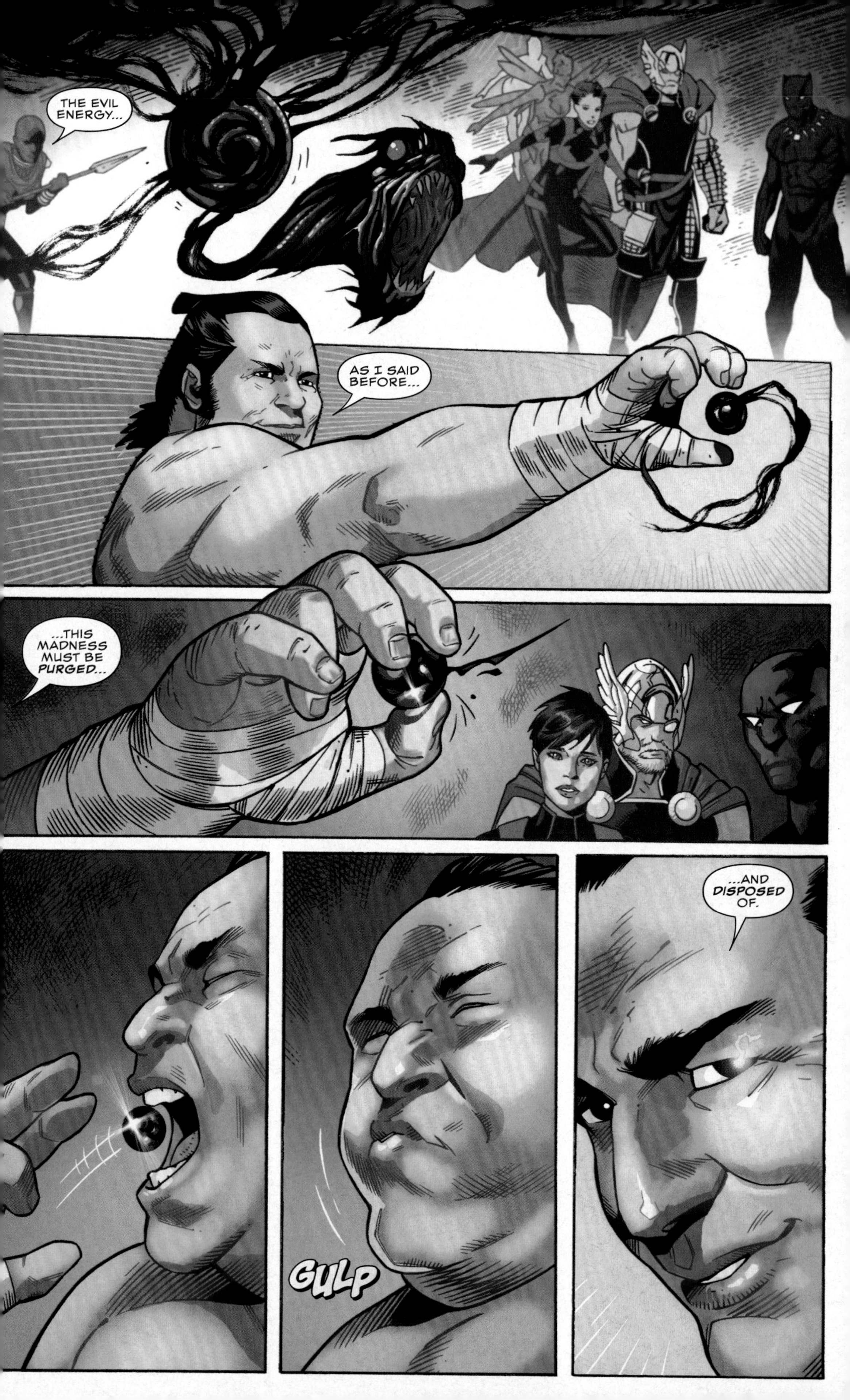
THE EVIL ENERGY...
AS I SAID BEFORE...
...THIS MADNESS MUST BE PURGED...
GULP
...AND DISPOSED OF.

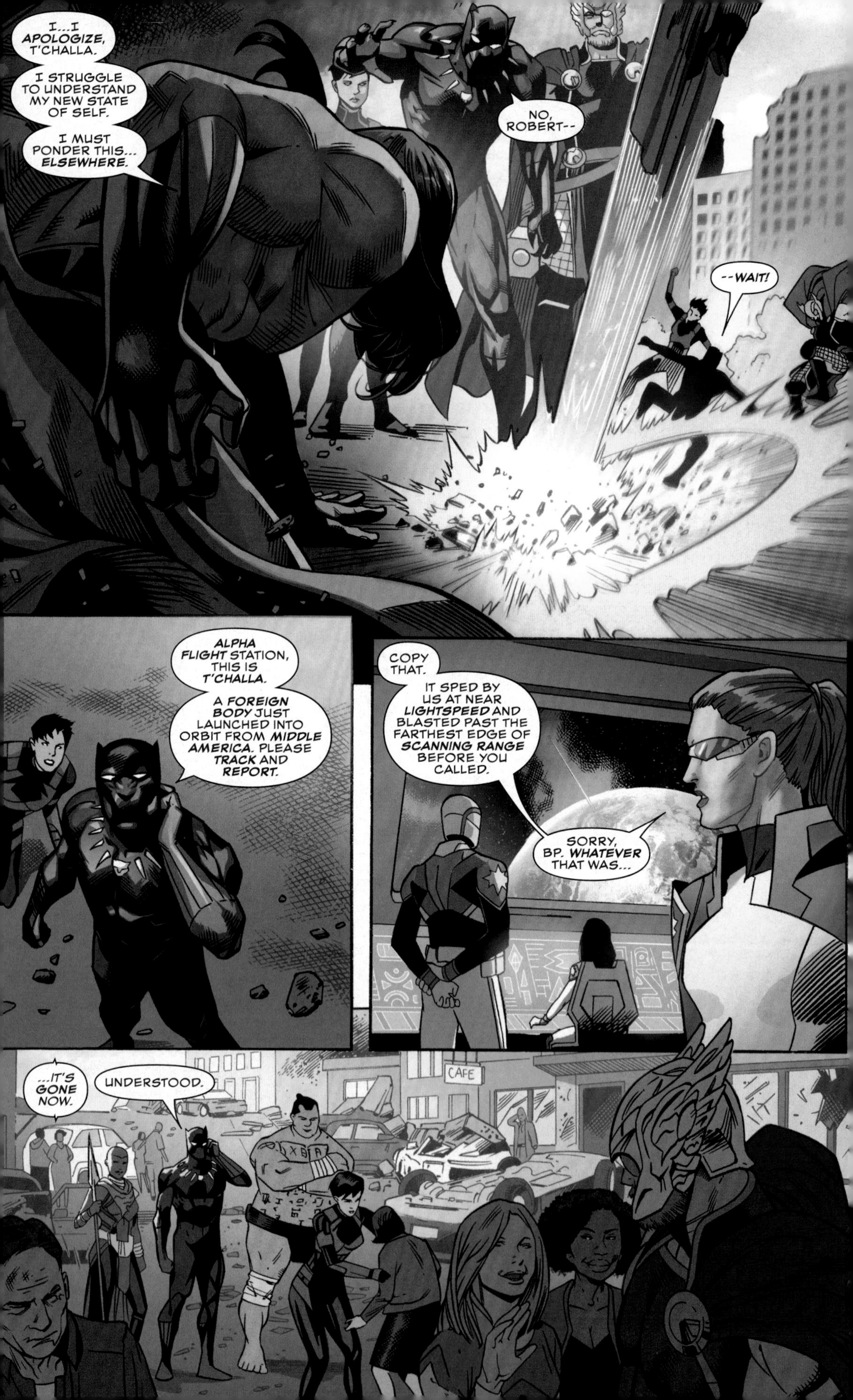
I...I APOLOGIZE, T'CHALLA.
I STRUGGLE TO UNDERSTAND MY NEW STATE OF SELF.
I MUST PONDER THIS... ELSEWHERE.
NO, ROBERT--
--WAIT!
ALPHA FLIGHT STATION, THIS IS T'CHALLA.
A FOREIGN BODY JUST LAUNCHED INTO ORBIT FROM MIDDLE AMERICA. PLEASE TRACK AND REPORT.
COPY THAT.
IT SPED BY US AT NEAR LIGHTSPEED AND BLASTED PAST THE FARTHEST EDGE OF SCANNING RANGE BEFORE YOU CALLED.
SORRY, BP. WHATEVER THAT WAS...
...IT'S GONE NOW.
UNDERSTOOD.
CAFE

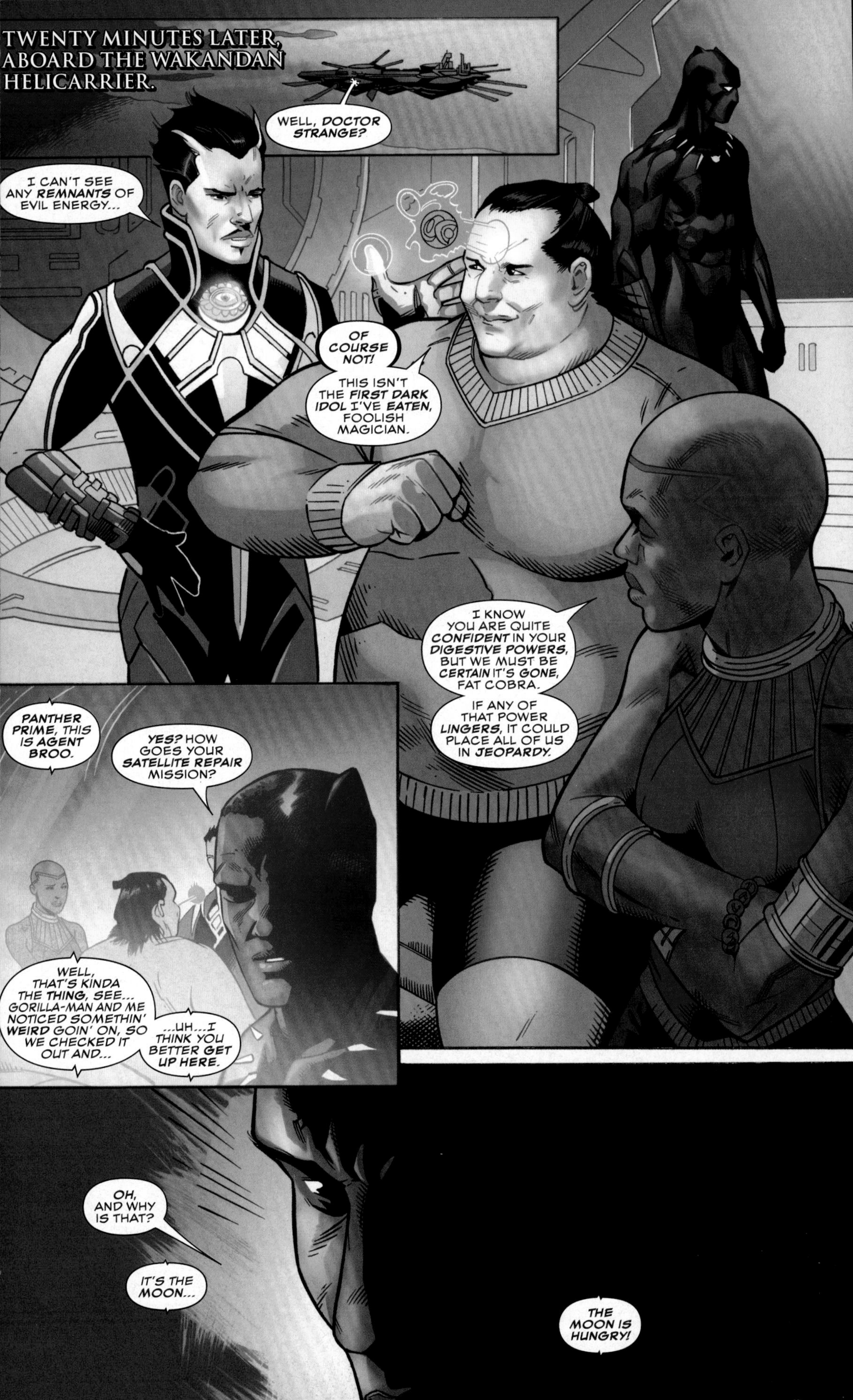

TWENTY MINUTES LATER, ABOARD THE WAKANDAN HELICARRIER.
WELL, DOCTOR STRANGE?
I CAN'T SEE ANY REMNANTS OF EVIL ENERGY...
OF COURSE NOT!
THIS ISN'T THE FIRST DARK IDOL I'VE EATEN, FOOLISH MAGICIAN.
I KNOW YOU ARE QUITE CONFIDENT IN YOUR DIGESTIVE POWERS, BUT WE MUST BE CERTAIN IT'S GONE, FAT COBRA.
IF ANY OF THAT POWER LINGERS, IT COULD PLACE ALL OF US IN JEOPARDY.
PANTHER PRIME, THIS IS AGENT BROO.
YES? HOW GOES YOUR SATELLITE REPAIR MISSION?
WELL, THAT'S KINDA THE THING, SEE... GORILLA-MAN AND ME NOTICED SOMETHIN' WEIRD GOIN' ON, SO WE CHECKED IT OUT AND...
...UH...I THINK YOU BETTER GET UP HERE.
OH, AND WHY IS THAT?
IT'S THE MOON...
THE MOON IS HUNGRY!

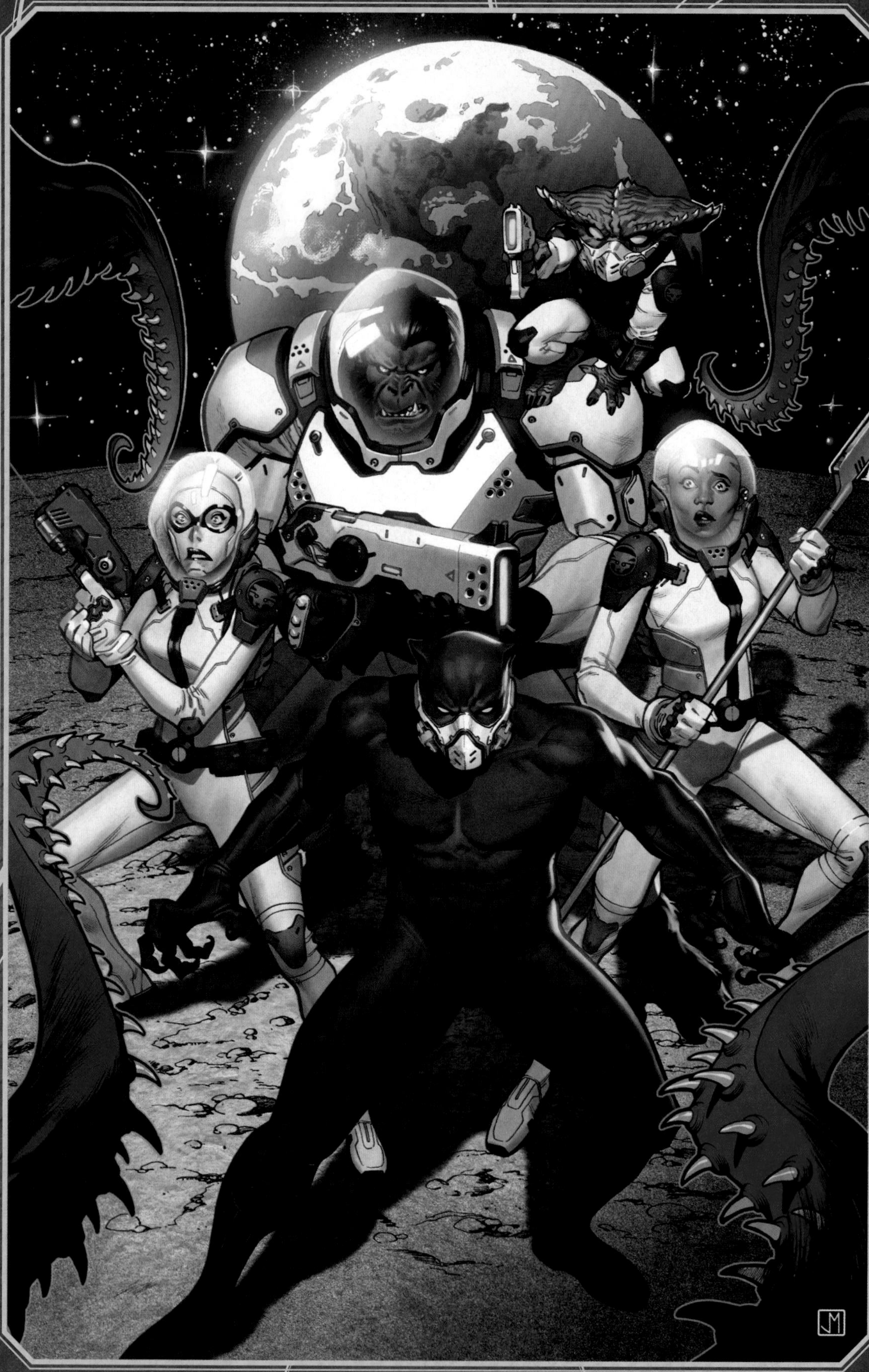

3

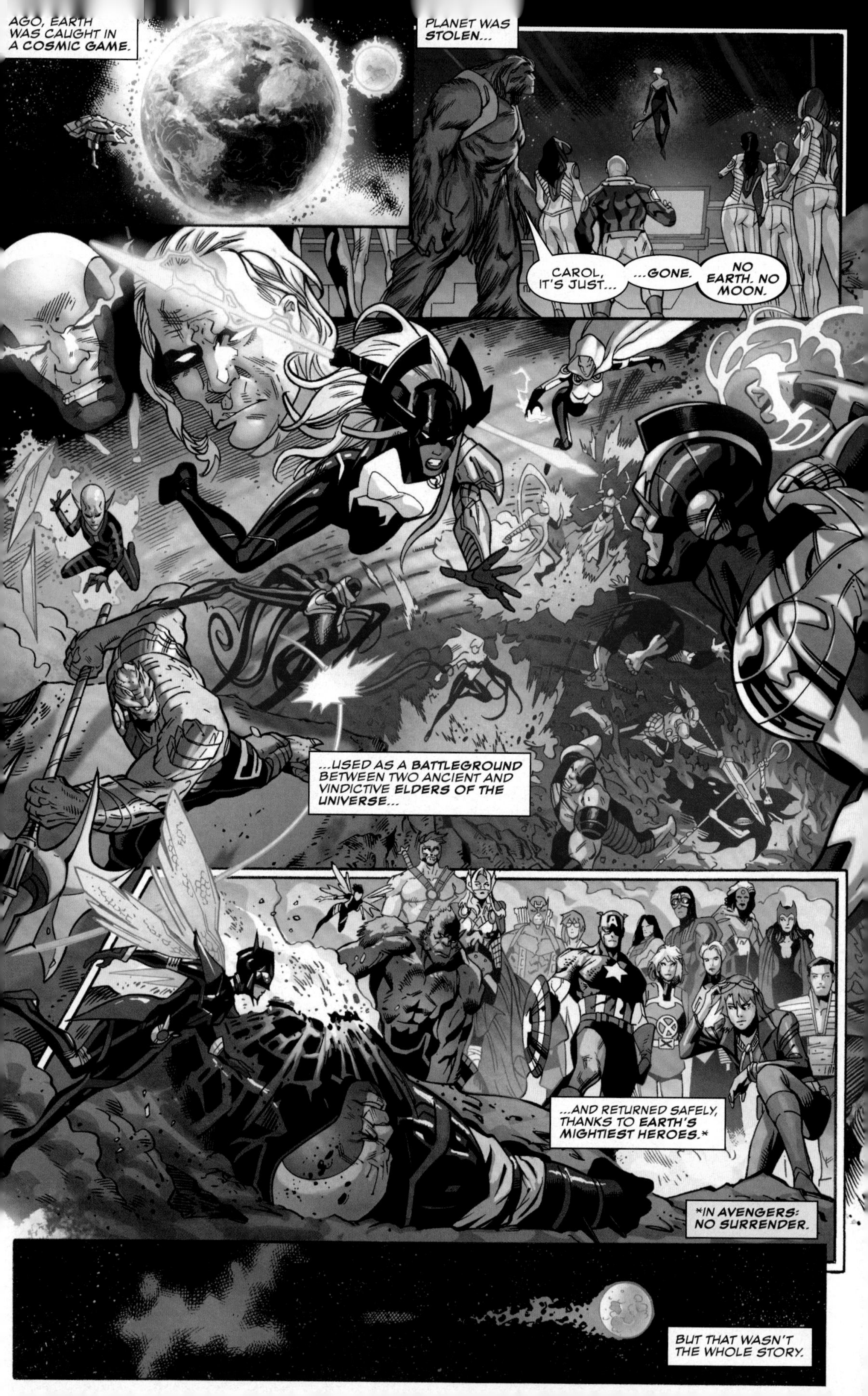

AGO, EARTH WAS CAUGHT IN A COSMIC GAME.
PLANET WAS STOLEN...
CAROL, IT'S JUST...
...GONE.
NO EARTH. NO MOON.
...USED AS A BATTLEGROUND BETWEEN TWO ANCIENT AND VINDICTIVE ELDERS OF THE UNIVERSE...
...AND RETURNED SAFELY, THANKS TO EARTH'S MIGHTIEST HEROES.*
*IN AVENGERS: NO SURRENDER.
BUT THAT WASN'T THE WHOLE STORY.

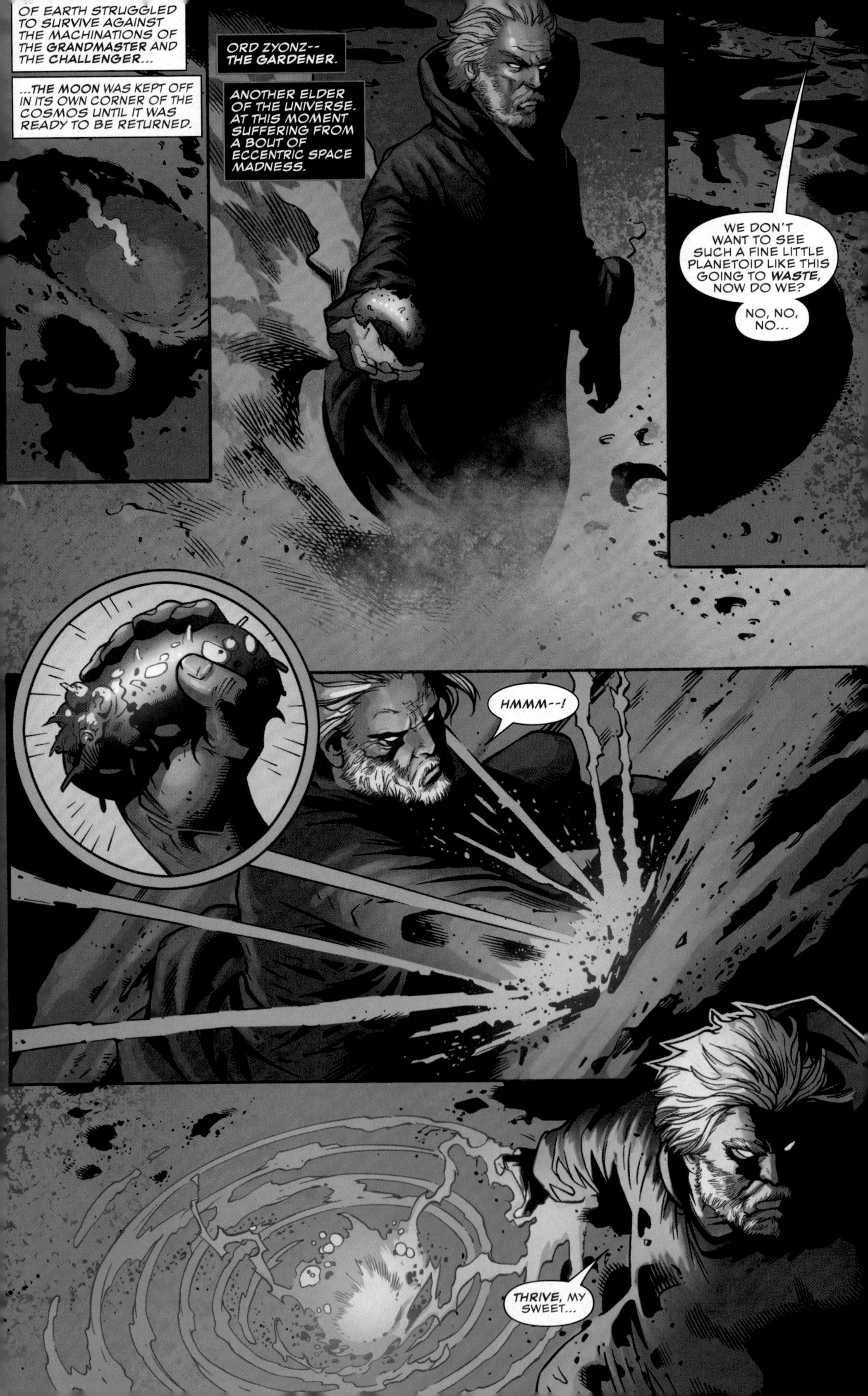
OF EARTH STRUGGLED TO SURVIVE AGAINST THE MACHINATIONS OF THE GRANDMASTER AND THE CHALLENGER...
...THE MOON WAS KEPT OFF IN ITS OWN CORNER OF THE COSMOS UNTIL IT WAS READY TO BE RETURNED.
ORD ZYONZ-- THE GARDENER.
ANOTHER ELDER OF THE UNIVERSE. AT THIS MOMENT SUFFERING FROM A BOUT OF ECCENTRIC SPACE MADNESS.
WE DON'T WANT TO SEE SUCH A FINE LITTLE PLANETOID LIKE THIS GOING TO WASTE, NOW DO WE?
NO, NO, NO...
HMMM--!
THRIVE, MY SWEET...

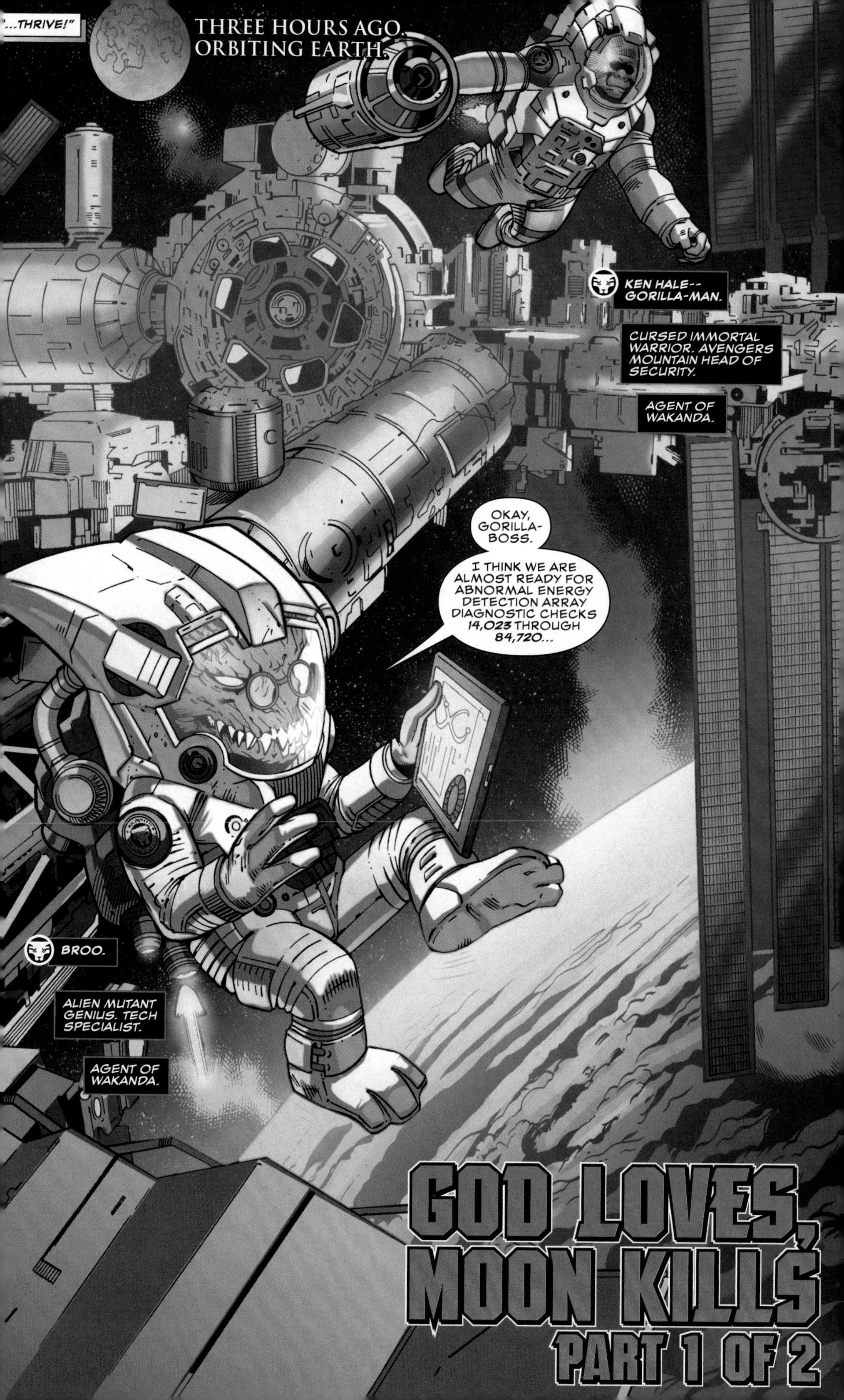
"...THRIVE!"
THREE HOURS AGO. ORBITING EARTH.
KEN HALE-- GORILLA-MAN.
CURSED IMMORTAL WARRIOR. AVENGERS MOUNTAIN HEAD OF SECURITY.
AGENT OF WAKANDA.
OKAY, GORILLA-BOSS.
I THINK WE ARE ALMOST READY FOR ABNORMAL ENERGY DETECTION ARRAY DIAGNOSTIC CHECKS 14,023 THROUGH 84,720...
BROO.
ALIEN MUTANT GENIUS. TECH SPECIALIST.
AGENT OF WAKANDA.
GOD LOVES, MOON KILLS
PART 1 OF 2

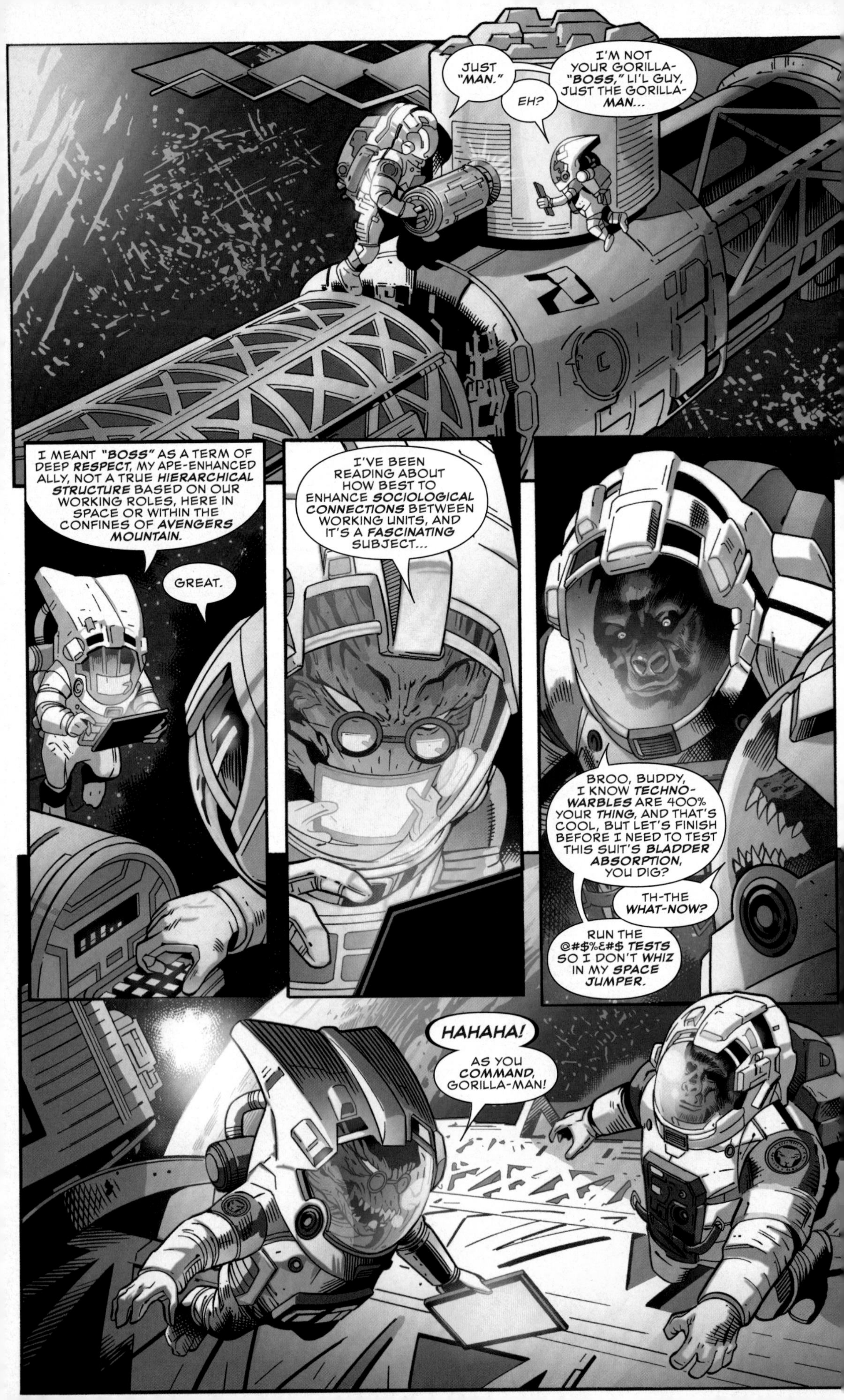
I'M NOT YOUR GORILLA-"BOSS," LI'L GUY, JUST THE GORILLA-MAN...
EH?
JUST "MAN."
I MEANT "BOSS" AS A TERM OF DEEP RESPECT, MY APE-ENHANCED ALLY, NOT A TRUE HIERARCHICAL STRUCTURE BASED ON OUR WORKING ROLES, HERE IN SPACE OR WITHIN THE CONFINES OF AVENGERS MOUNTAIN.
GREAT.
I'VE BEEN READING ABOUT HOW BEST TO ENHANCE SOCIOLOGICAL CONNECTIONS BETWEEN WORKING UNITS, AND IT'S A FASCINATING SUBJECT...
BROO, BUDDY, I KNOW TECHNO-WARBLES ARE 400% YOUR THING, AND THAT'S COOL, BUT LET'S FINISH BEFORE I NEED TO TEST THIS SUIT'S BLADDER ABSORPTION, YOU DIG?
TH-THE WHAT-NOW?
RUN THE @#$%&#$ TESTS SO I DON'T WHIZ IN MY SPACE JUMPER.
HAHAHA!
AS YOU COMMAND, GORILLA-MAN!

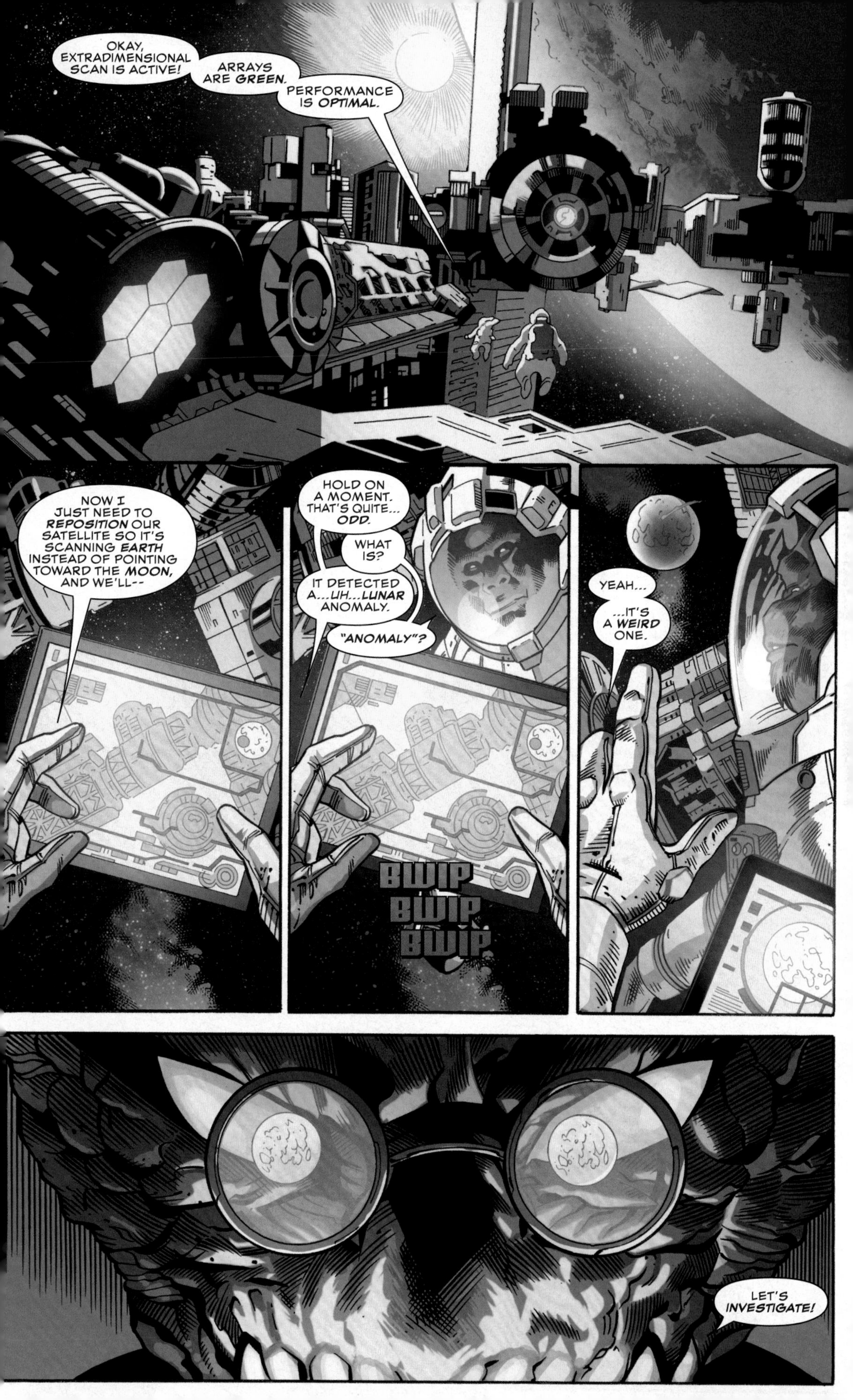
OKAY, EXTRADIMENSIONAL SCAN IS ACTIVE!
ARRAYS ARE GREEN.
PERFORMANCE IS OPTIMAL.
NOW I JUST NEED TO REPOSITION OUR SATELLITE SO IT'S SCANNING EARTH INSTEAD OF POINTING TOWARD THE MOON, AND WE'LL--
HOLD ON A MOMENT. THAT'S QUITE... ODD.
WHAT IS?
IT DETECTED A...UH...LUNAR ANOMALY.
"ANOMALY"?
BWIP
BWIP
BWIP
YEAH...
...IT'S A WEIRD ONE.
LET'S INVESTIGATE!

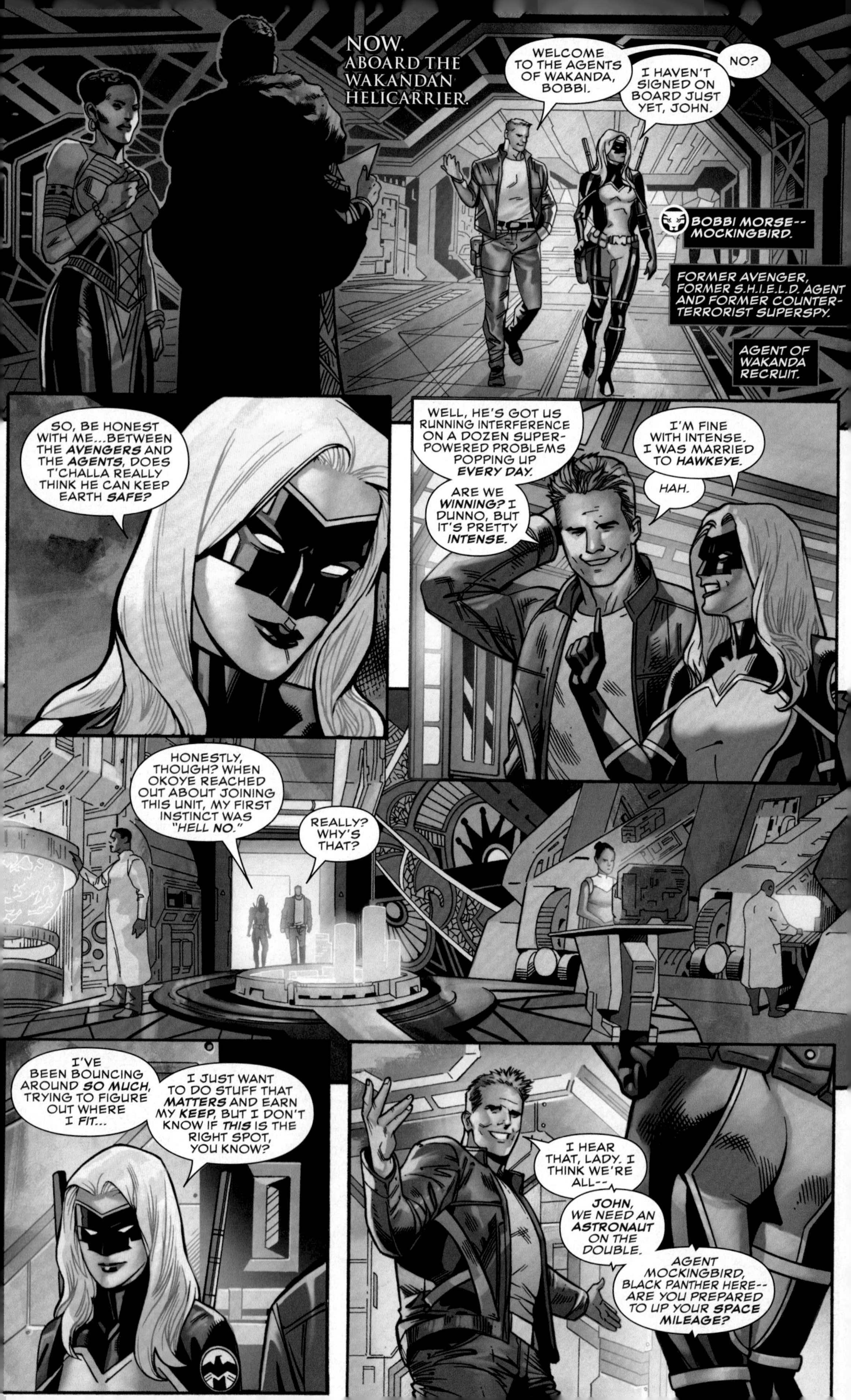

NOW. ABOARD THE WAKANDAN HELICARRIER.
WELCOME TO THE AGENTS OF WAKANDA, BOBBI.
I HAVEN'T SIGNED ON BOARD JUST YET, JOHN.
NO?
BOBBI MORSE--MOCKINGBIRD.
FORMER AVENGER, FORMER S.H.I.E.L.D. AGENT AND FORMER COUNTER-TERRORIST SUPERSPY.
AGENT OF WAKANDA RECRUIT.
SO, BE HONEST WITH ME...BETWEEN THE AVENGERS AND THE AGENTS, DOES T'CHALLA REALLY THINK HE CAN KEEP EARTH SAFE?
WELL, HE'S GOT US RUNNING INTERFERENCE ON A DOZEN SUPER-POWERED PROBLEMS POPPING UP EVERY DAY.
ARE WE WINNING? I DUNNO, BUT IT'S PRETTY INTENSE.
I'M FINE WITH INTENSE. I WAS MARRIED TO HAWKEYE.
HAH.
HONESTLY, THOUGH? WHEN OKOYE REACHED OUT ABOUT JOINING THIS UNIT, MY FIRST INSTINCT WAS "HELL NO."
REALLY? WHY'S THAT?
I'VE BEEN BOUNCING AROUND SO MUCH, TRYING TO FIGURE OUT WHERE I FIT...
I JUST WANT TO DO STUFF THAT MATTERS AND EARN MY KEEP, BUT I DON'T KNOW IF THIS IS THE RIGHT SPOT, YOU KNOW?
I HEAR THAT, LADY. I THINK WE'RE ALL--
JOHN, WE NEED AN ASTRONAUT ON THE DOUBLE.
AGENT MOCKINGBIRD, BLACK PANTHER HERE--ARE YOU PREPARED TO UP YOUR SPACE MILEAGE?

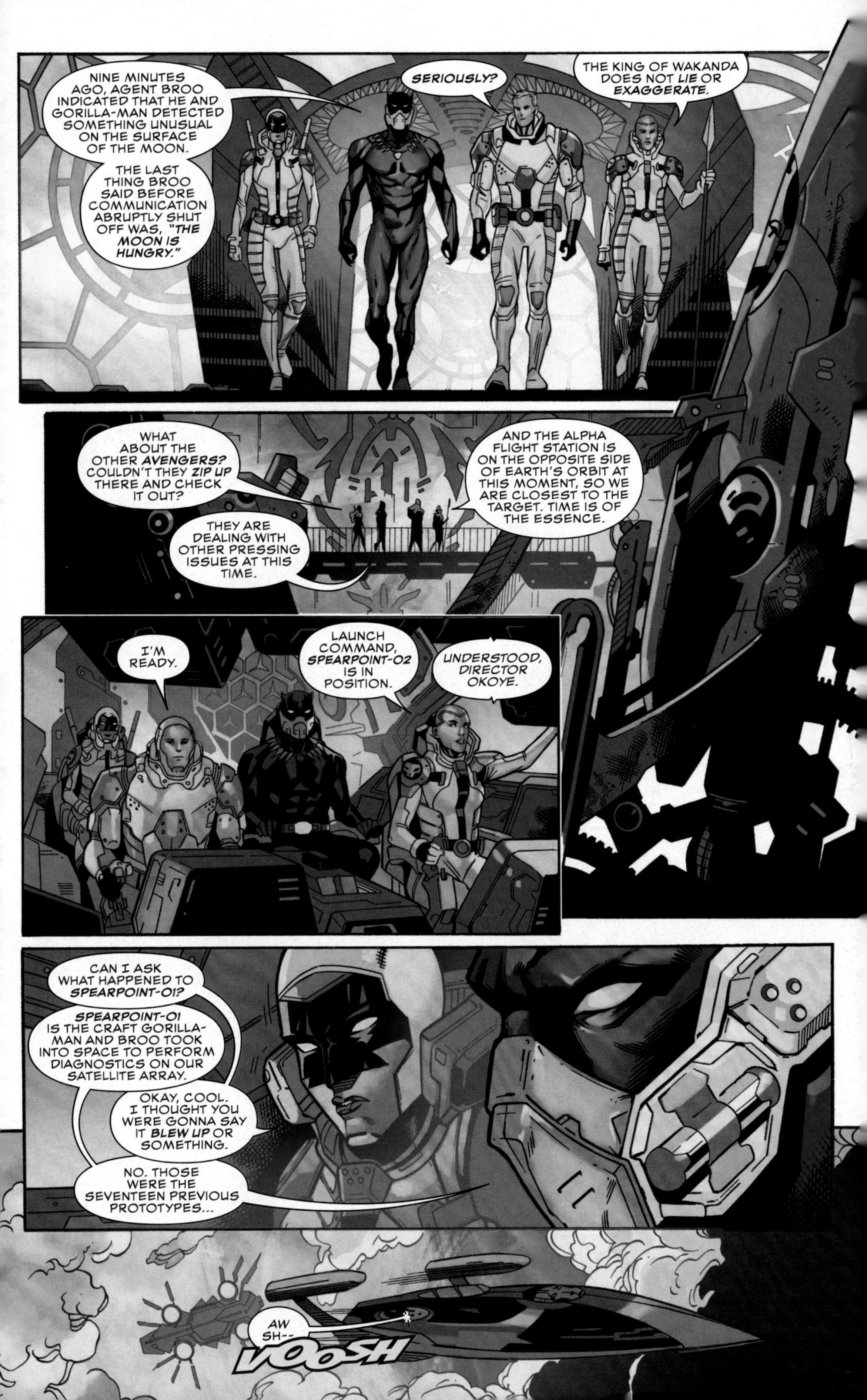
NINE MINUTES AGO, AGENT BROO INDICATED THAT HE AND GORILLA-MAN DETECTED SOMETHING UNUSUAL ON THE SURFACE OF THE MOON.
THE LAST THING BROO SAID BEFORE COMMUNICATION ABRUPTLY SHUT OFF WAS, "THE MOON IS HUNGRY."
SERIOUSLY?
THE KING OF WAKANDA DOES NOT LIE OR EXAGGERATE.
WHAT ABOUT THE OTHER AVENGERS? COULDN'T THEY ZIP UP THERE AND CHECK IT OUT?
THEY ARE DEALING WITH OTHER PRESSING ISSUES AT THIS TIME.
AND THE ALPHA FLIGHT STATION IS ON THE OPPOSITE SIDE OF EARTH'S ORBIT AT THIS MOMENT, SO WE ARE CLOSEST TO THE TARGET. TIME IS OF THE ESSENCE.
I'M READY.
LAUNCH COMMAND, SPEARPOINT-02 IS IN POSITION.
UNDERSTOOD, DIRECTOR OKOYE.
CAN I ASK WHAT HAPPENED TO SPEARPOINT-01?
SPEARPOINT-01 IS THE CRAFT GORILLA-MAN AND BROO TOOK INTO SPACE TO PERFORM DIAGNOSTICS ON OUR SATELLITE ARRAY.
OKAY, COOL. I THOUGHT YOU WERE GONNA SAY IT BLEW UP OR SOMETHING.
NO. THOSE WERE THE SEVENTEEN PREVIOUS PROTOTYPES...
AW SH--
VOOSH

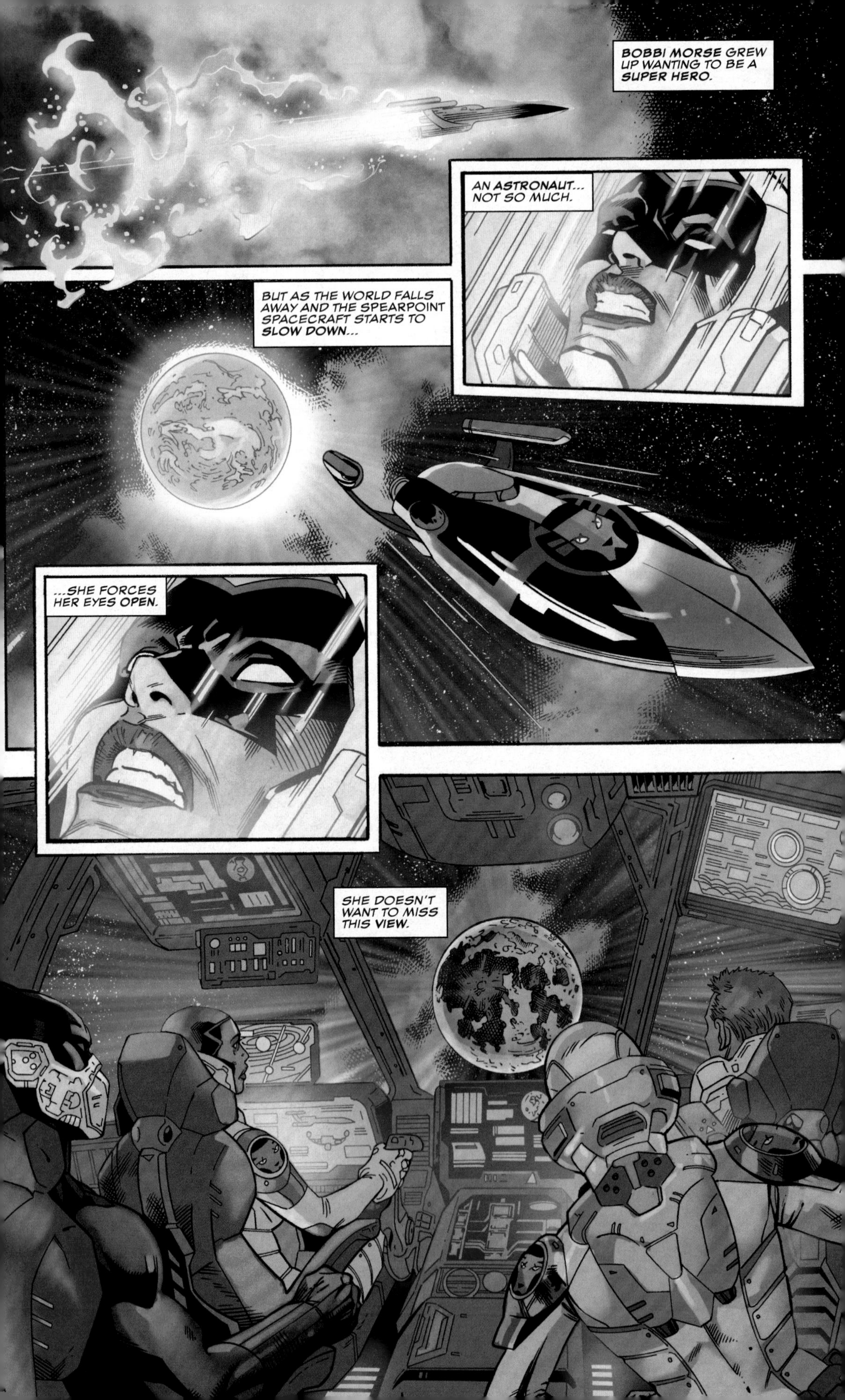
BOBBI MORSE GREW UP WANTING TO BE A SUPER HERO.
AN ASTRONAUT... NOT SO MUCH.
BUT AS THE WORLD FALLS AWAY AND THE SPEARPOINT SPACECRAFT STARTS TO SLOW DOWN...
...SHE FORCES HER EYES OPEN.
SHE DOESN'T WANT TO MISS THIS VIEW.

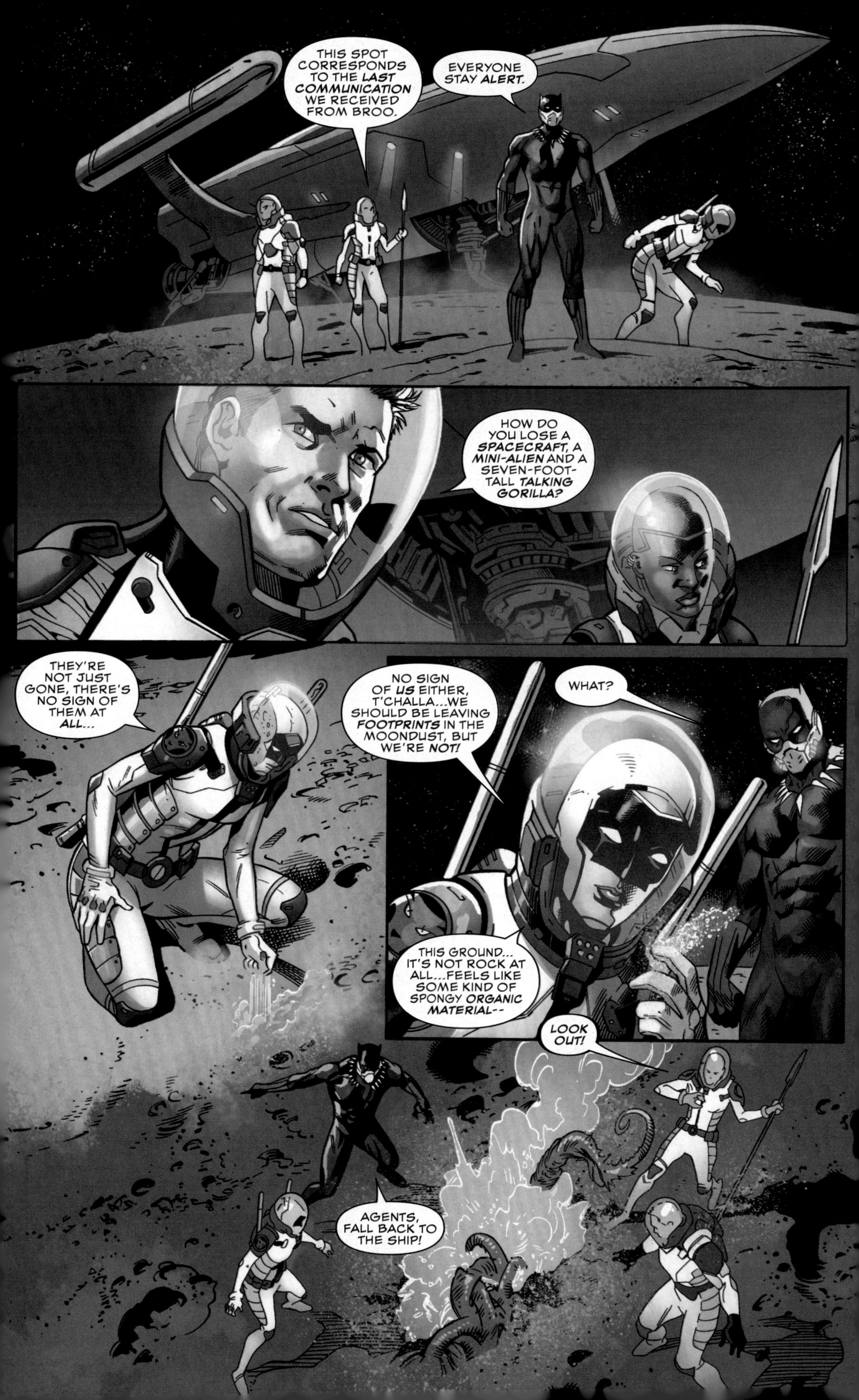

THIS SPOT CORRESPONDS TO THE *LAST COMMUNICATION* WE RECEIVED FROM BROO.
EVERYONE STAY *ALERT.*
HOW DO YOU LOSE A *SPACECRAFT*, A *MINI-ALIEN* AND A SEVEN-FOOT-TALL *TALKING GORILLA?*
THEY'RE NOT JUST GONE, THERE'S NO SIGN OF THEM AT *ALL...*
NO SIGN OF *US* EITHER, T'CHALLA...WE SHOULD BE LEAVING *FOOTPRINTS* IN THE MOONDUST, BUT WE'RE *NOT!*
WHAT?
THIS GROUND... IT'S NOT ROCK AT ALL...FEELS LIKE SOME KIND OF SPONGY *ORGANIC MATERIAL--*
LOOK OUT!
AGENTS, FALL BACK TO THE SHIP!

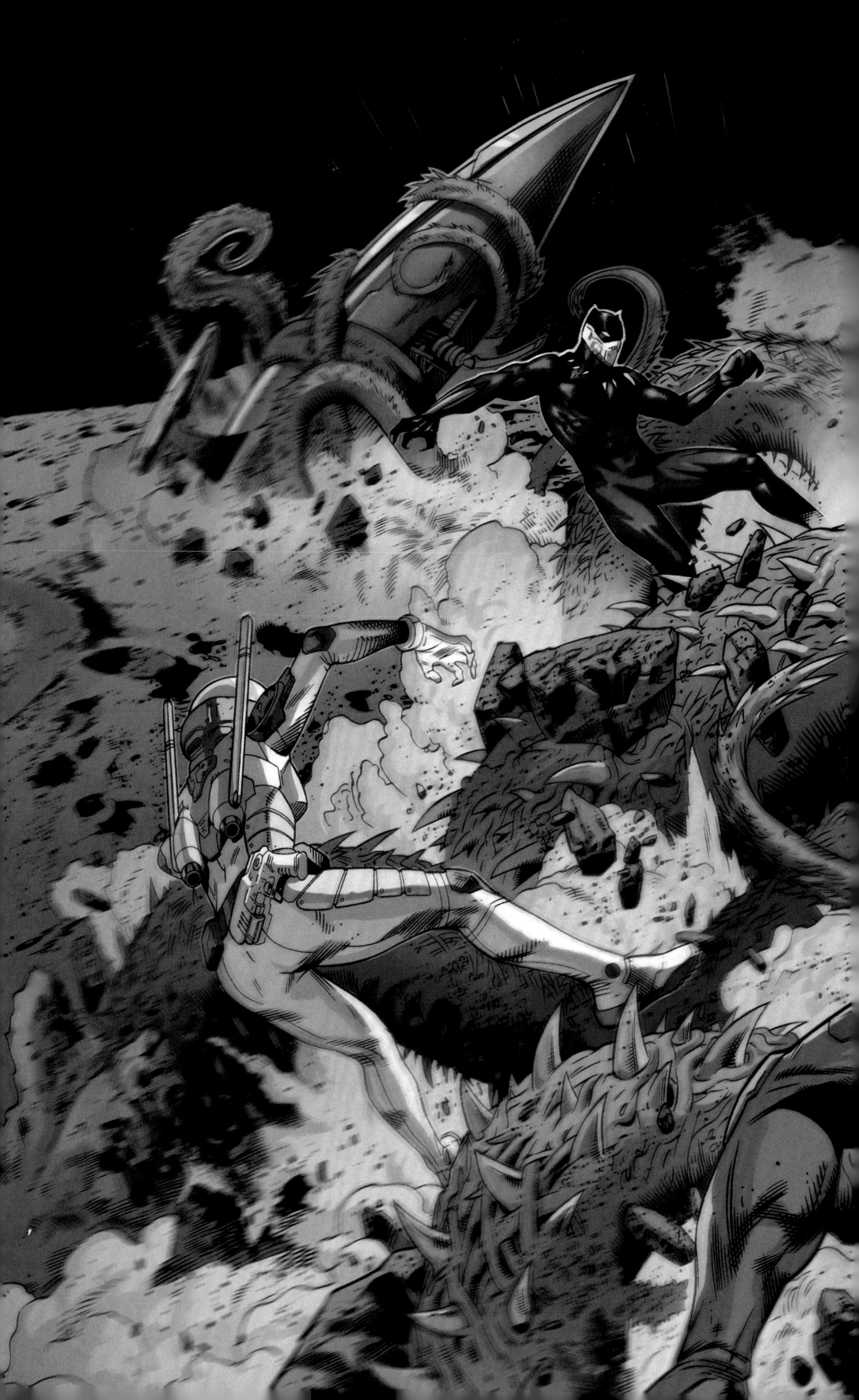

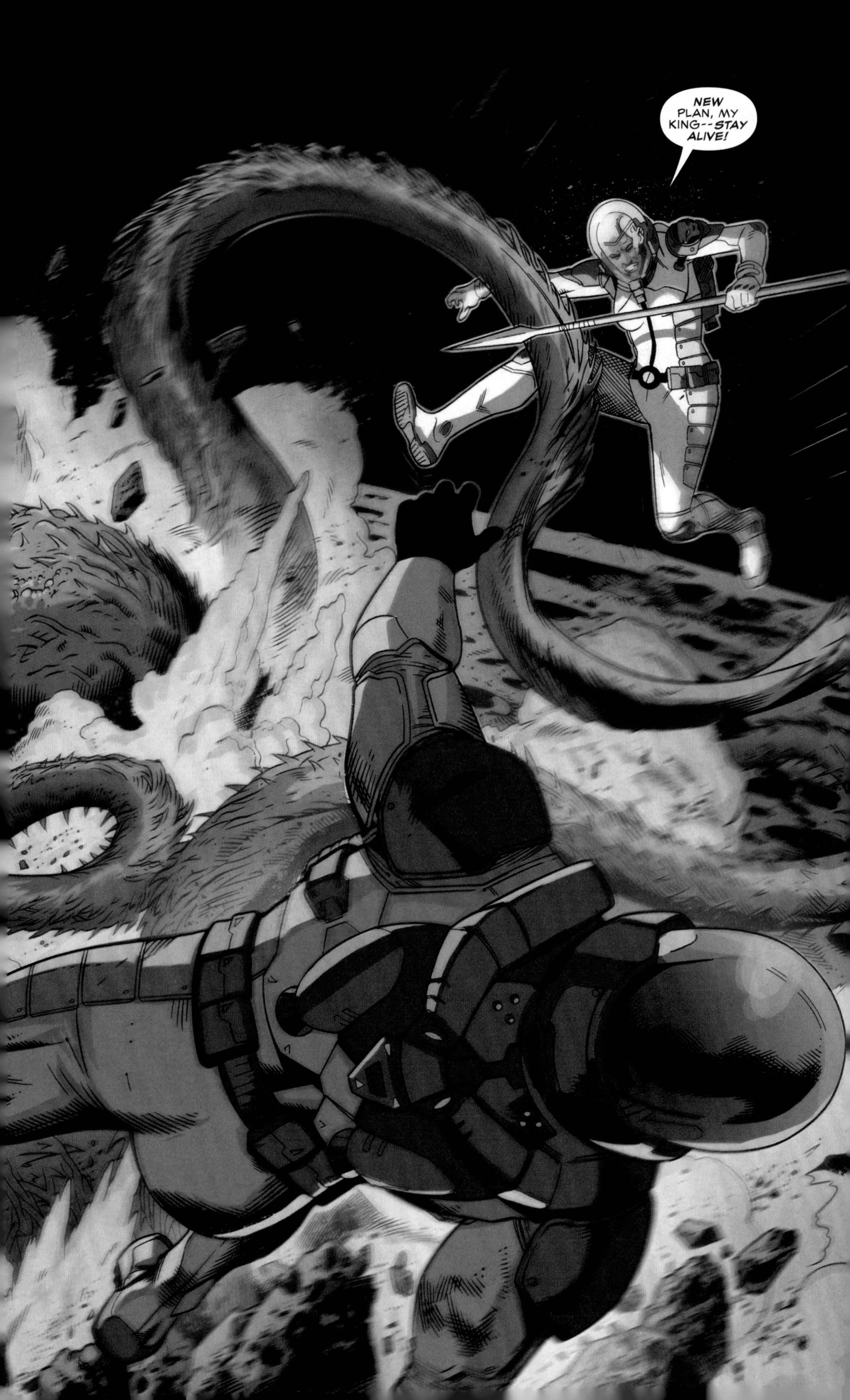
NEW PLAN, MY KING--STAY ALIVE!

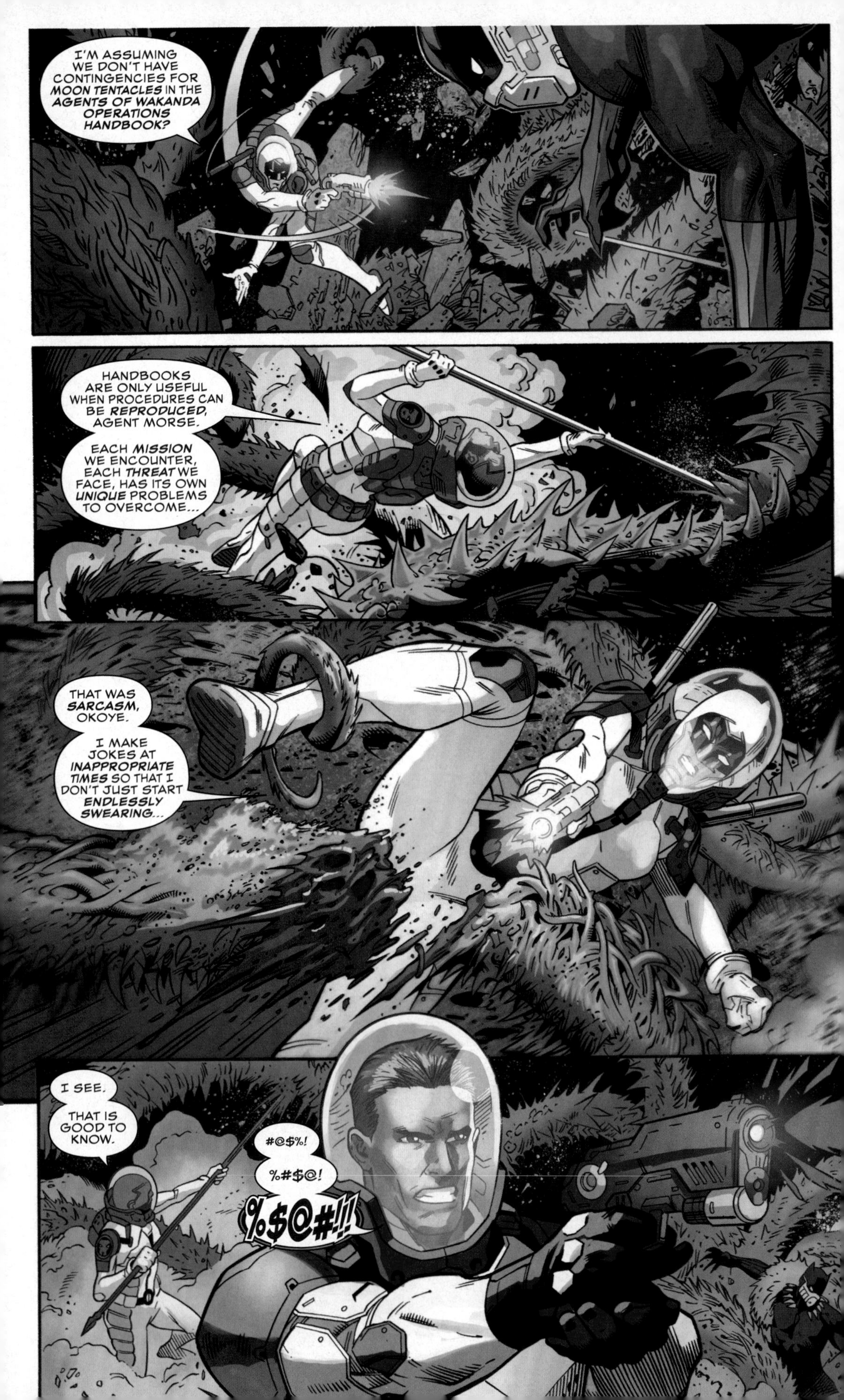
I'M ASSUMING WE DON'T HAVE CONTINGENCIES FOR MOON TENTACLES IN THE AGENTS OF WAKANDA OPERATIONS HANDBOOK?
HANDBOOKS ARE ONLY USEFUL WHEN PROCEDURES CAN BE REPRODUCED, AGENT MORSE.
EACH MISSION WE ENCOUNTER, EACH THREAT WE FACE, HAS ITS OWN UNIQUE PROBLEMS TO OVERCOME...
THAT WAS SARCASM, OKOYE.
I MAKE JOKES AT INAPPROPRIATE TIMES SO THAT I DON'T JUST START ENDLESSLY SWEARING...
I SEE.
THAT IS GOOD TO KNOW.
#@$%!
%#$@!
%$@#!!!

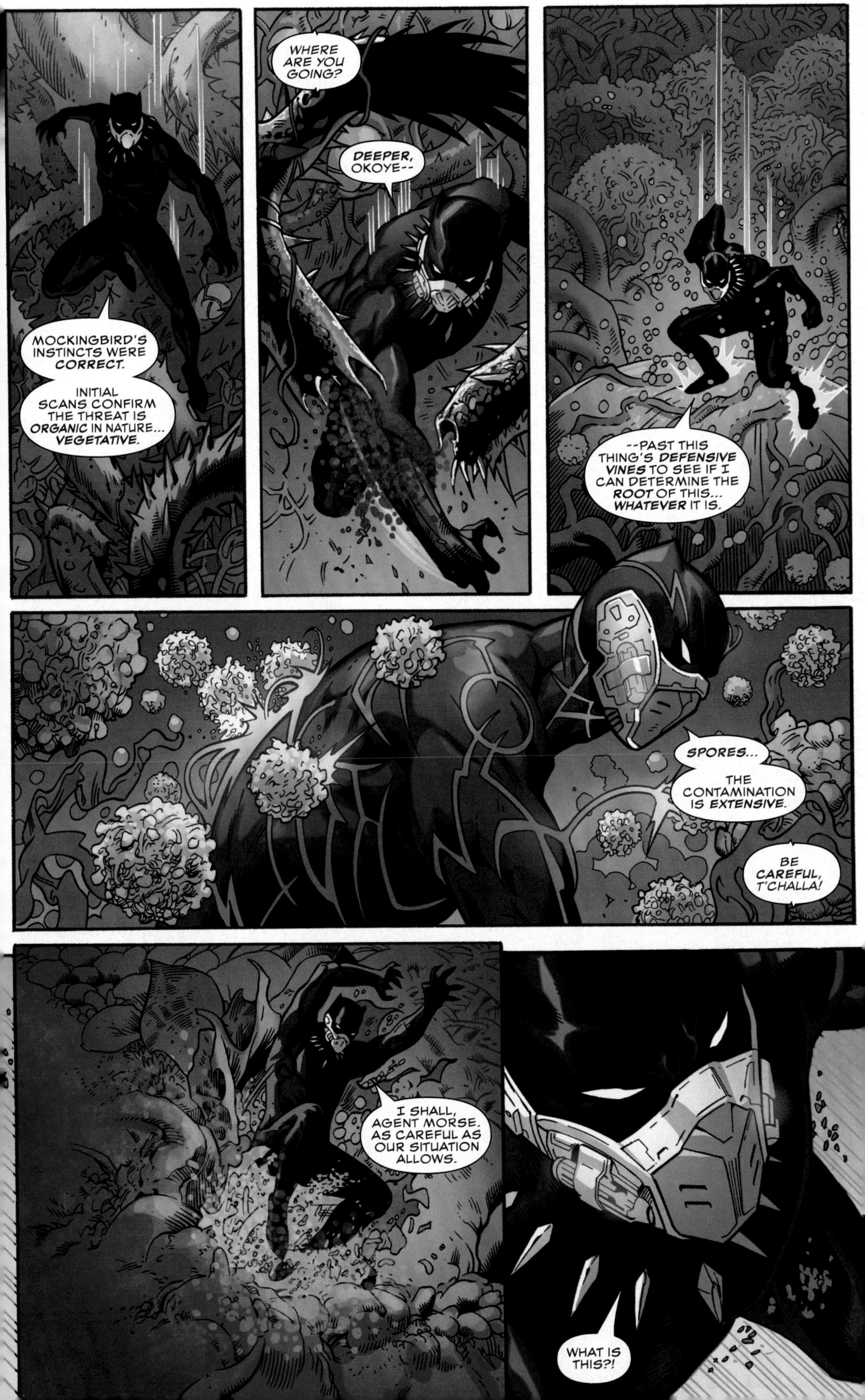
MOCKINGBIRD'S INSTINCTS WERE CORRECT.
INITIAL SCANS CONFIRM THE THREAT IS ORGANIC IN NATURE... VEGETATIVE.
WHERE ARE YOU GOING?
DEEPER, OKOYE--
--PAST THIS THING'S DEFENSIVE VINES TO SEE IF I CAN DETERMINE THE ROOT OF THIS... WHATEVER IT IS.
SPORES...
THE CONTAMINATION IS EXTENSIVE.
BE CAREFUL, T'CHALLA!
I SHALL, AGENT MORSE. AS CAREFUL AS OUR SITUATION ALLOWS.
WHAT IS THIS?!

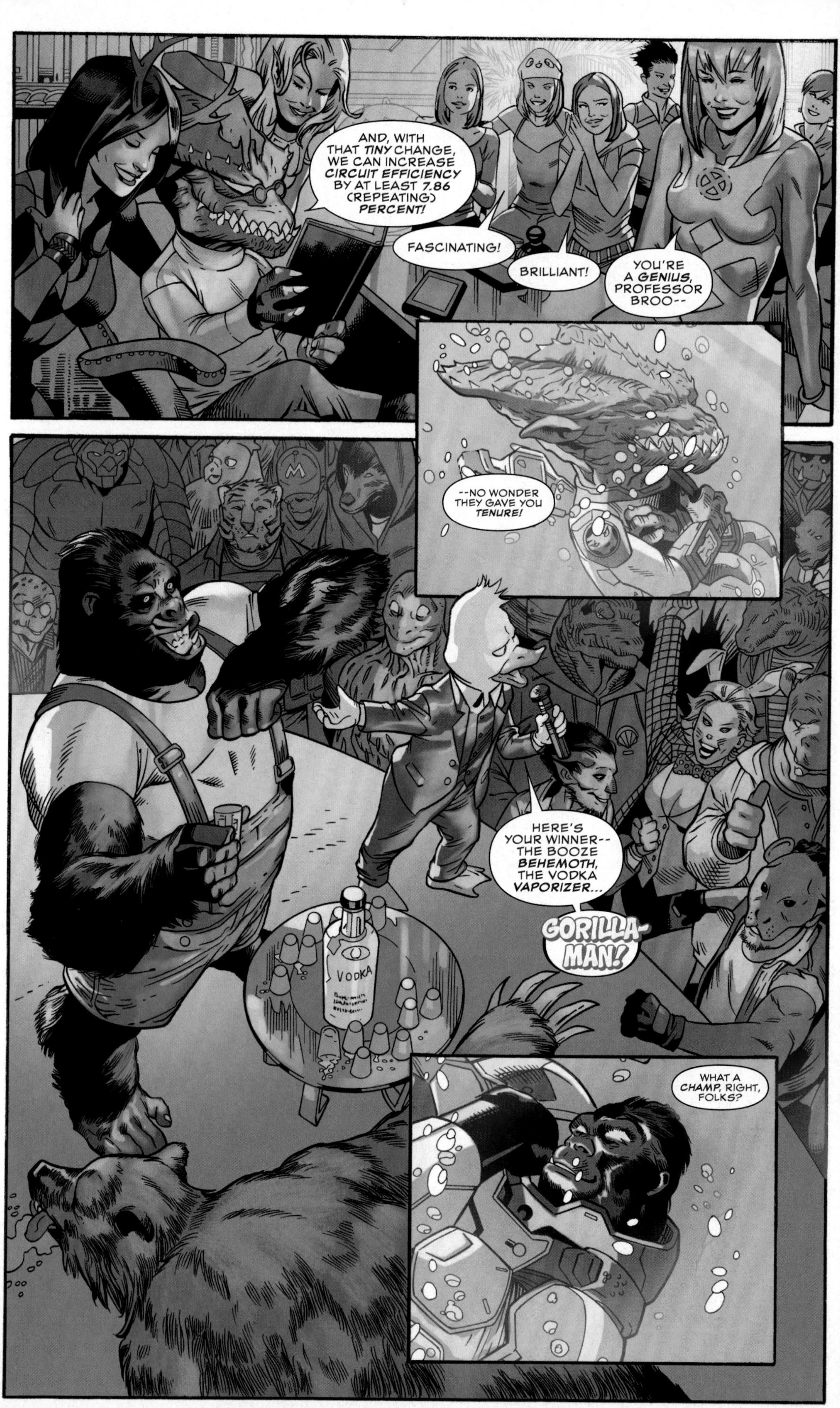
AND, WITH THAT TINY CHANGE, WE CAN INCREASE CIRCUIT EFFICIENCY BY AT LEAST 7.86 (REPEATING) PERCENT!
FASCINATING!
BRILLIANT!
YOU'RE A GENIUS, PROFESSOR BROO--
--NO WONDER THEY GAVE YOU TENURE!
HERE'S YOUR WINNER-- THE BOOZE BEHEMOTH, THE VODKA VAPORIZER...
GORILLA-MAN!
VODKA
WHAT A CHAMP, RIGHT, FOLKS?

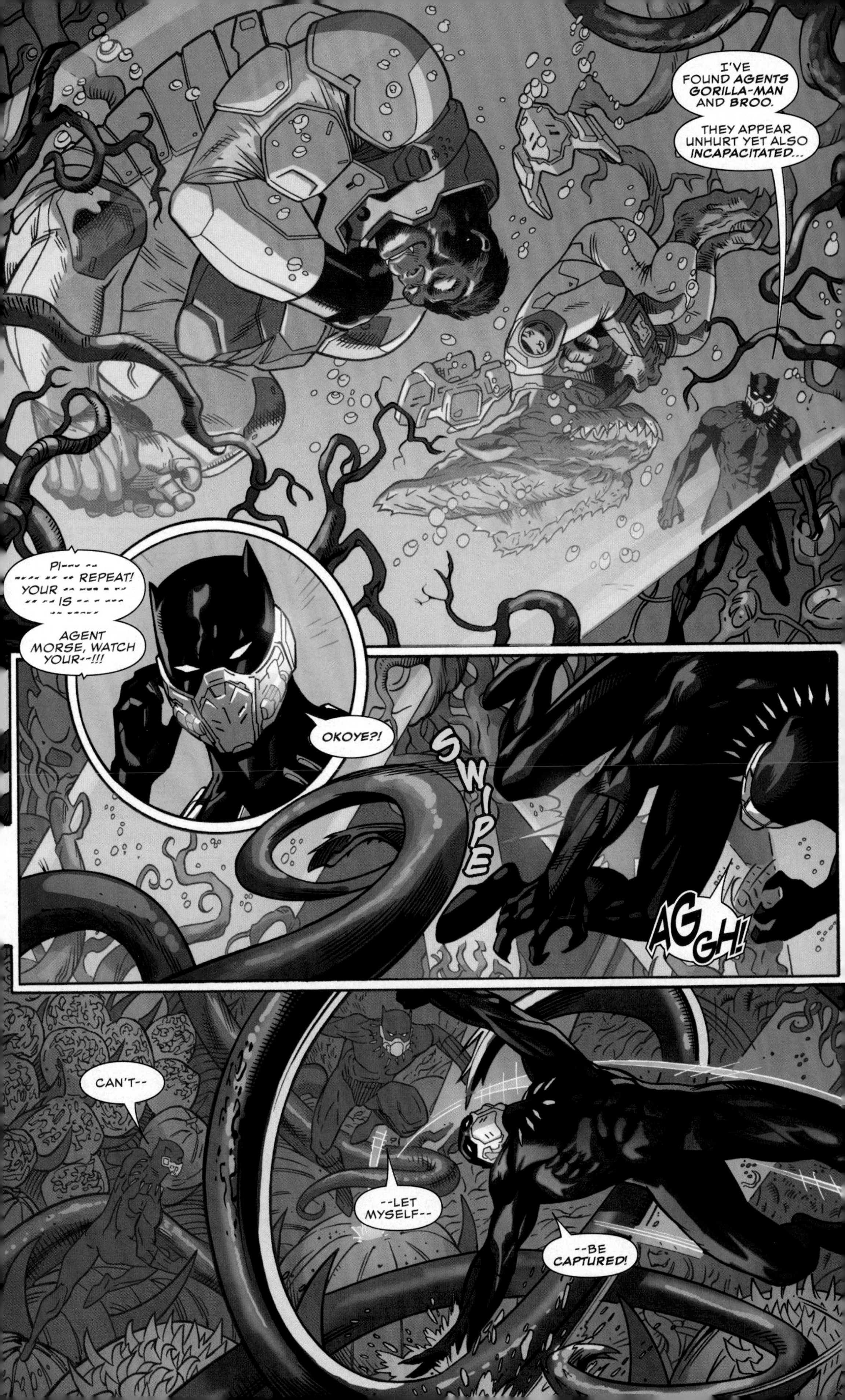
I'VE FOUND AGENTS GORILLA-MAN AND BROO.
THEY APPEAR UNHURT YET ALSO INCAPACITATED...
PI REPEAT! YOUR IS
AGENT MORSE, WATCH YOUR--!!!
OKOYE?!
SWIPE
AGGH!!
CAN'T--
--LET MYSELF--
--BE CAPTURED!

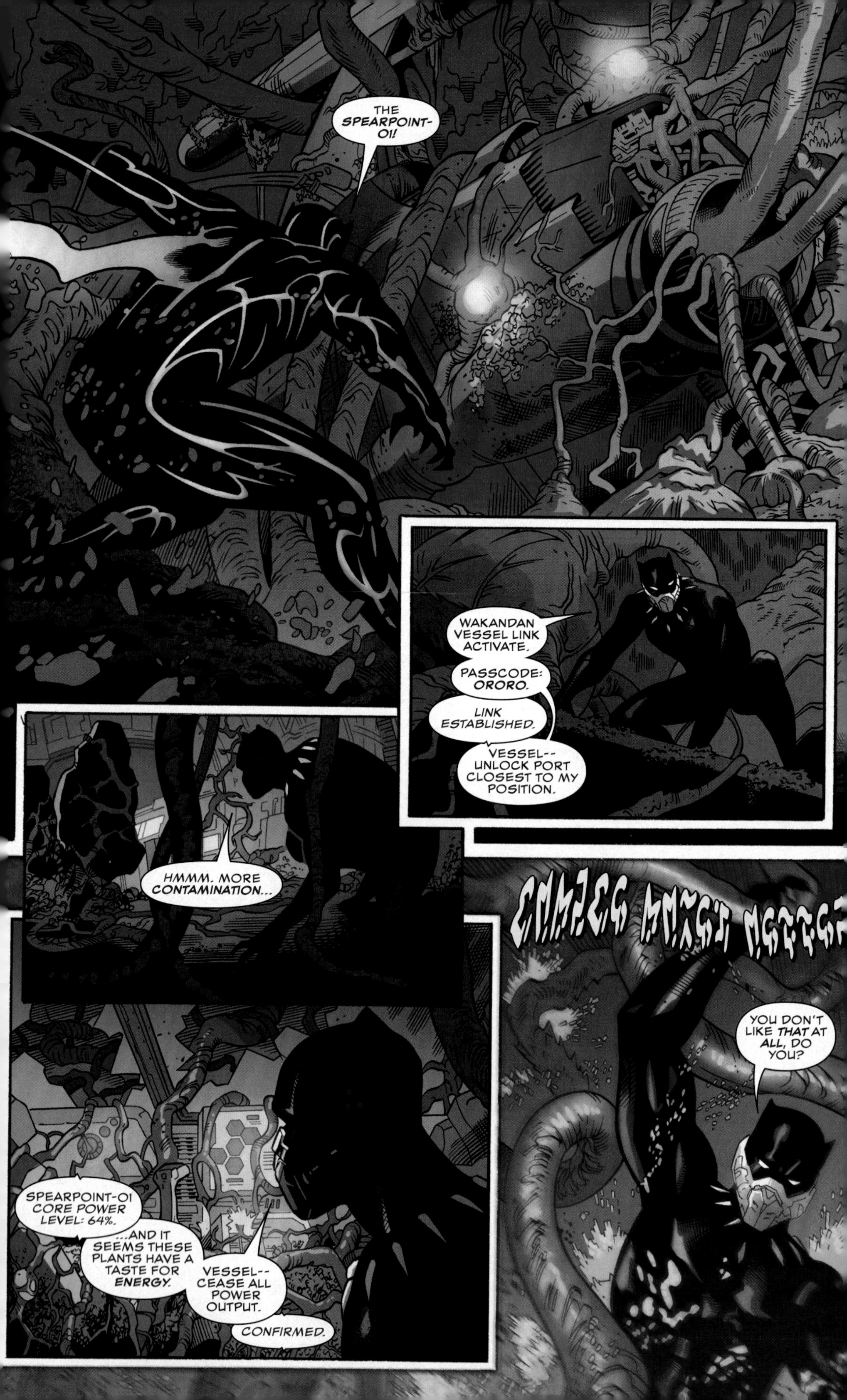
THE SPEARPOINT-01!
WAKANDAN VESSEL LINK ACTIVATE.
PASSCODE: ORORO.
LINK ESTABLISHED.
VESSEL-- UNLOCK PORT CLOSEST TO MY POSITION.
HMMM. MORE CONTAMINATION...
SPEARPOINT-01 CORE POWER LEVEL: 64%.
...AND IT SEEMS THESE PLANTS HAVE A TASTE FOR ENERGY.
VESSEL-- CEASE ALL POWER OUTPUT.
CONFIRMED.
YOU DON'T LIKE THAT AT ALL, DO YOU?

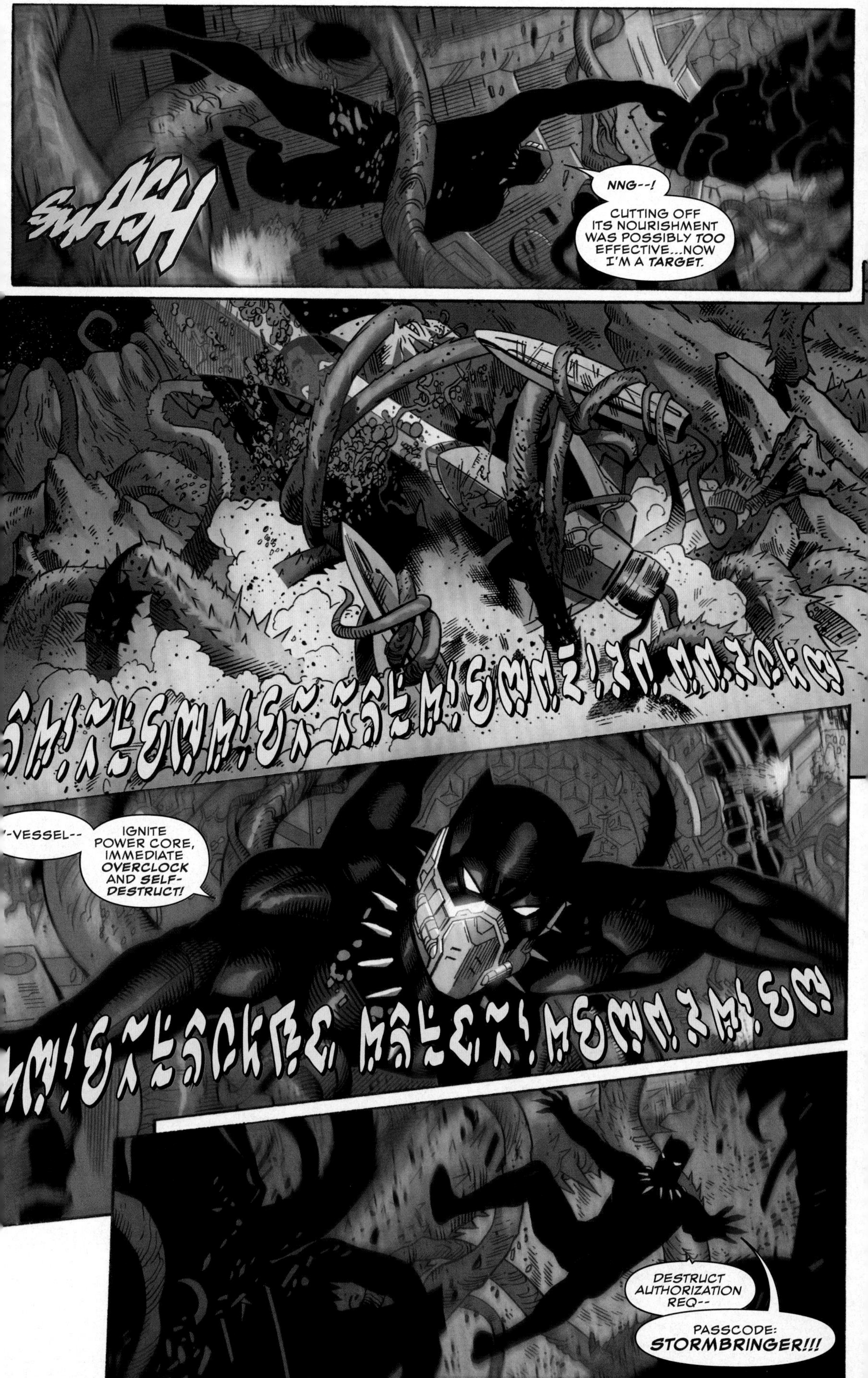

SWASH
NNG--!
CUTTING OFF ITS NOURISHMENT WAS POSSIBLY TOO EFFECTIVE...NOW I'M A TARGET.
-VESSEL--
IGNITE POWER CORE, IMMEDIATE OVERCLOCK AND SELF-DESTRUCT!
DESTRUCT AUTHORIZATION REQ--
PASSCODE: STORMBRINGER!!!

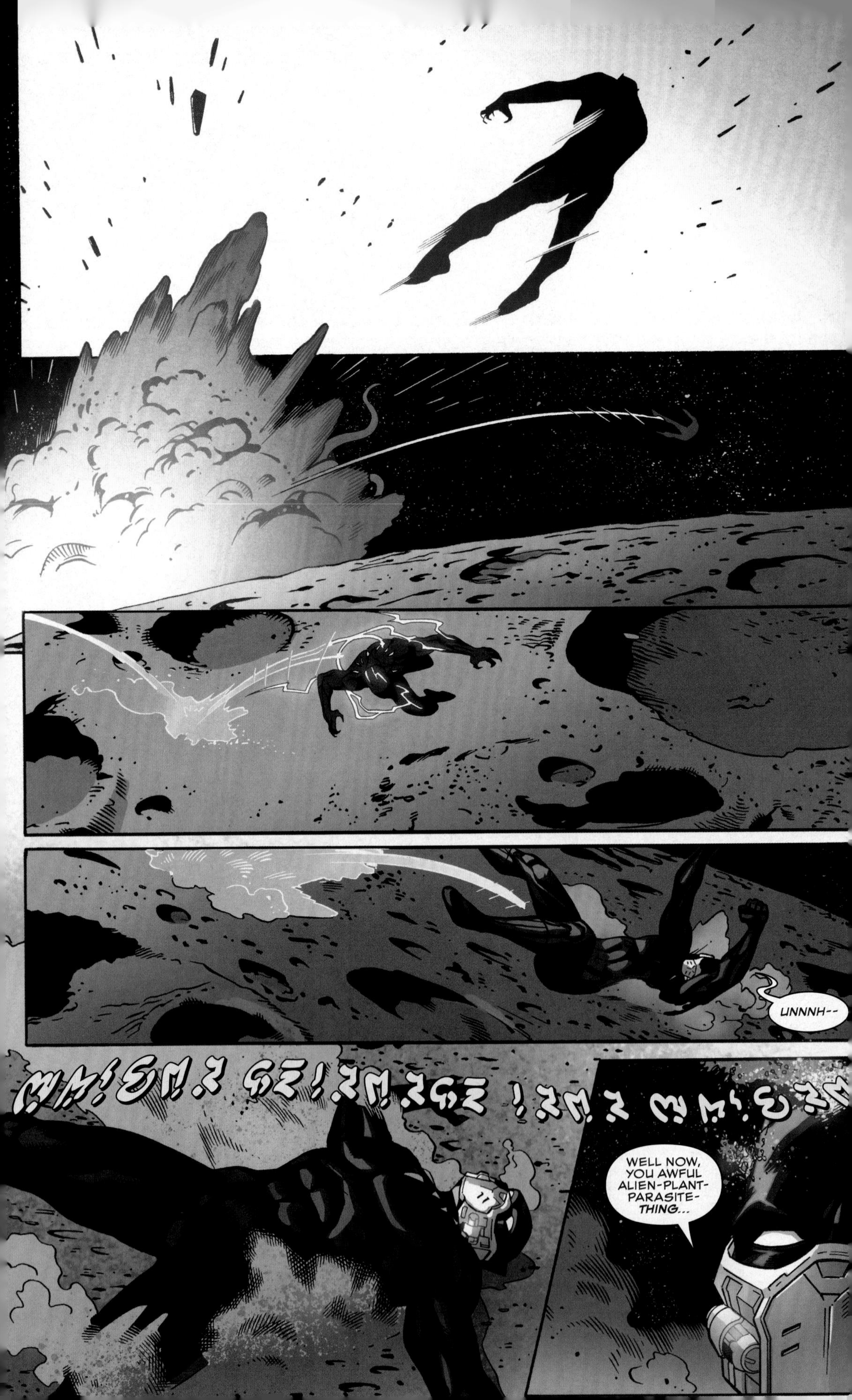
UNNNH--
WELL NOW, YOU AWFUL ALIEN-PLANT-PARASITE-THING...

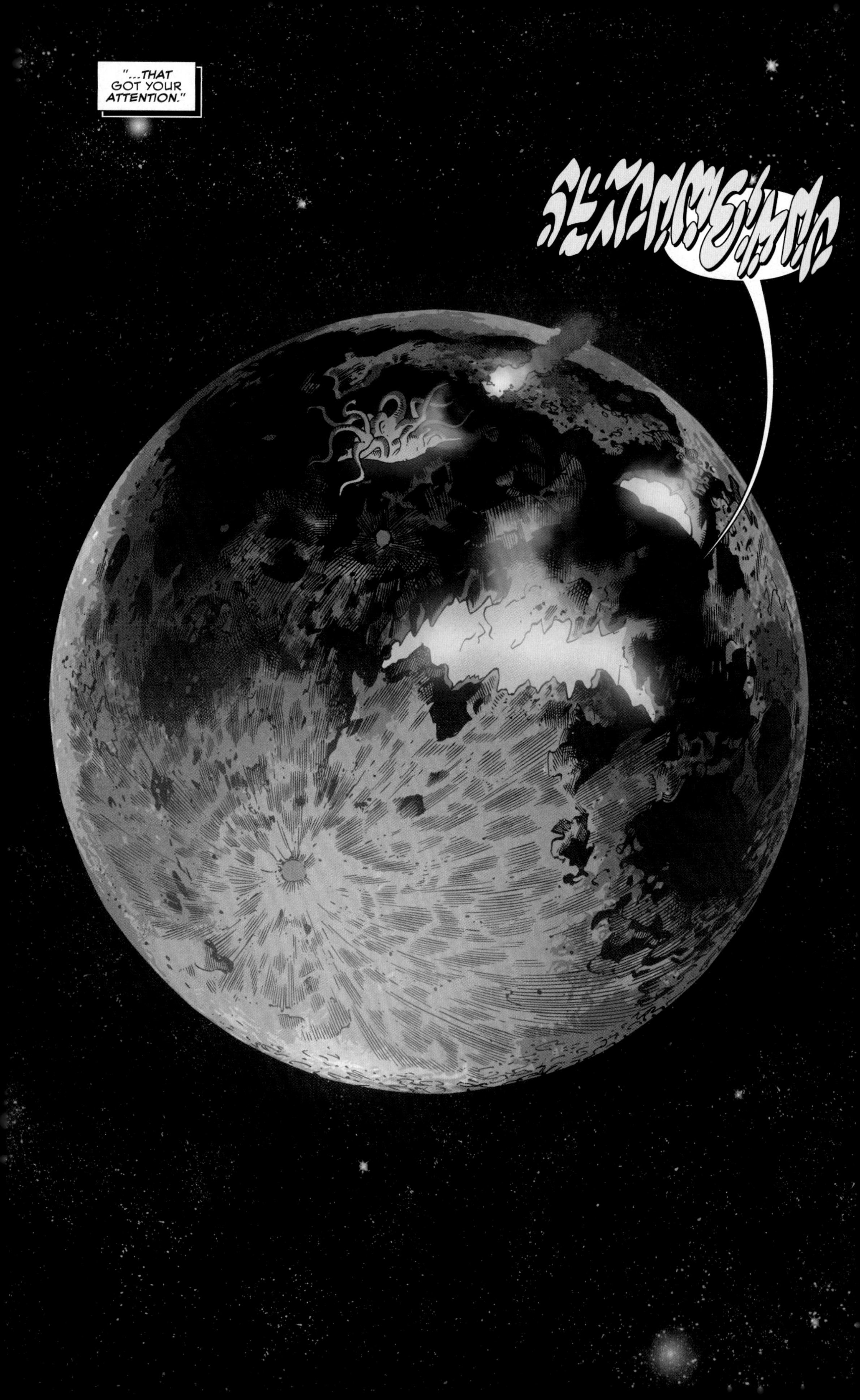
"...THAT GOT YOUR ATTENTION."

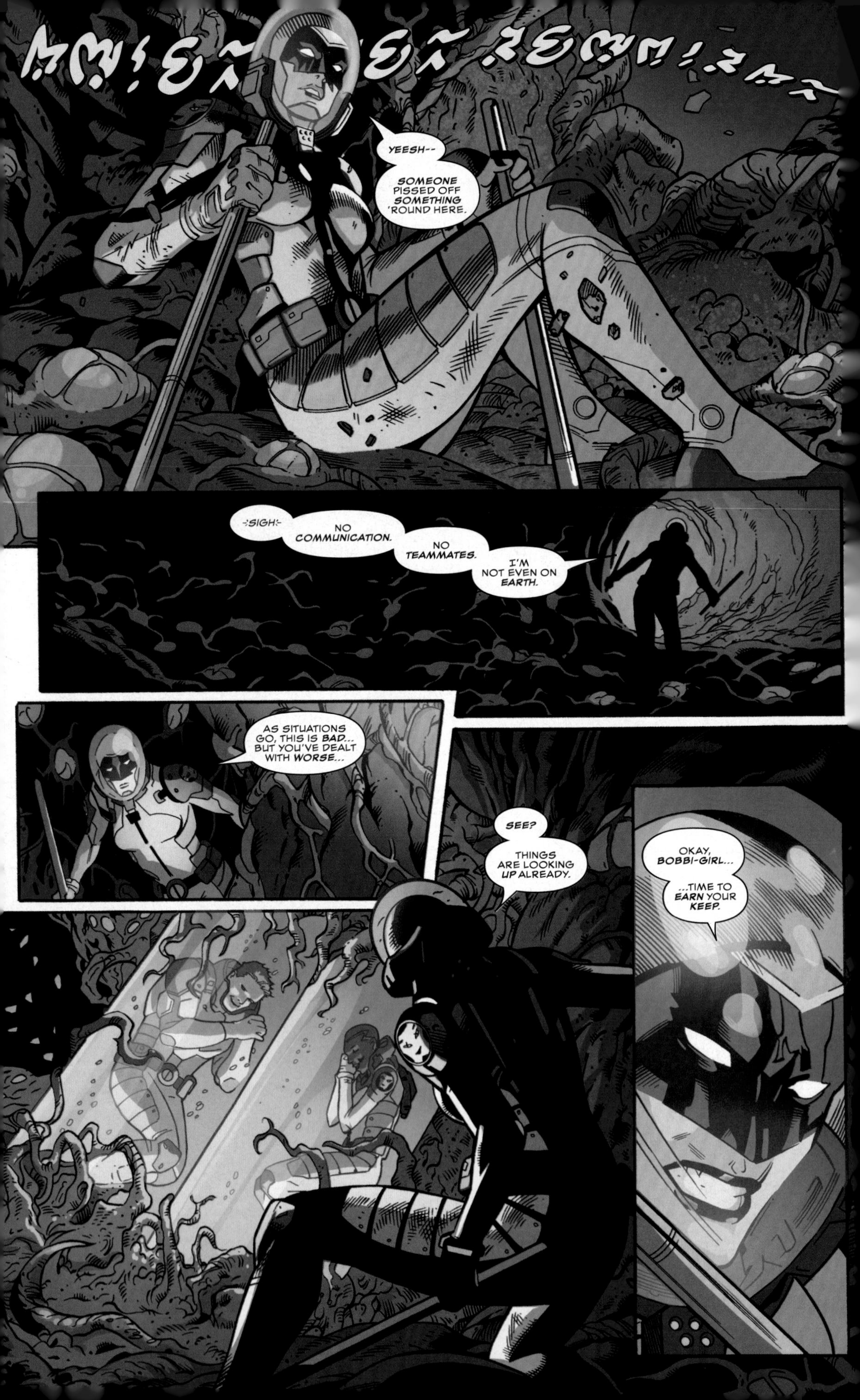
YEESH--
SOMEONE PISSED OFF SOMETHING 'ROUND HERE.
-SIGH-
NO COMMUNICATION.
NO TEAMMATES.
I'M NOT EVEN ON EARTH.
AS SITUATIONS GO, THIS IS BAD... BUT YOU'VE DEALT WITH WORSE...
SEE?
THINGS ARE LOOKING UP ALREADY.
OKAY, BOBBI-GIRL...
...TIME TO EARN YOUR KEEP.

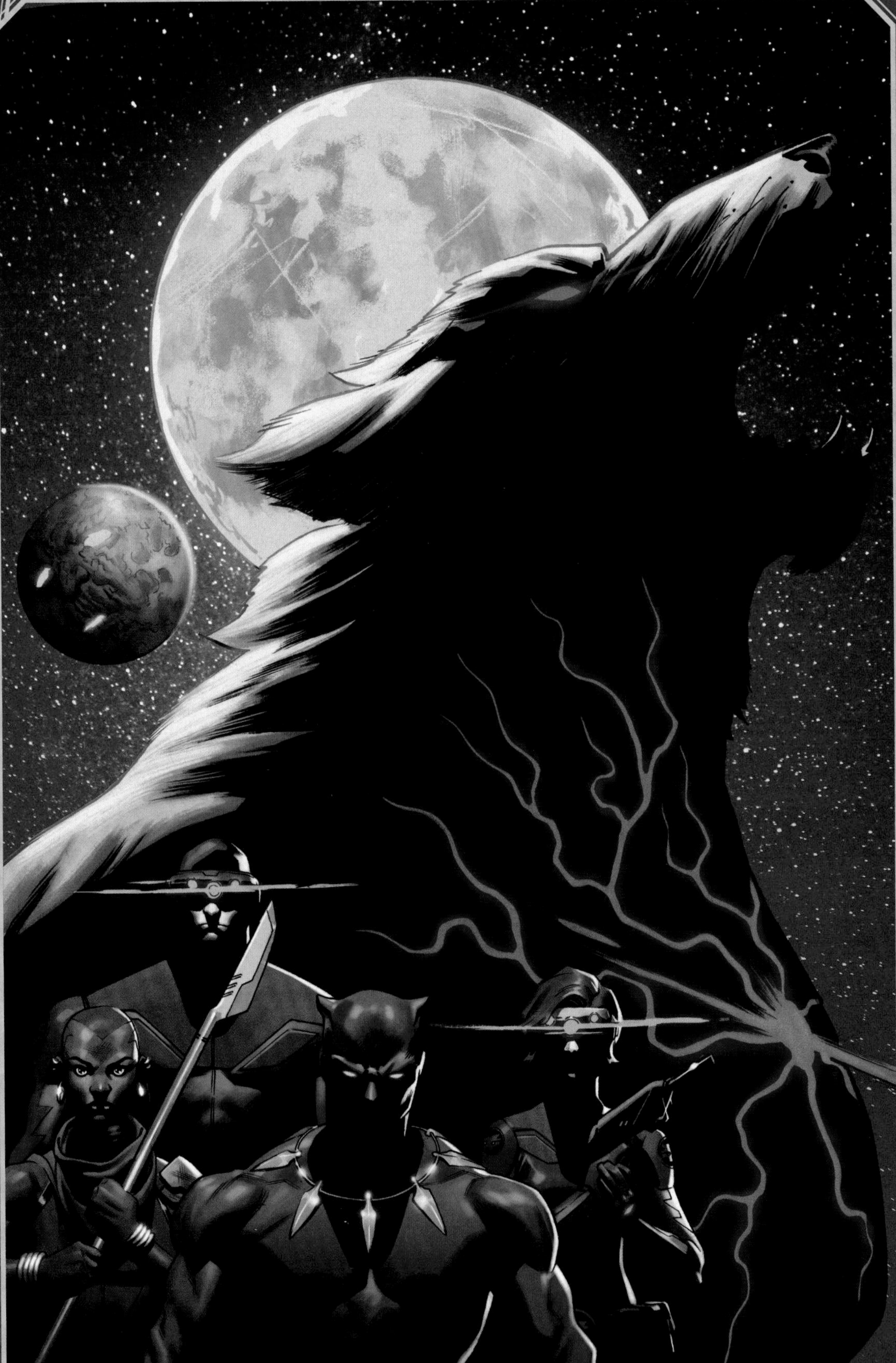

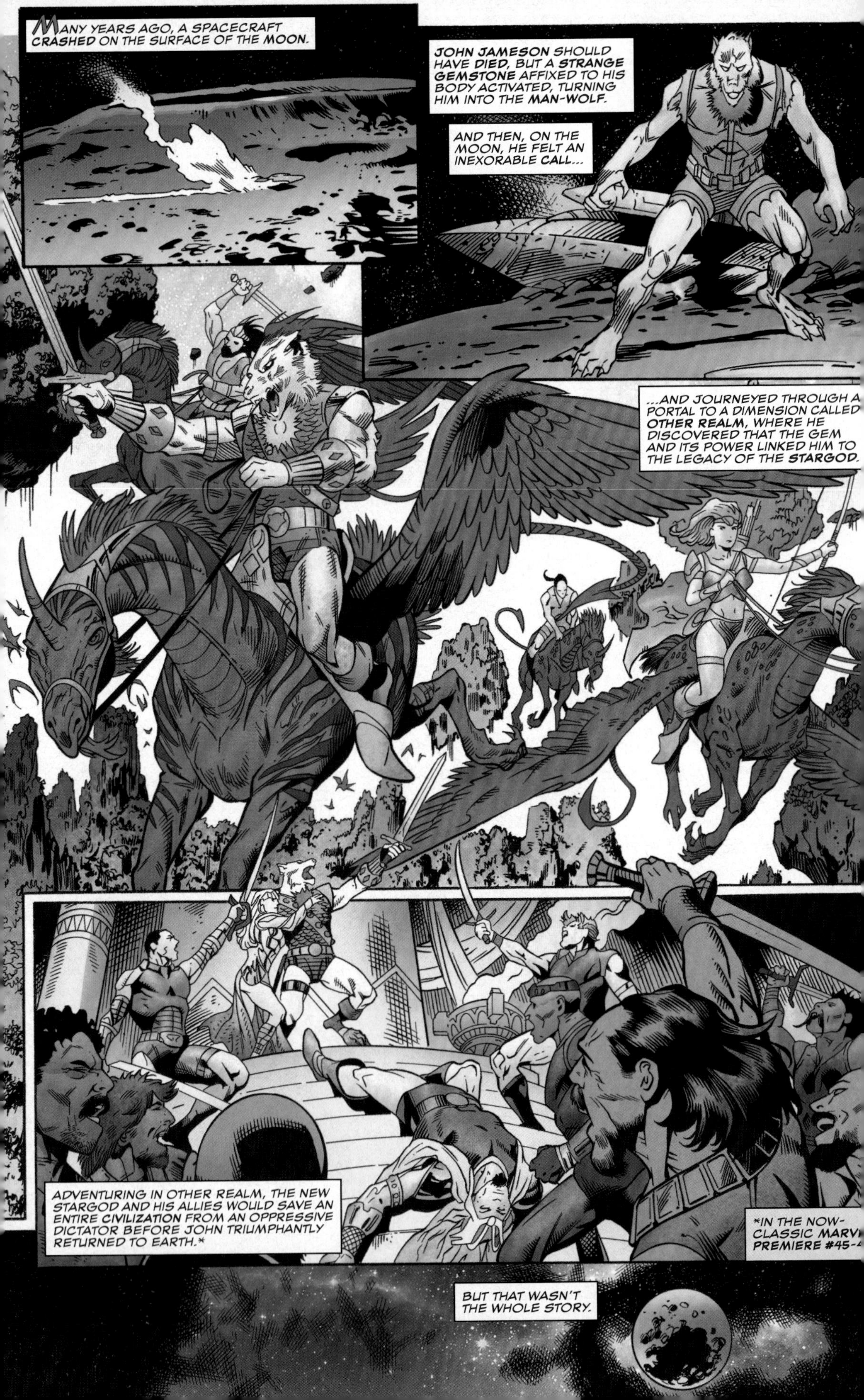
MANY YEARS AGO, A SPACECRAFT CRASHED ON THE SURFACE OF THE MOON.
JOHN JAMESON SHOULD HAVE DIED, BUT A STRANGE GEMSTONE AFFIXED TO HIS BODY ACTIVATED, TURNING HIM INTO THE MAN-WOLF.
AND THEN, ON THE MOON, HE FELT AN INEXORABLE CALL...
...AND JOURNEYED THROUGH A PORTAL TO A DIMENSION CALLED OTHER REALM, WHERE HE DISCOVERED THAT THE GEM AND ITS POWER LINKED HIM TO THE LEGACY OF THE STARGOD.
ADVENTURING IN OTHER REALM, THE NEW STARGOD AND HIS ALLIES WOULD SAVE AN ENTIRE CIVILIZATION FROM AN OPPRESSIVE DICTATOR BEFORE JOHN TRIUMPHANTLY RETURNED TO EARTH.*
*IN THE NOW-CLASSIC MARV PREMIERE #45-
BUT THAT WASN'T THE WHOLE STORY.

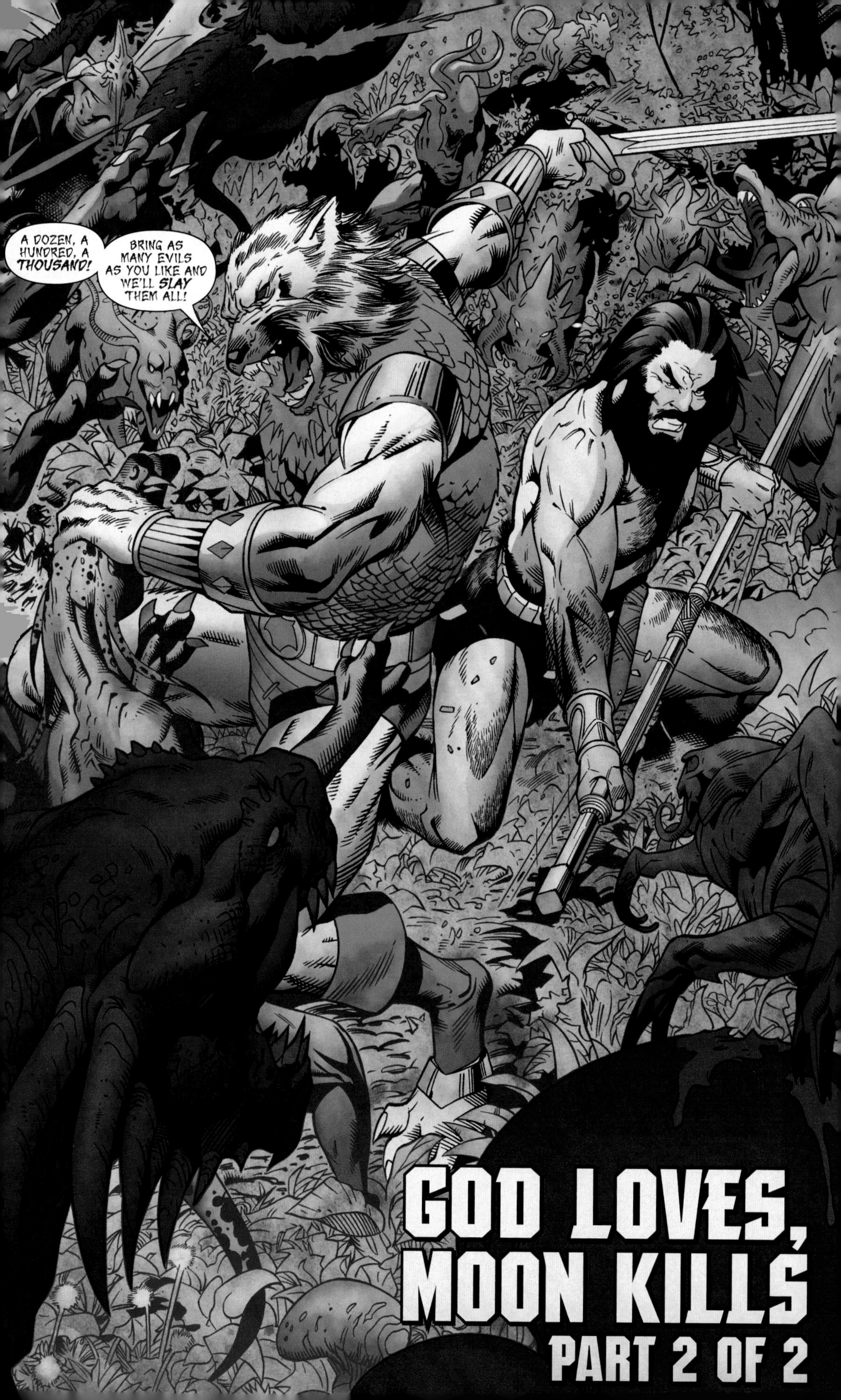
A DOZEN, A HUNDRED, A THOUSAND!
BRING AS MANY EVILS AS YOU LIKE AND WE'LL SLAY THEM ALL!
GOD LOVES, MOON KILLS
PART 2 OF 2

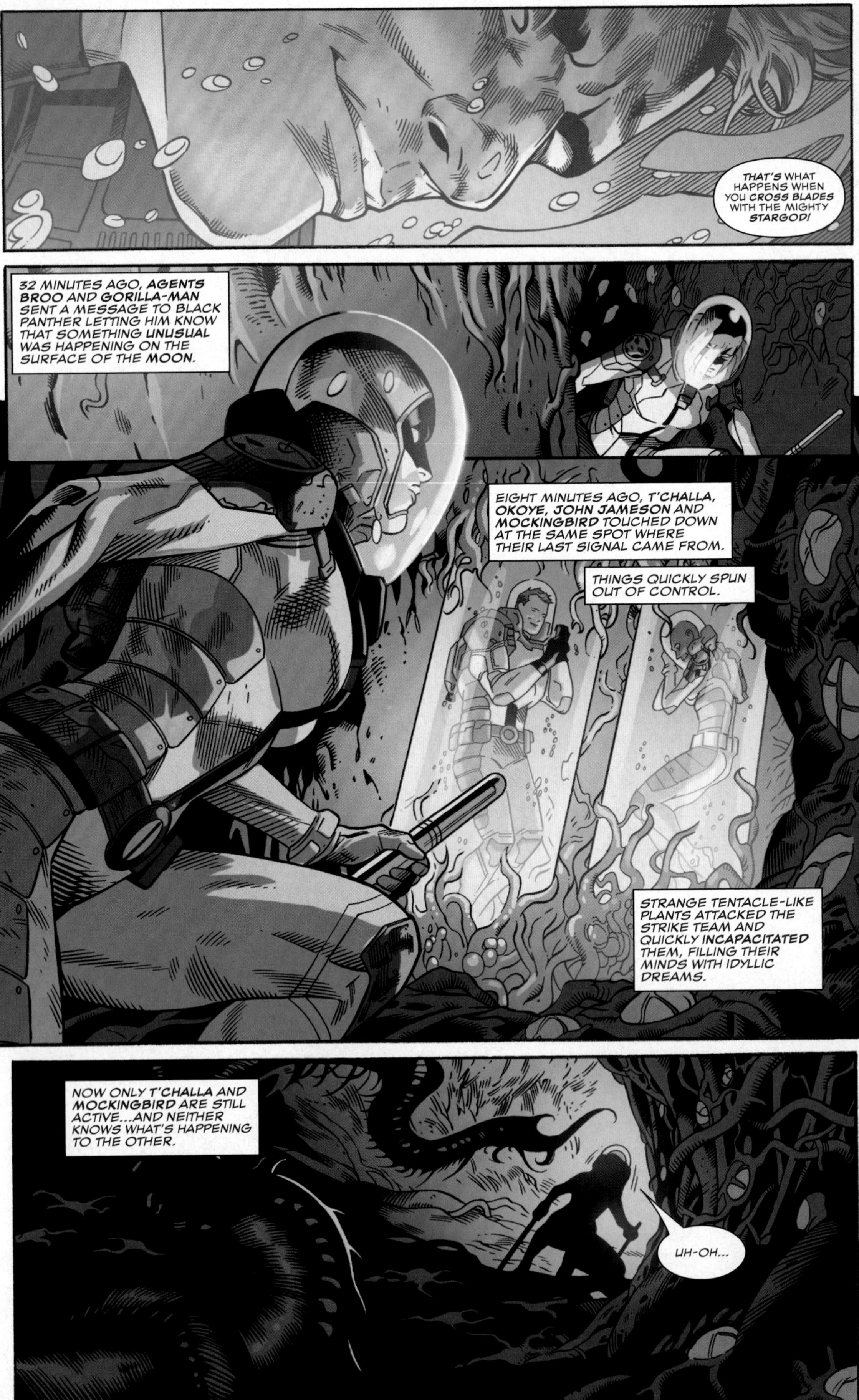

THAT'S WHAT HAPPENS WHEN YOU CROSS BLADES WITH THE MIGHTY STARGOD!
32 MINUTES AGO, AGENTS BROO AND GORILLA-MAN SENT A MESSAGE TO BLACK PANTHER LETTING HIM KNOW THAT SOMETHING UNUSUAL WAS HAPPENING ON THE SURFACE OF THE MOON.
EIGHT MINUTES AGO, T'CHALLA, OKOYE, JOHN JAMESON AND MOCKINGBIRD TOUCHED DOWN AT THE SAME SPOT WHERE THEIR LAST SIGNAL CAME FROM.
THINGS QUICKLY SPUN OUT OF CONTROL.
STRANGE TENTACLE-LIKE PLANTS ATTACKED THE STRIKE TEAM AND QUICKLY INCAPACITATED THEM, FILLING THEIR MINDS WITH IDYLLIC DREAMS.
NOW ONLY T'CHALLA AND MOCKINGBIRD ARE STILL ACTIVE...AND NEITHER KNOWS WHAT'S HAPPENING TO THE OTHER.
UH-OH...

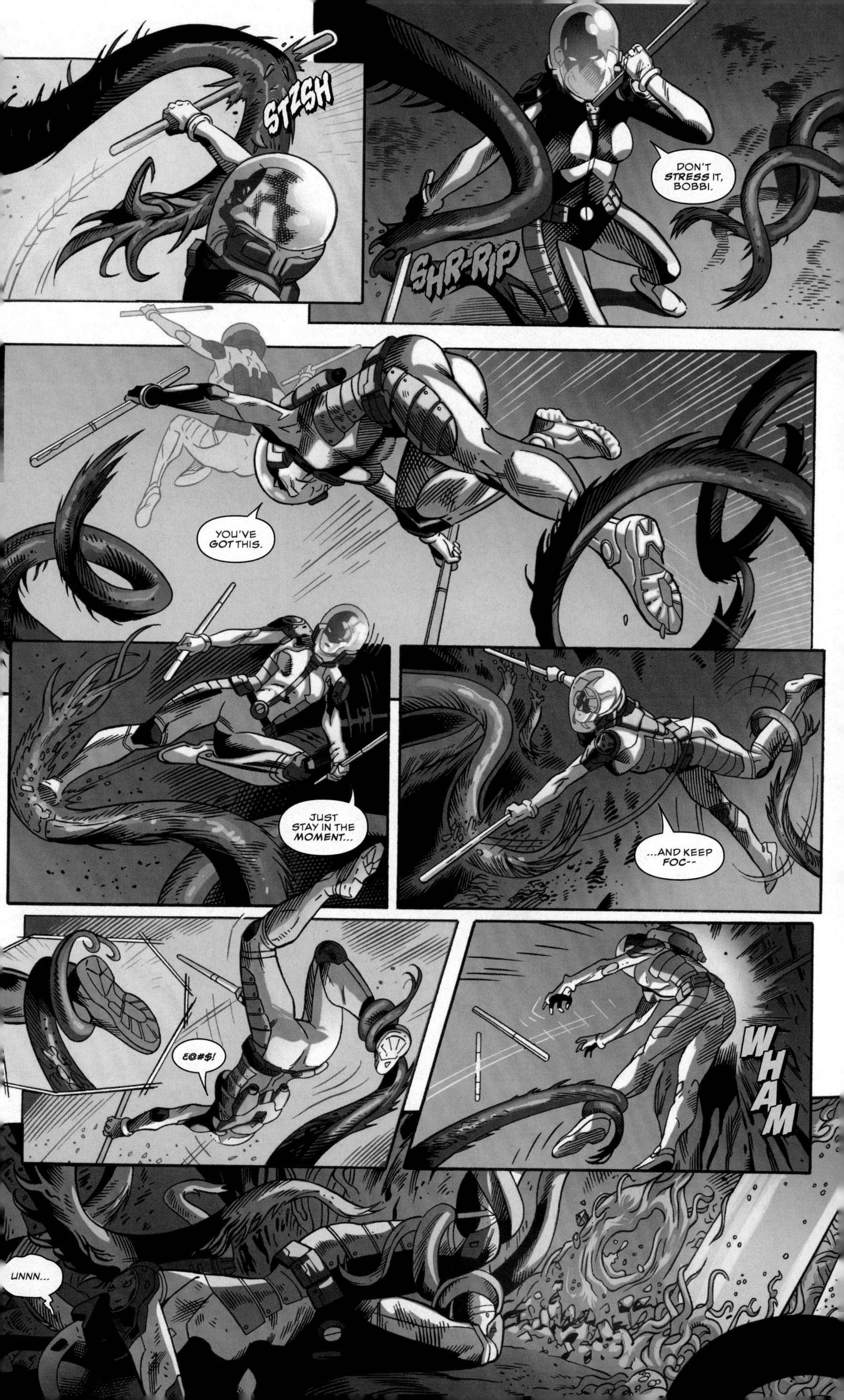
STZSH
DON'T STRESS IT, BOBBI.
SHR-RIP
YOU'VE GOT THIS.
JUST STAY IN THE MOMENT...
...AND KEEP FOC--
&@#$!
WHAM
UNNN...

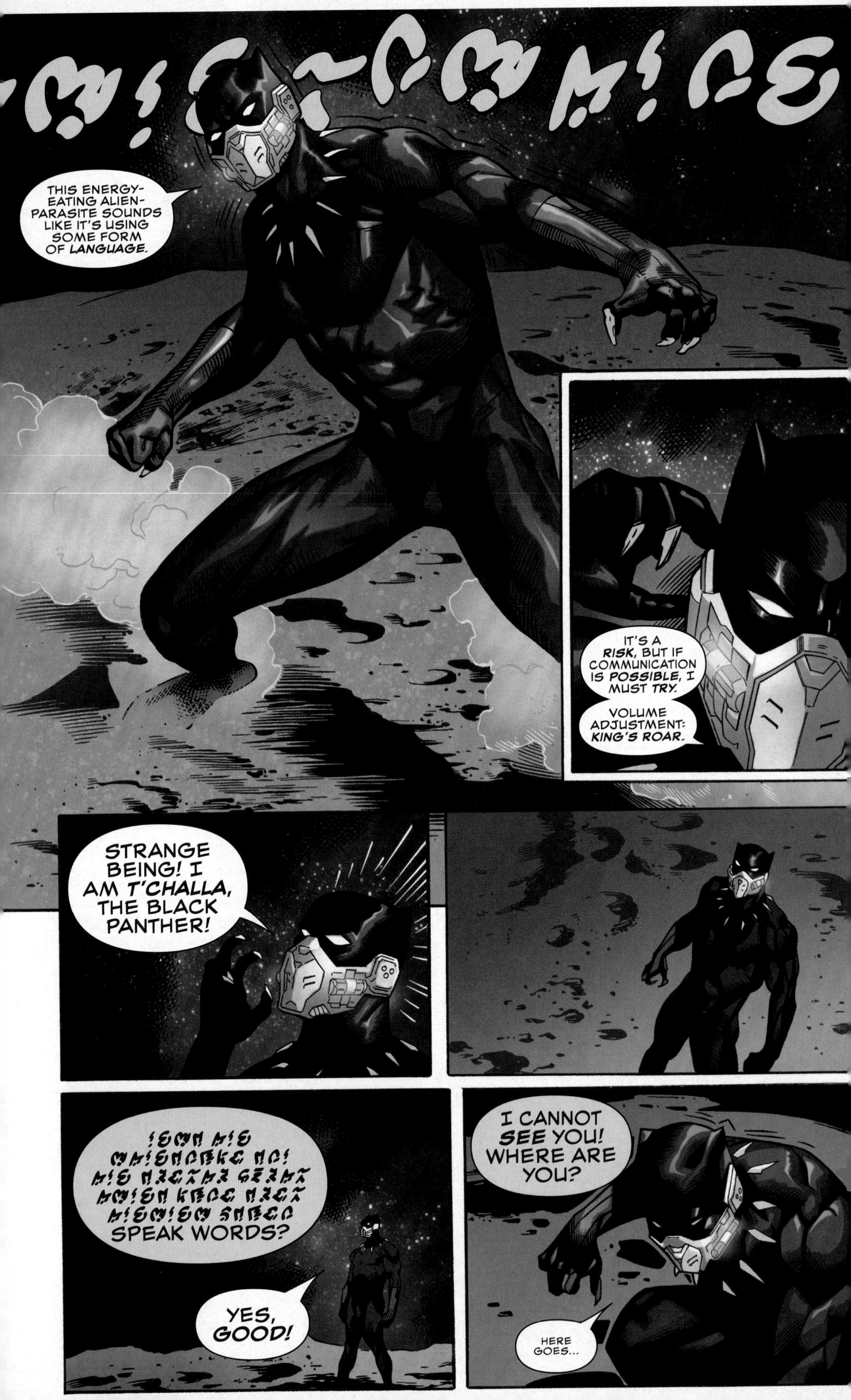

THIS ENERGY-EATING ALIEN-PARASITE SOUNDS LIKE IT'S USING SOME FORM OF LANGUAGE.
IT'S A RISK, BUT IF COMMUNICATION IS POSSIBLE, I MUST TRY.
VOLUME ADJUSTMENT: KING'S ROAR.
STRANGE BEING! I AM T'CHALLA, THE BLACK PANTHER!
SPEAK WORDS?
YES, GOOD!
I CANNOT SEE YOU! WHERE ARE YOU?
HERE GOES...

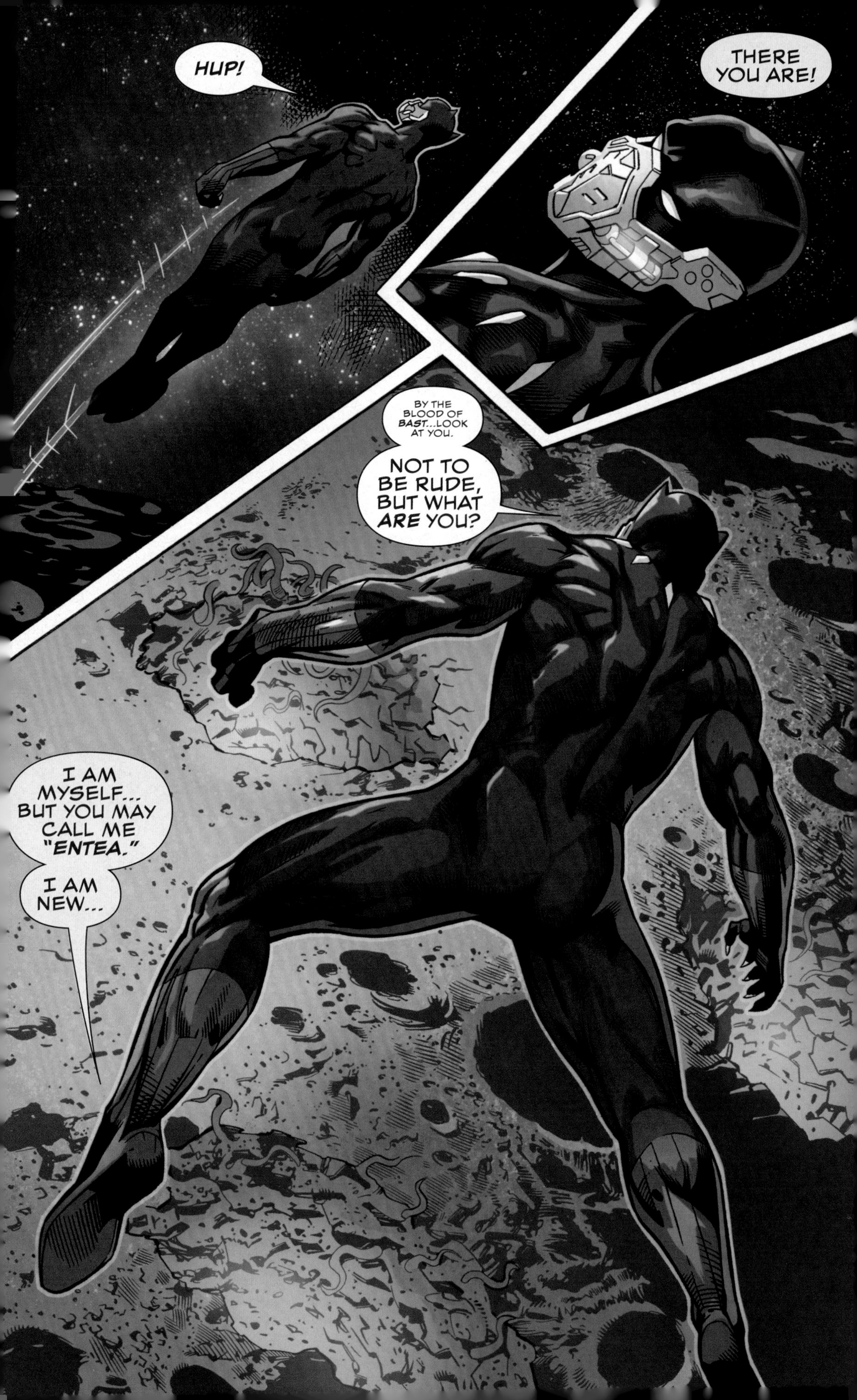
HUP!
THERE YOU ARE!
BY THE BLOOD OF BAST...LOOK AT YOU.
NOT TO BE RUDE, BUT WHAT ARE YOU?
I AM MYSELF... BUT YOU MAY CALL ME "ENTEA."
I AM NEW...

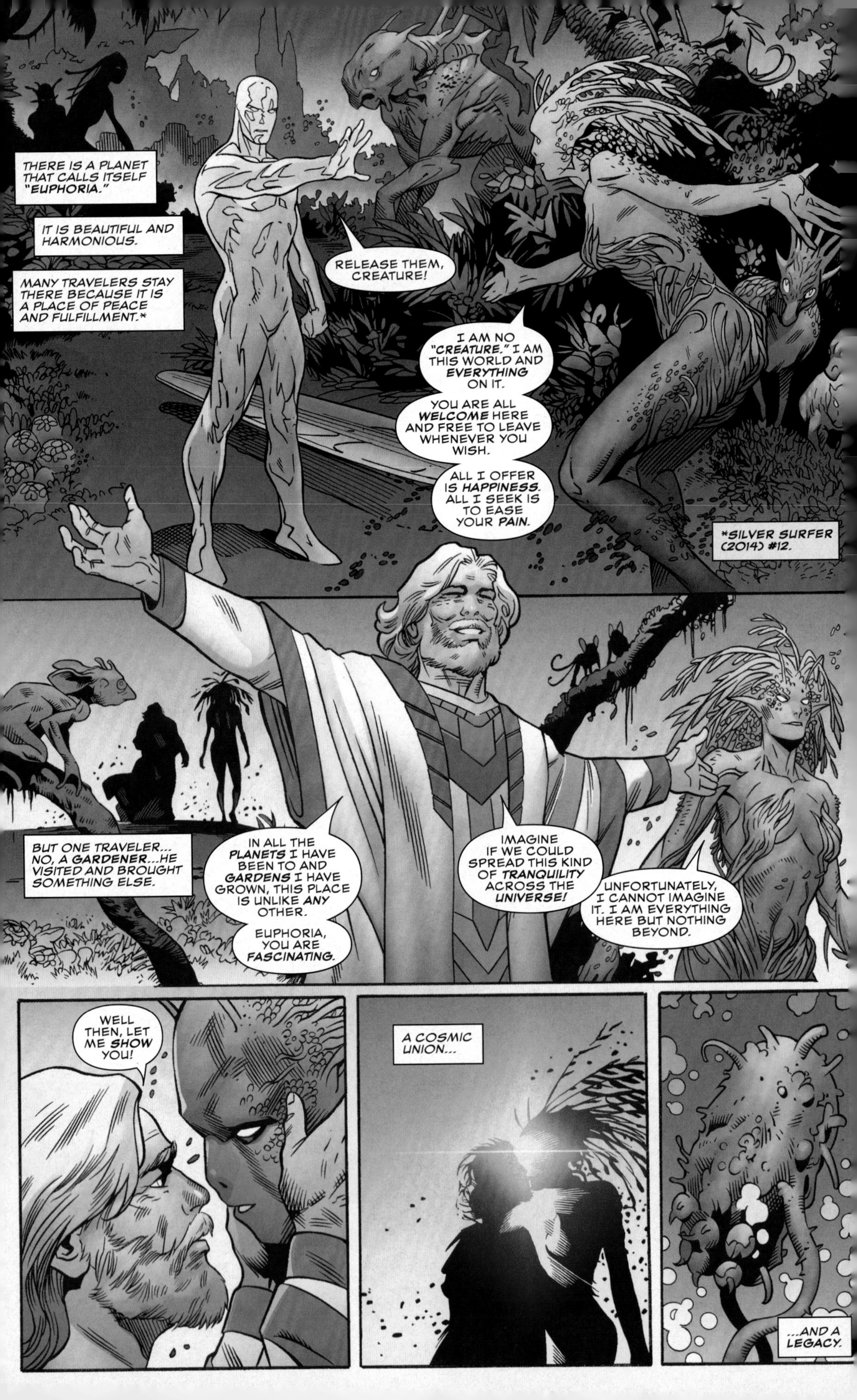
THERE IS A PLANET THAT CALLS ITSELF "EUPHORIA."
IT IS BEAUTIFUL AND HARMONIOUS.
MANY TRAVELERS STAY THERE BECAUSE IT IS A PLACE OF PEACE AND FULFILLMENT.*
RELEASE THEM, CREATURE!
I AM NO "CREATURE." I AM THIS WORLD AND EVERYTHING ON IT.
YOU ARE ALL WELCOME HERE AND FREE TO LEAVE WHENEVER YOU WISH.
ALL I OFFER IS HAPPINESS. ALL I SEEK IS TO EASE YOUR PAIN.
*SILVER SURFER (2014) #12.
BUT ONE TRAVELER... NO, A GARDENER...HE VISITED AND BROUGHT SOMETHING ELSE.
IN ALL THE PLANETS I HAVE BEEN TO AND GARDENS I HAVE GROWN, THIS PLACE IS UNLIKE ANY OTHER.
EUPHORIA, YOU ARE FASCINATING.
IMAGINE IF WE COULD SPREAD THIS KIND OF TRANQUILITY ACROSS THE UNIVERSE!
UNFORTUNATELY, I CANNOT IMAGINE IT. I AM EVERYTHING HERE BUT NOTHING BEYOND.
WELL THEN, LET ME SHOW YOU!
A COSMIC UNION...
...AND A LEGACY.

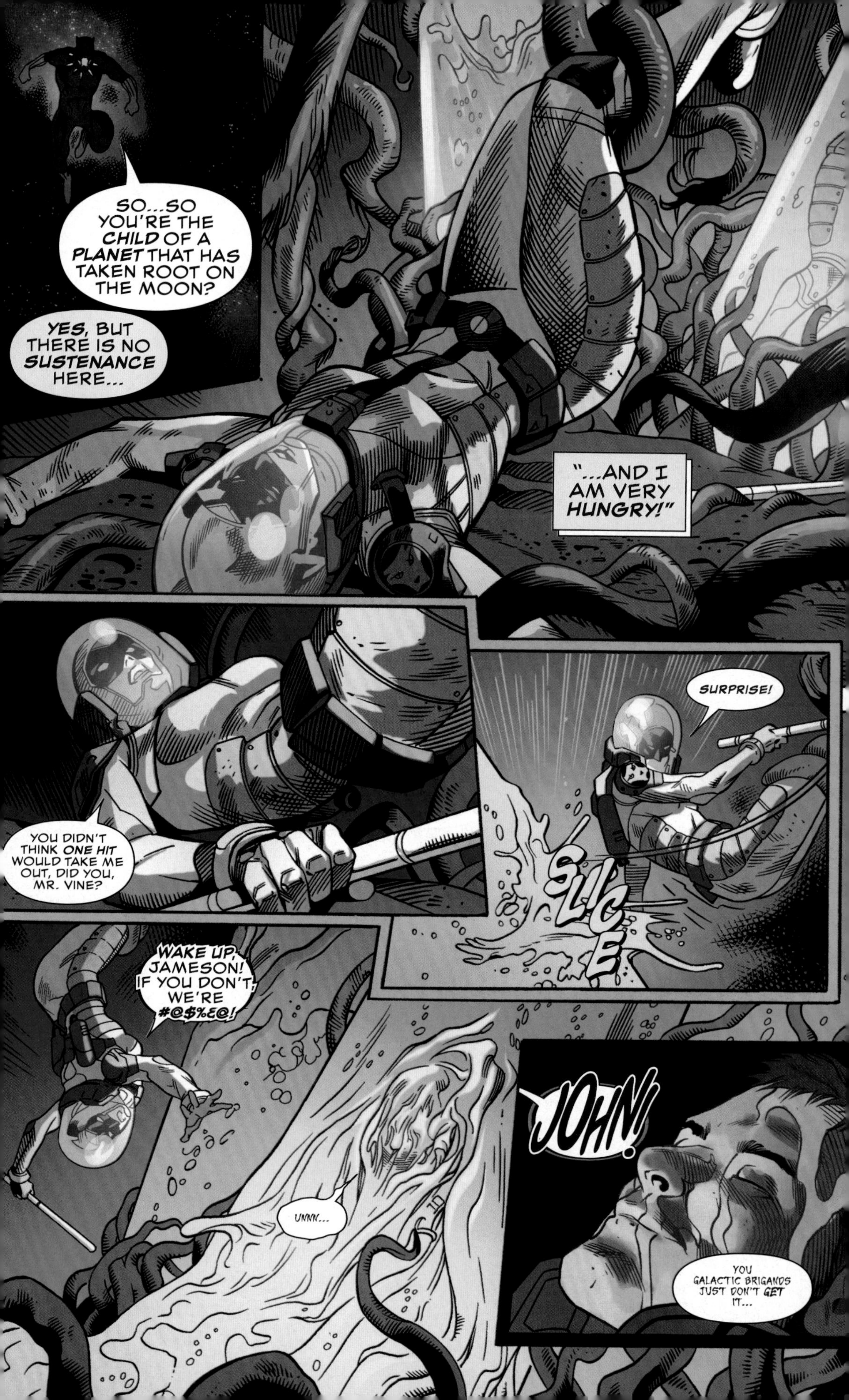
SO...SO YOU'RE THE CHILD OF A PLANET THAT HAS TAKEN ROOT ON THE MOON?
YES, BUT THERE IS NO SUSTENANCE HERE...
"...AND I AM VERY HUNGRY!"
YOU DIDN'T THINK ONE HIT WOULD TAKE ME OUT, DID YOU, MR. VINE?
SURPRISE!
SLICE
WAKE UP, JAMESON! IF YOU DON'T, WE'RE #@$%&@!
UNNN...
JOHN!
YOU GALACTIC BRIGANDS JUST DON'T GET IT...

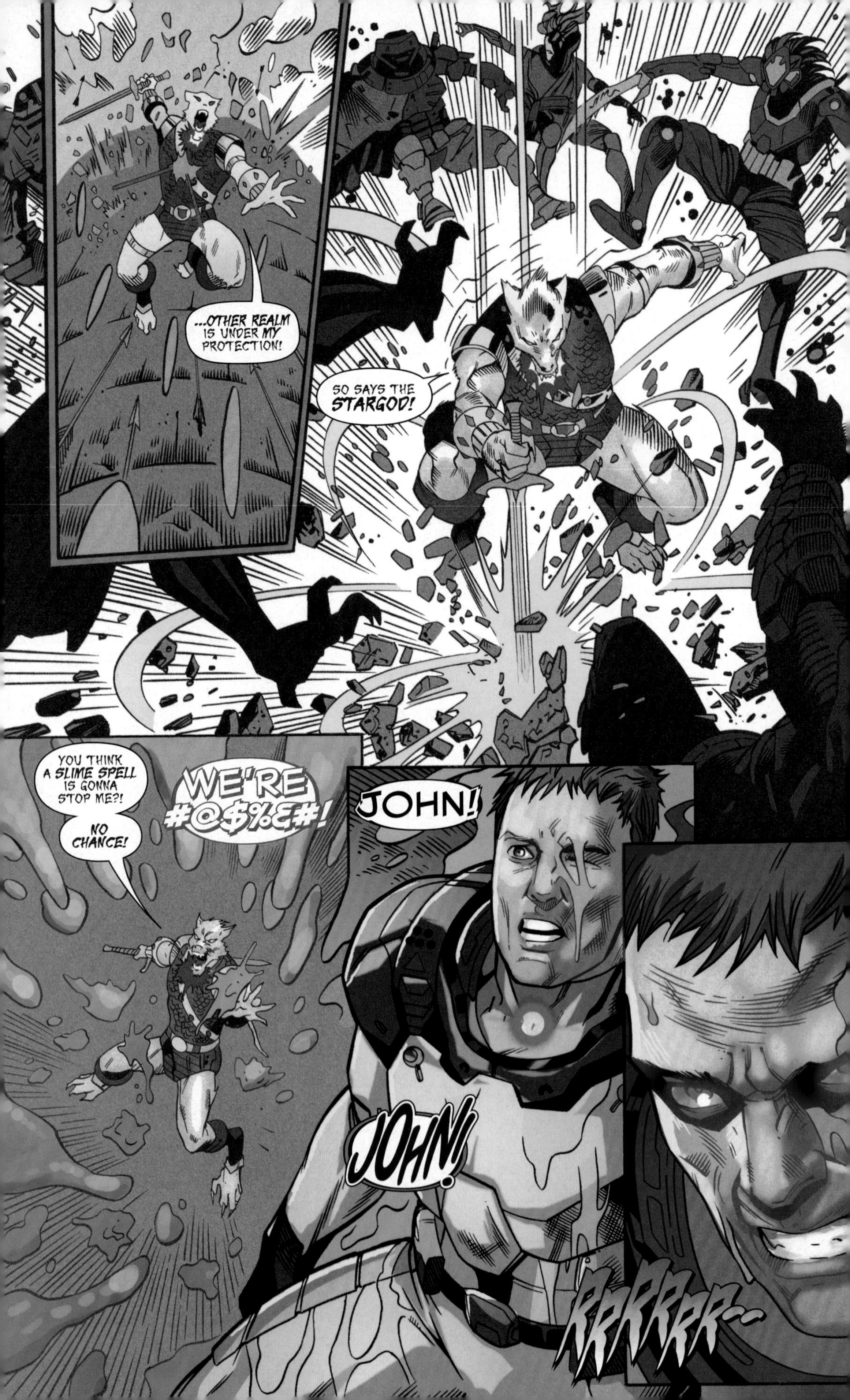
...OTHER REALM IS UNDER MY PROTECTION!
SO SAYS THE STARGOD!
YOU THINK A SLIME SPELL IS GONNA STOP ME?!
NO CHANCE!
WE'RE #@$%&#!
JOHN!
JOHN!
RRRRRR--

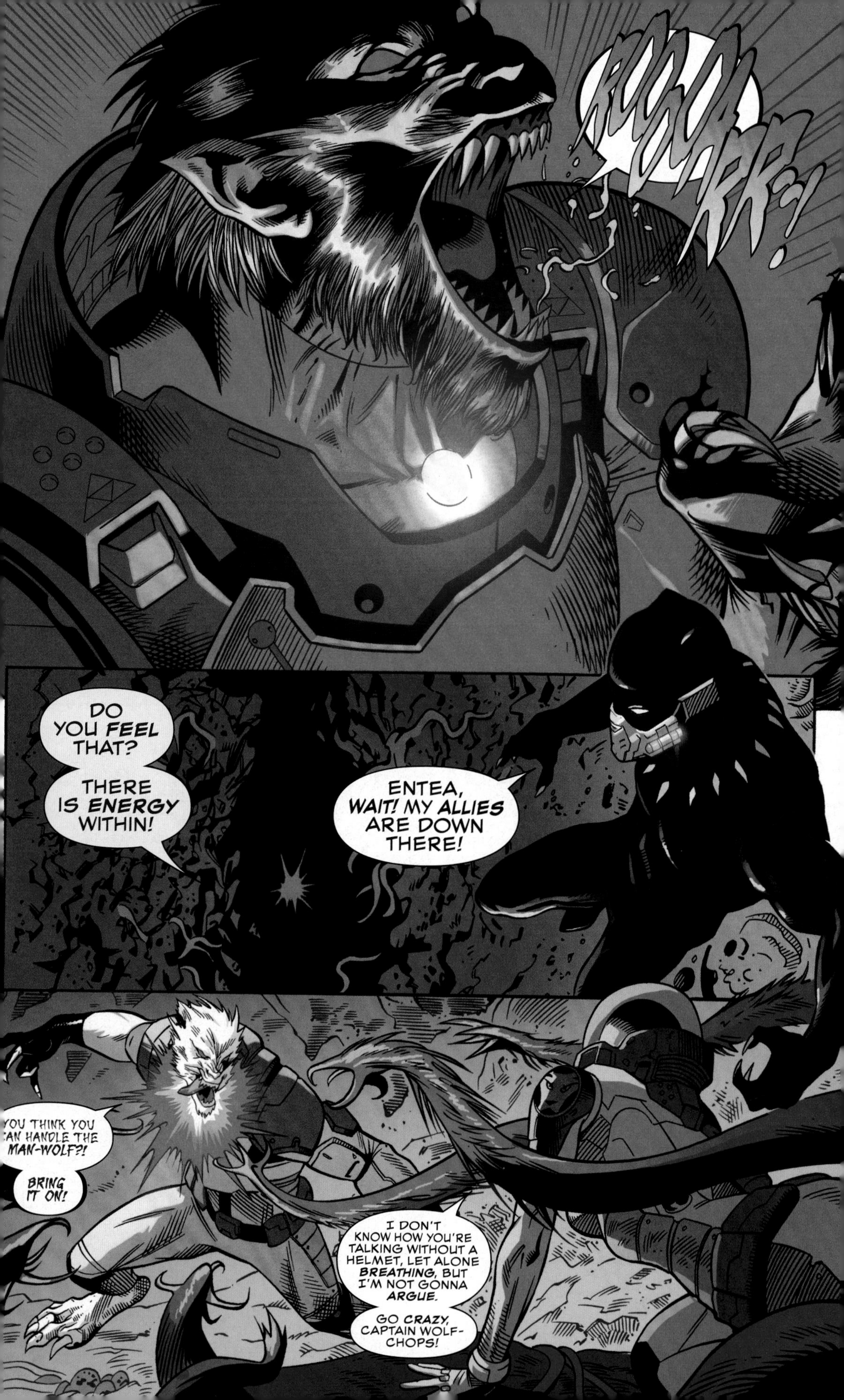

RRROOAARR?!
DO YOU FEEL THAT?
THERE IS ENERGY WITHIN!
ENTEA, WAIT! MY ALLIES ARE DOWN THERE!
YOU THINK YOU CAN HANDLE THE MAN-WOLF?!
BRING IT ON!
I DON'T KNOW HOW YOU'RE TALKING WITHOUT A HELMET, LET ALONE BREATHING, BUT I'M NOT GONNA ARGUE.
GO CRAZY, CAPTAIN WOLF-CHOPS!

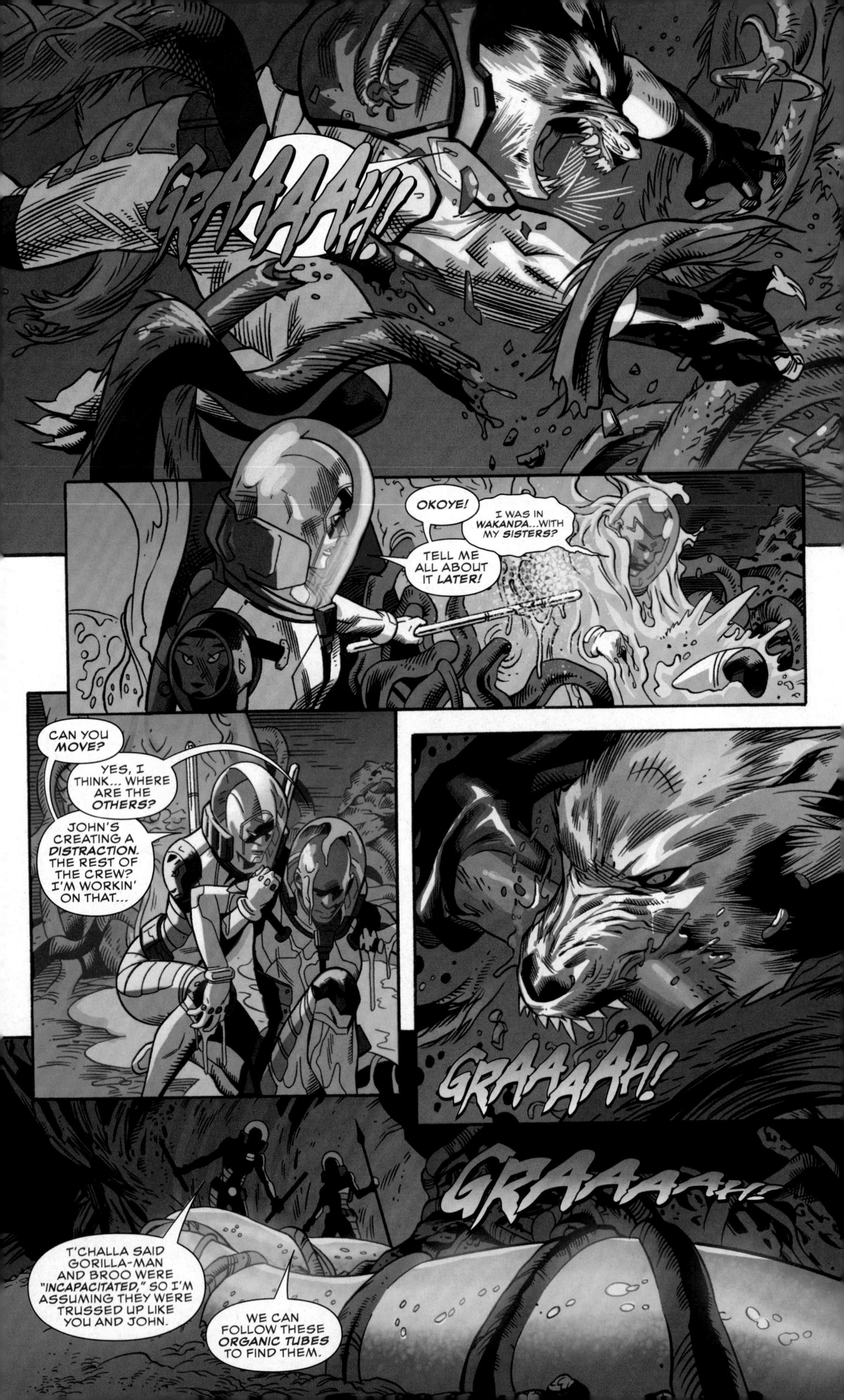
GRAAAAH!!
OKOYE!
I WAS IN WAKANDA...WITH MY SISTERS?
TELL ME ALL ABOUT IT LATER!
CAN YOU MOVE?
YES, I THINK... WHERE ARE THE OTHERS?
JOHN'S CREATING A DISTRACTION. THE REST OF THE CREW? I'M WORKIN' ON THAT...
GRAAAAH!
GRAAAAAH!!
T'CHALLA SAID GORILLA-MAN AND BROO WERE "INCAPACITATED," SO I'M ASSUMING THEY WERE TRUSSED UP LIKE YOU AND JOHN.
WE CAN FOLLOW THESE ORGANIC TUBES TO FIND THEM.

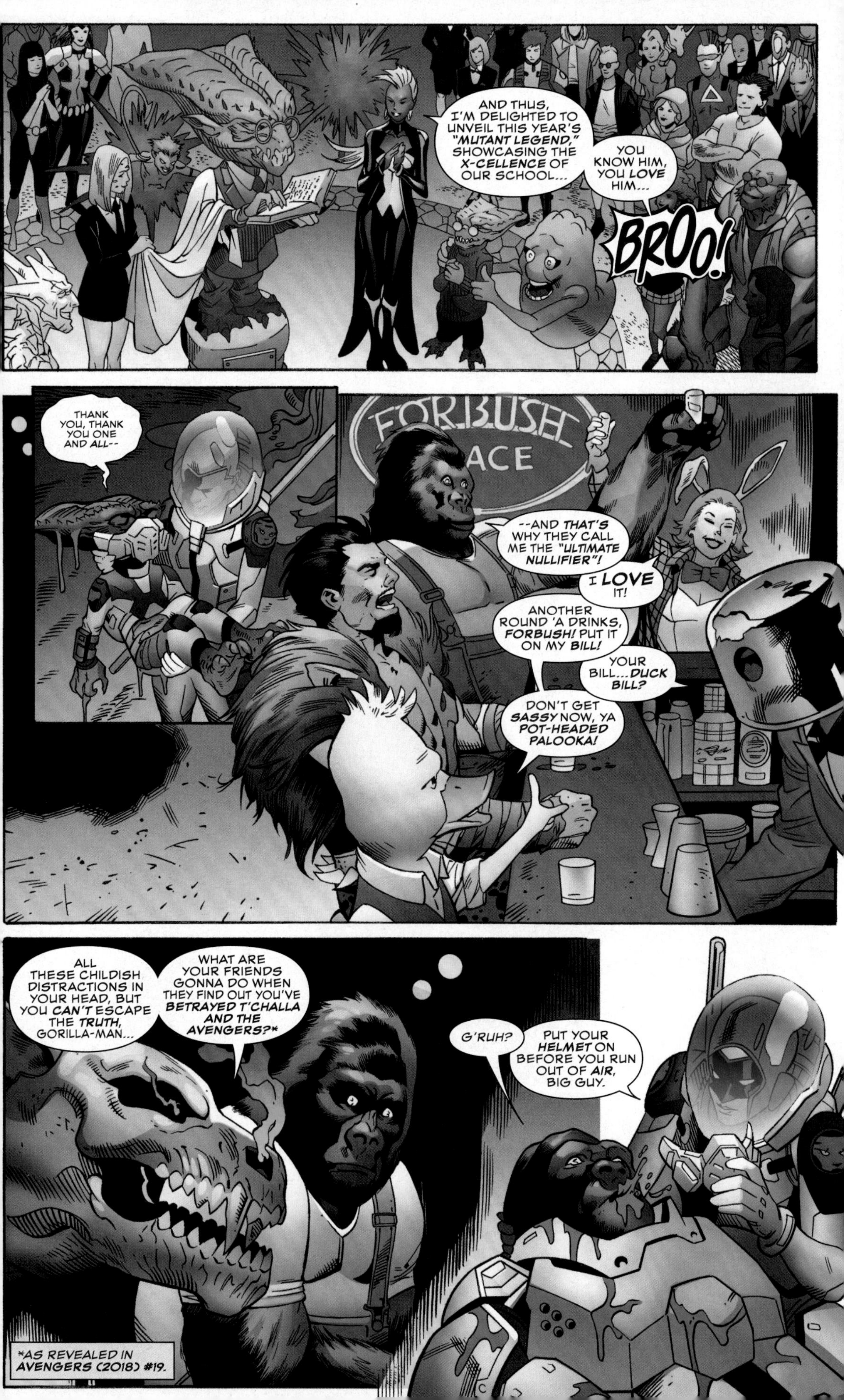
AND THUS, I'M DELIGHTED TO UNVEIL THIS YEAR'S "MUTANT LEGEND," SHOWCASING THE X-CELLENCE OF OUR SCHOOL...
YOU KNOW HIM, YOU LOVE HIM...
BROO!
FORBUSH
ACE
THANK YOU, THANK YOU ONE AND ALL--
--AND THAT'S WHY THEY CALL ME THE "ULTIMATE NULLIFIER"!
I LOVE IT!
ANOTHER ROUND 'A DRINKS, FORBUSH! PUT IT ON MY BILL!
YOUR BILL...DUCK BILL?
DON'T GET SASSY NOW, YA POT-HEADED PALOOKA!
ALL THESE CHILDISH DISTRACTIONS IN YOUR HEAD, BUT YOU CAN'T ESCAPE THE TRUTH, GORILLA-MAN...
WHAT ARE YOUR FRIENDS GONNA DO WHEN THEY FIND OUT YOU'VE BETRAYED T'CHALLA AND THE AVENGERS?*
G'RUH?
PUT YOUR HELMET ON BEFORE YOU RUN OUT OF AIR, BIG GUY.
*AS REVEALED IN AVENGERS (2018) #19.

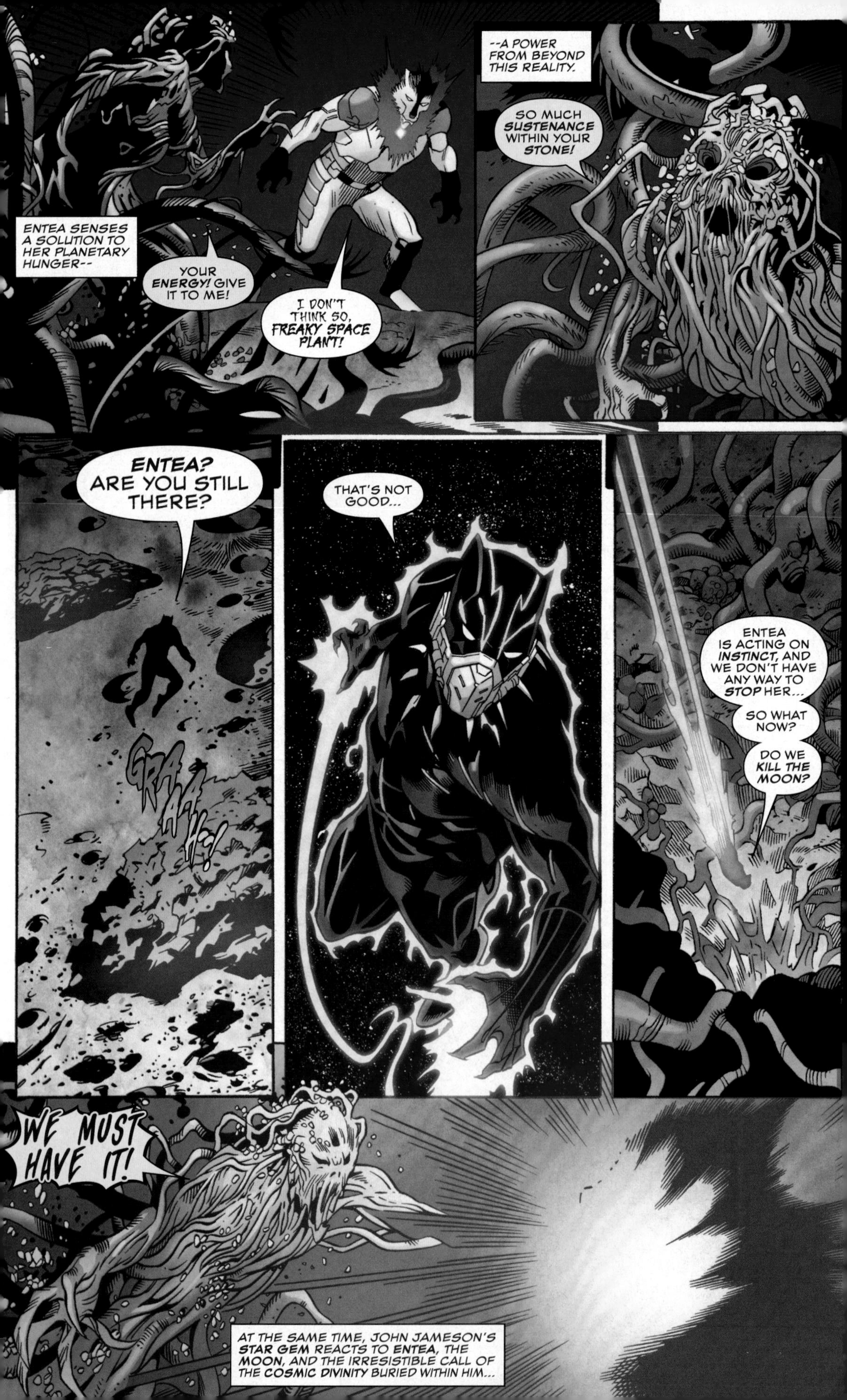

ENTEA SENSES A SOLUTION TO HER PLANETARY HUNGER--
YOUR ENERGY! GIVE IT TO ME!
I DON'T THINK SO, FREAKY SPACE PLANT!
--A POWER FROM BEYOND THIS REALITY.
SO MUCH SUSTENANCE WITHIN YOUR STONE!
ENTEA? ARE YOU STILL THERE?
GRAAAH!
THAT'S NOT GOOD...
ENTEA IS ACTING ON INSTINCT, AND WE DON'T HAVE ANY WAY TO STOP HER...
SO WHAT NOW?
DO WE KILL THE MOON?
WE MUST HAVE IT!
AT THE SAME TIME, JOHN JAMESON'S STAR GEM REACTS TO ENTEA, THE MOON, AND THE IRRESISTIBLE CALL OF THE COSMIC DIVINITY BURIED WITHIN HIM...

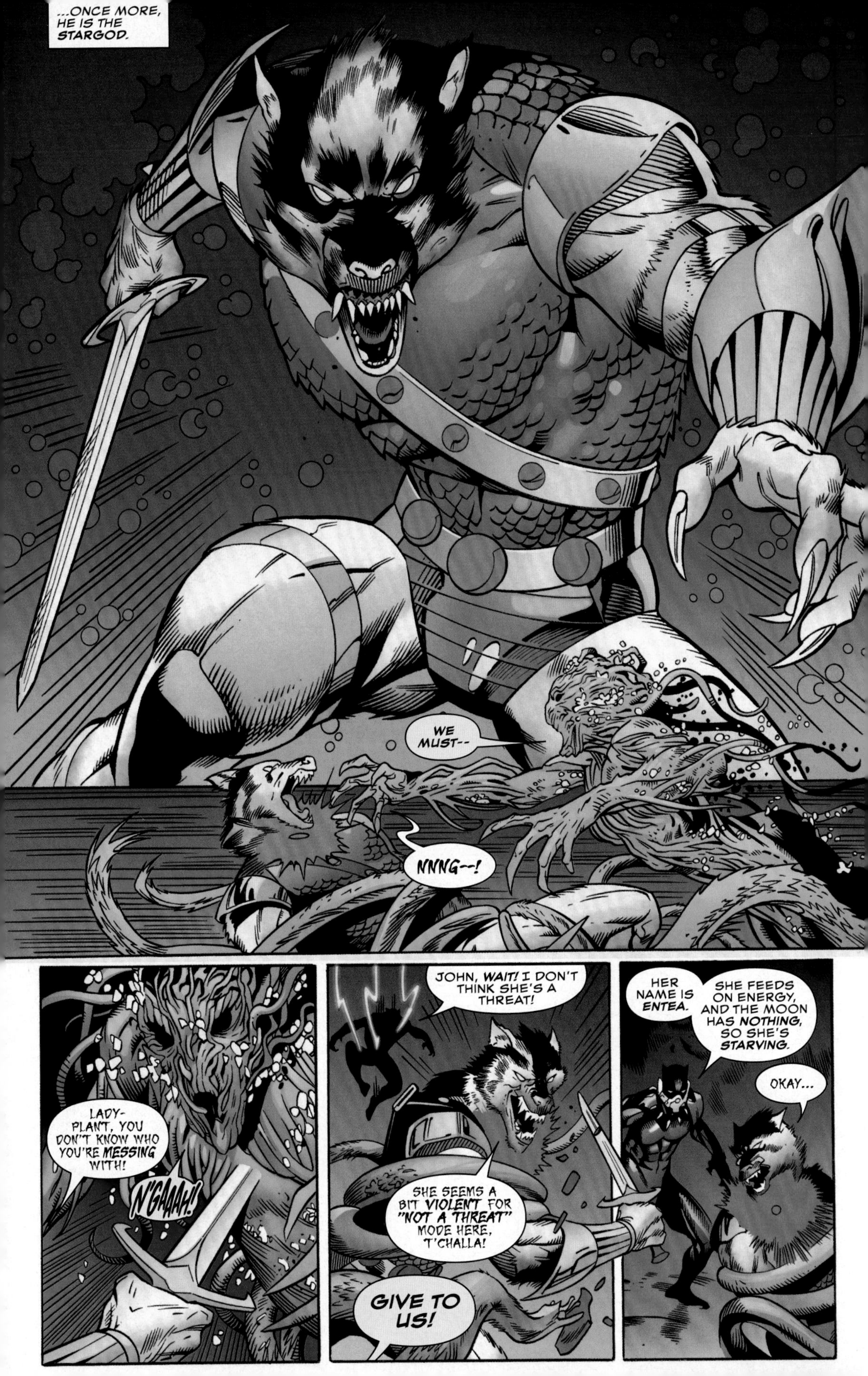
...ONCE MORE, HE IS THE STARGOD.
WE MUST--
NNNG--!
LADY-PLANT, YOU DON'T KNOW WHO YOU'RE MESSING WITH!
N'GAAAH!
JOHN, WAIT! I DON'T THINK SHE'S A THREAT!
SHE SEEMS A BIT VIOLENT FOR "NOT A THREAT" MODE HERE, T'CHALLA!
GIVE TO US!
HER NAME IS ENTEA.
SHE FEEDS ON ENERGY, AND THE MOON HAS NOTHING, SO SHE'S STARVING.
OKAY...

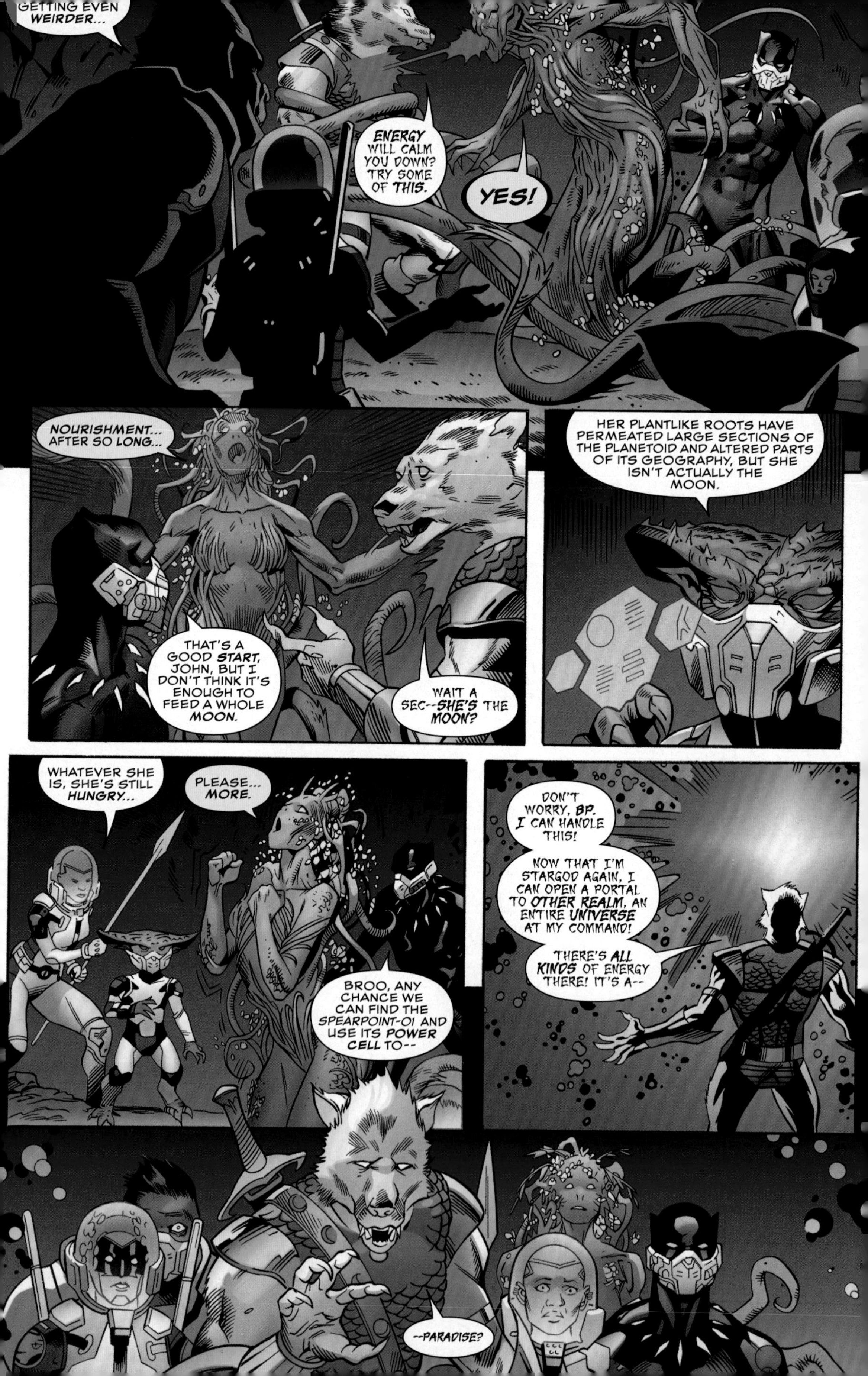
GETTING EVEN WEIRDER...
ENERGY WILL CALM YOU DOWN? TRY SOME OF THIS.
YES!
NOURISHMENT... AFTER SO LONG...
THAT'S A GOOD START, JOHN, BUT I DON'T THINK IT'S ENOUGH TO FEED A WHOLE MOON.
WAIT A SEC--SHE'S THE MOON?
HER PLANTLIKE ROOTS HAVE PERMEATED LARGE SECTIONS OF THE PLANETOID AND ALTERED PARTS OF ITS GEOGRAPHY, BUT SHE ISN'T ACTUALLY THE MOON.
WHATEVER SHE IS, SHE'S STILL HUNGRY...
PLEASE... MORE.
BROO, ANY CHANCE WE CAN FIND THE SPEARPOINT-01 AND USE ITS POWER CELL TO--
DON'T WORRY, BP. I CAN HANDLE THIS!
NOW THAT I'M STARGOD AGAIN, I CAN OPEN A PORTAL TO OTHER REALM, AN ENTIRE UNIVERSE AT MY COMMAND!
THERE'S ALL KINDS OF ENERGY THERE! IT'S A--
--PARADISE?

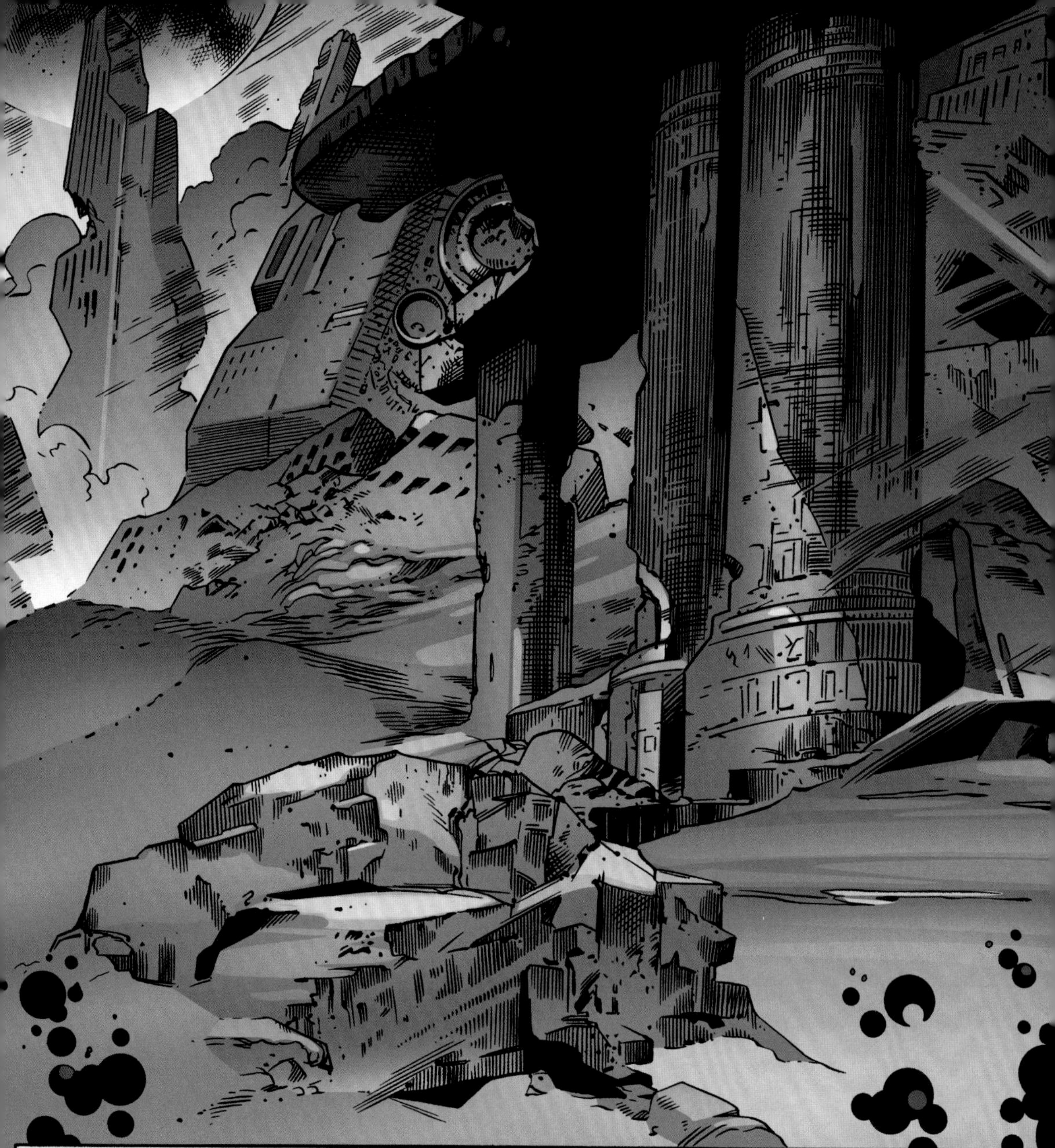

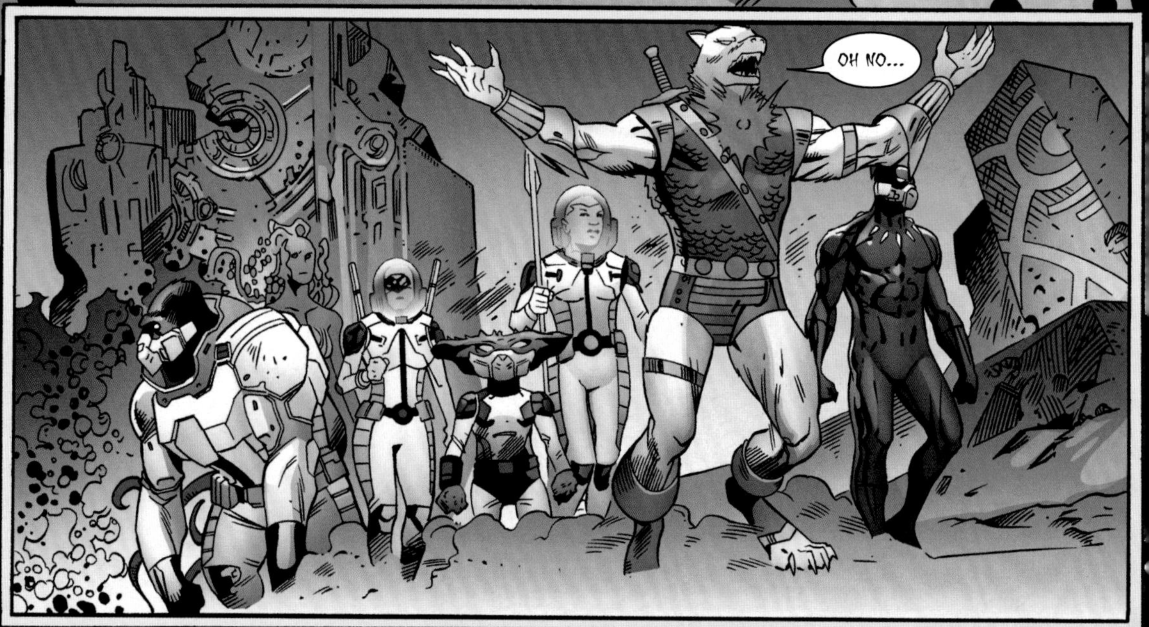
OH NO...

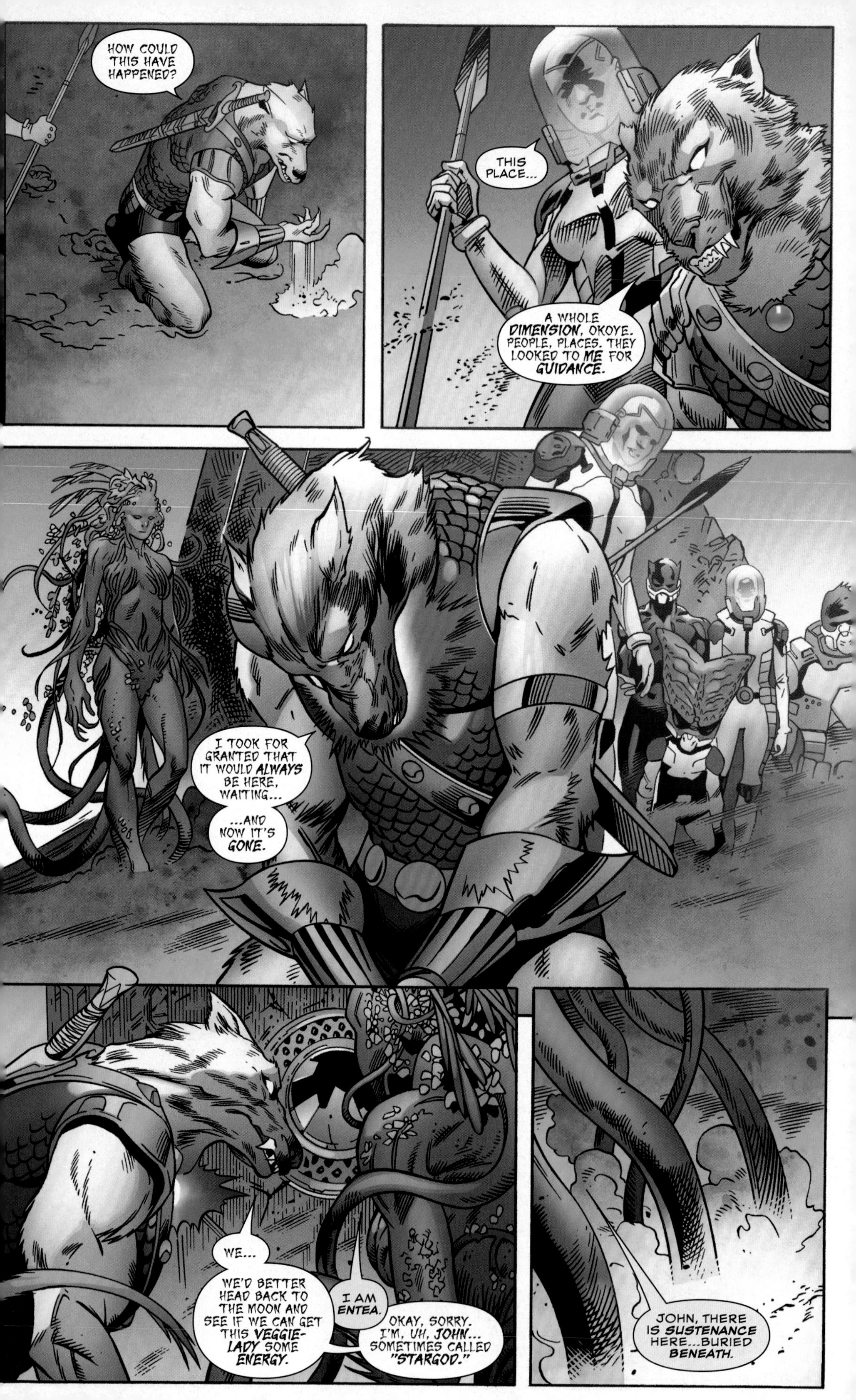
HOW COULD THIS HAVE HAPPENED?
THIS PLACE...
A WHOLE DIMENSION, OKOYE. PEOPLE, PLACES. THEY LOOKED TO ME FOR GUIDANCE.
I TOOK FOR GRANTED THAT IT WOULD ALWAYS BE HERE, WAITING...
...AND NOW IT'S GONE.
WE...
WE'D BETTER HEAD BACK TO THE MOON AND SEE IF WE CAN GET THIS VEGGIE-LADY SOME ENERGY.
I AM ENTEA.
OKAY, SORRY. I'M, UH, JOHN... SOMETIMES CALLED "STARGOD."
JOHN, THERE IS SUSTENANCE HERE...BURIED BENEATH.

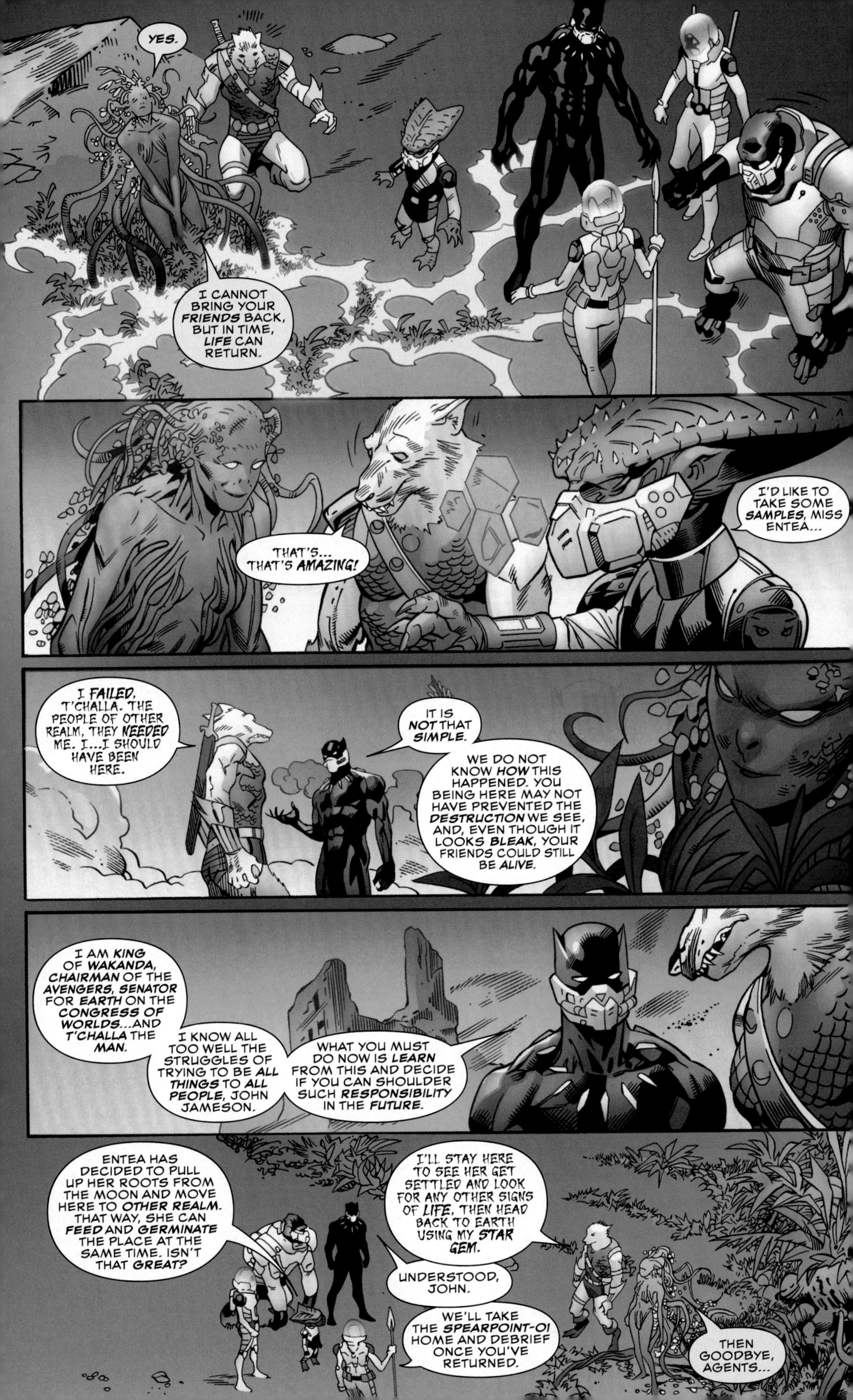
YES.
I CANNOT BRING YOUR FRIENDS BACK, BUT IN TIME, LIFE CAN RETURN.
THAT'S... THAT'S AMAZING!
I'D LIKE TO TAKE SOME SAMPLES, MISS ENTEA...
I FAILED, T'CHALLA. THE PEOPLE OF OTHER REALM, THEY NEEDED ME. I...I SHOULD HAVE BEEN HERE.
IT IS NOT THAT SIMPLE.
WE DO NOT KNOW HOW THIS HAPPENED. YOU BEING HERE MAY NOT HAVE PREVENTED THE DESTRUCTION WE SEE, AND, EVEN THOUGH IT LOOKS BLEAK, YOUR FRIENDS COULD STILL BE ALIVE.
I AM KING OF WAKANDA, CHAIRMAN OF THE AVENGERS, SENATOR FOR EARTH ON THE CONGRESS OF WORLDS...AND T'CHALLA THE MAN.
I KNOW ALL TOO WELL THE STRUGGLES OF TRYING TO BE ALL THINGS TO ALL PEOPLE, JOHN JAMESON.
WHAT YOU MUST DO NOW IS LEARN FROM THIS AND DECIDE IF YOU CAN SHOULDER SUCH RESPONSIBILITY IN THE FUTURE.
ENTEA HAS DECIDED TO PULL UP HER ROOTS FROM THE MOON AND MOVE HERE TO OTHER REALM. THAT WAY, SHE CAN FEED AND GERMINATE THE PLACE AT THE SAME TIME. ISN'T THAT GREAT?
I'LL STAY HERE TO SEE HER GET SETTLED AND LOOK FOR ANY OTHER SIGNS OF LIFE, THEN HEAD BACK TO EARTH USING MY STAR GEM.
UNDERSTOOD, JOHN.
WE'LL TAKE THE SPEARPOINT-01 HOME AND DEBRIEF ONCE YOU'VE RETURNED.
THEN GOODBYE, AGENTS...

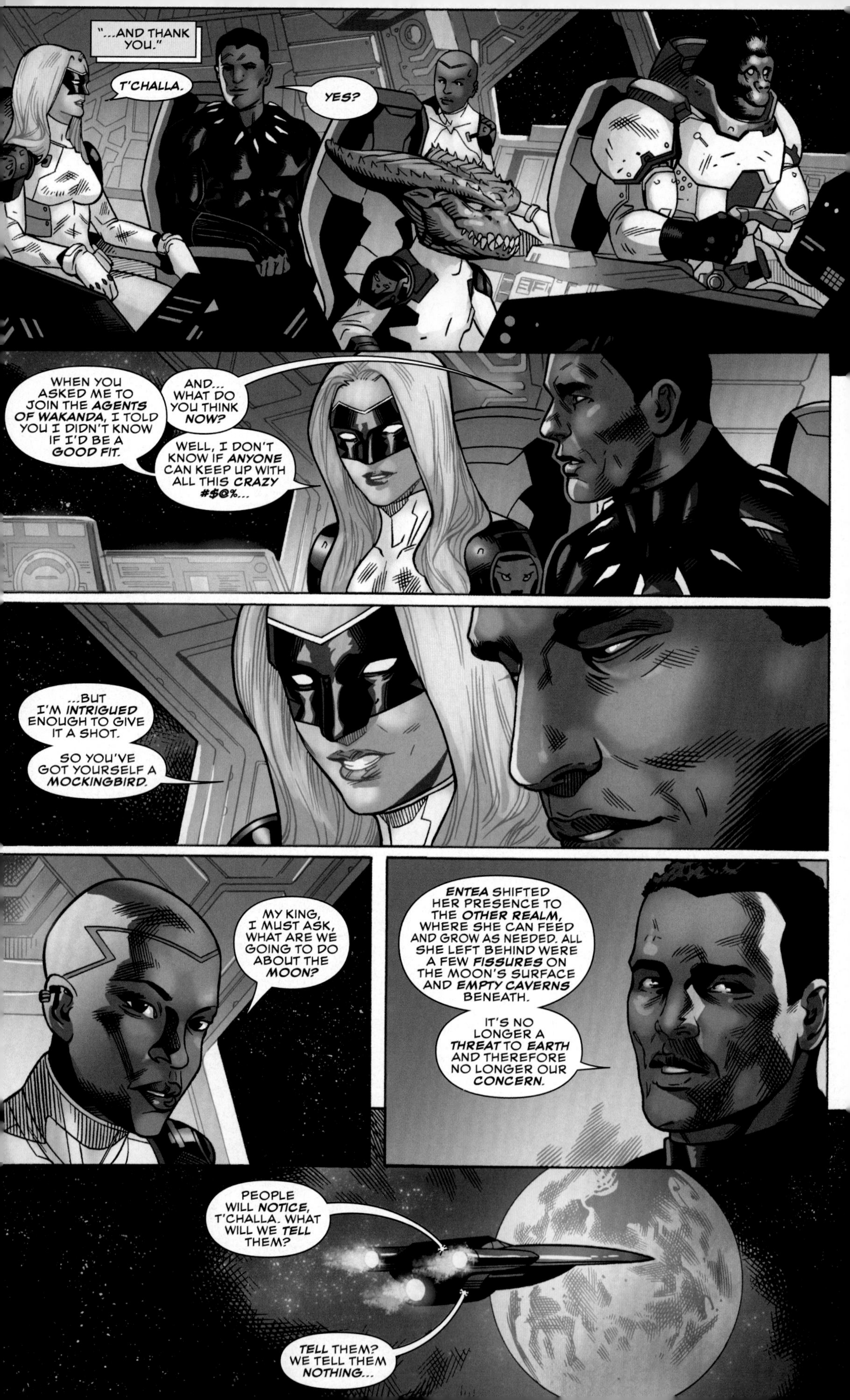
"...AND THANK YOU."
T'CHALLA.
YES?
WHEN YOU ASKED ME TO JOIN THE AGENTS OF WAKANDA, I TOLD YOU I DIDN'T KNOW IF I'D BE A GOOD FIT.
AND... WHAT DO YOU THINK NOW?
WELL, I DON'T KNOW IF ANYONE CAN KEEP UP WITH ALL THIS CRAZY #$@%...
...BUT I'M INTRIGUED ENOUGH TO GIVE IT A SHOT.
SO YOU'VE GOT YOURSELF A MOCKINGBIRD.
MY KING, I MUST ASK, WHAT ARE WE GOING TO DO ABOUT THE MOON?
ENTEA SHIFTED HER PRESENCE TO THE OTHER REALM, WHERE SHE CAN FEED AND GROW AS NEEDED. ALL SHE LEFT BEHIND WERE A FEW FISSURES ON THE MOON'S SURFACE AND EMPTY CAVERNS BENEATH.
IT'S NO LONGER A THREAT TO EARTH AND THEREFORE NO LONGER OUR CONCERN.
PEOPLE WILL NOTICE, T'CHALLA. WHAT WILL WE TELL THEM?
TELL THEM? WE TELL THEM NOTHING...

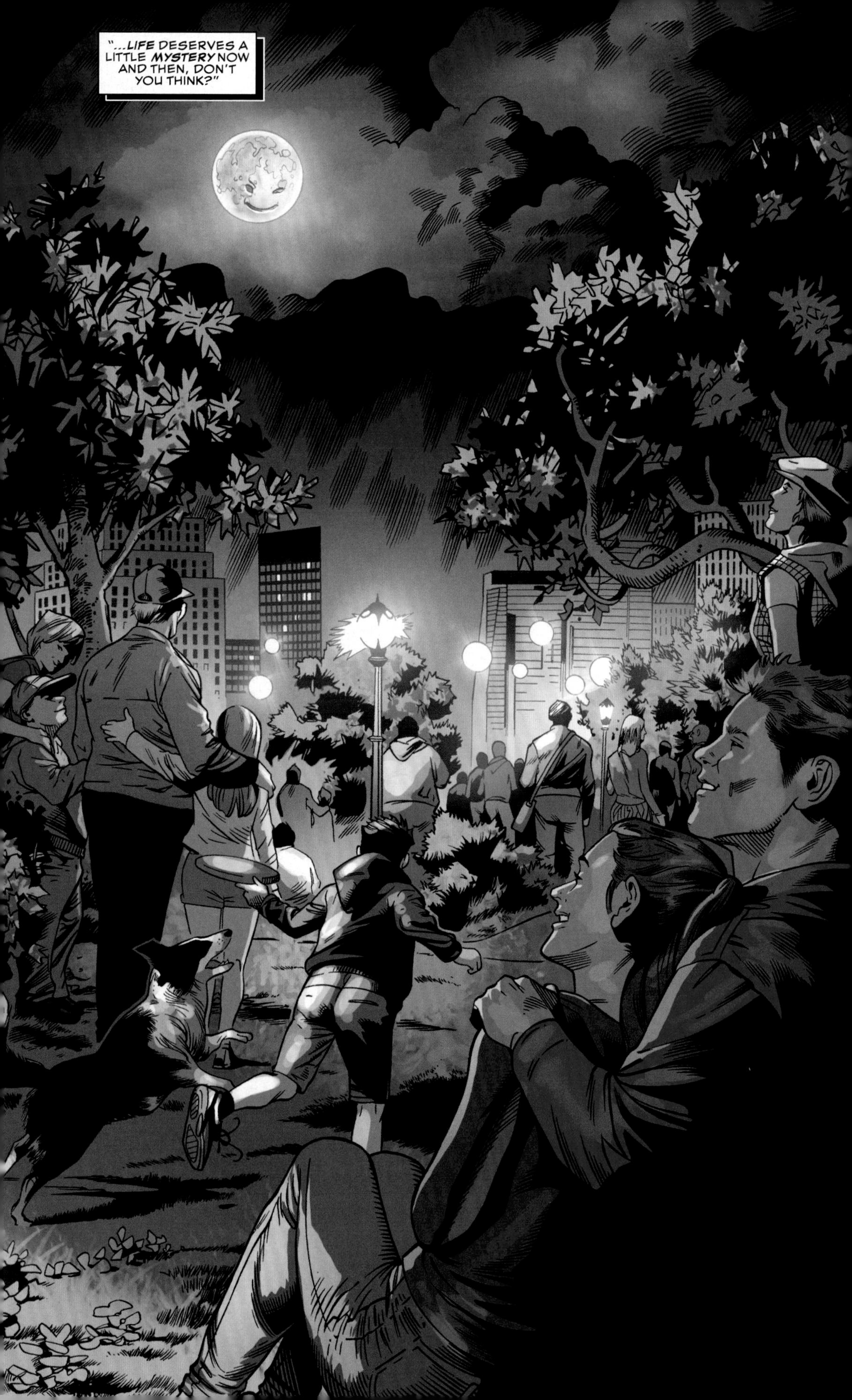
"...LIFE DESERVES A LITTLE MYSTERY NOW AND THEN, DON'T YOU THINK?"

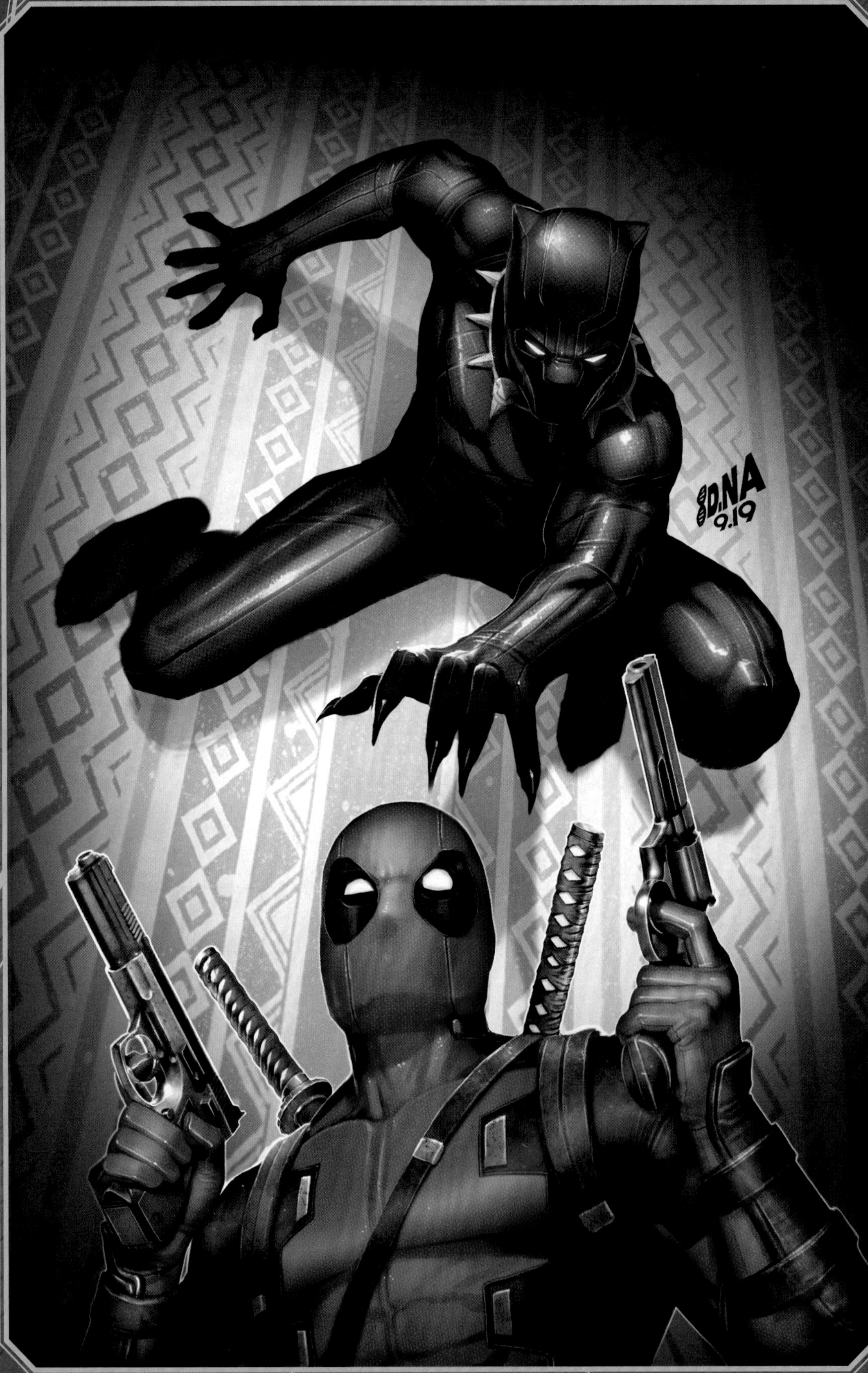
D.NA
9.19

5

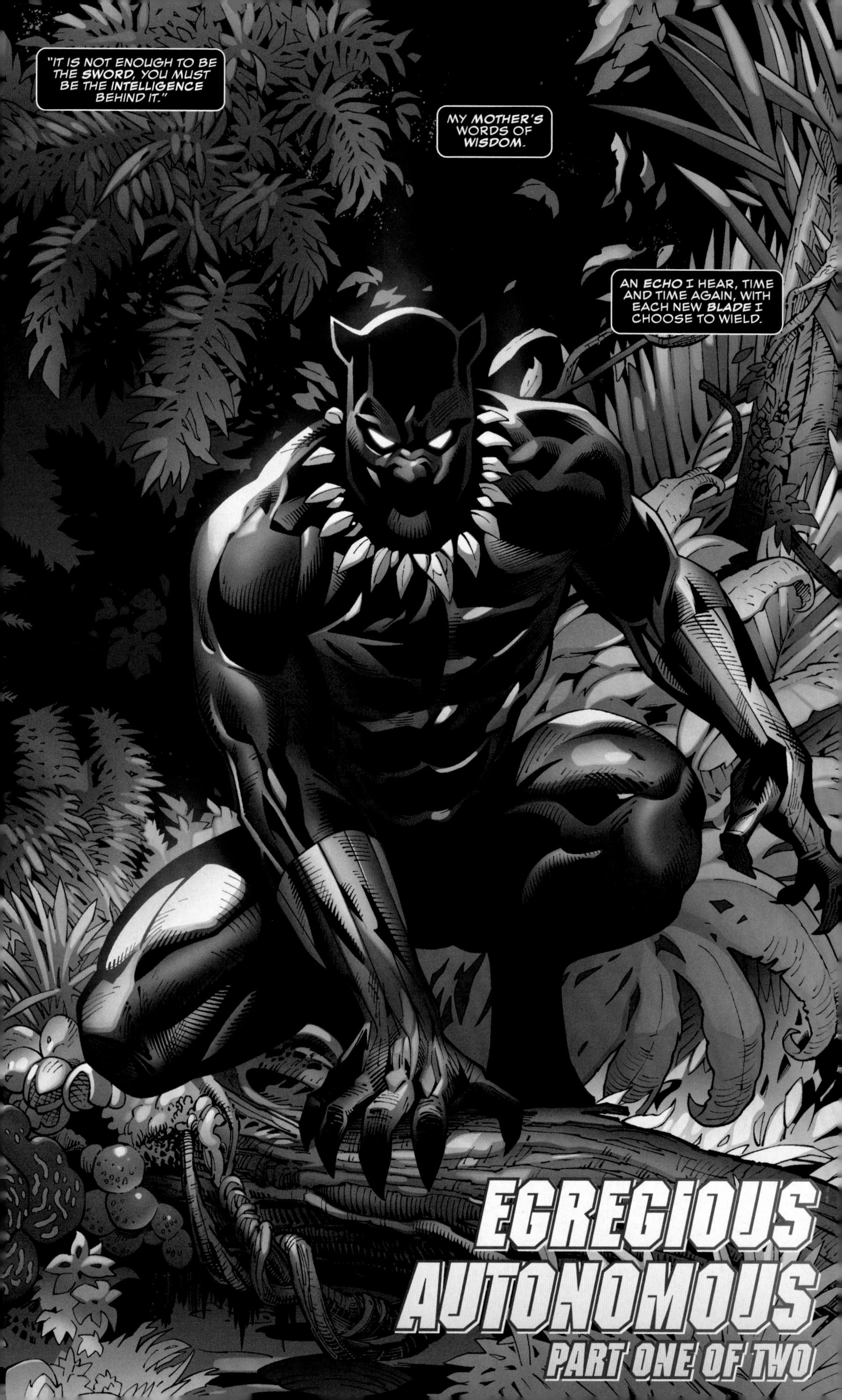
"IT IS NOT ENOUGH TO BE THE SWORD, YOU MUST BE THE INTELLIGENCE BEHIND IT."
MY MOTHER'S WORDS OF WISDOM.
AN ECHO I HEAR, TIME AND TIME AGAIN, WITH EACH NEW BLADE I CHOOSE TO WIELD.
EGREGIOUS AUTONOMOUS
PART ONE OF TWO

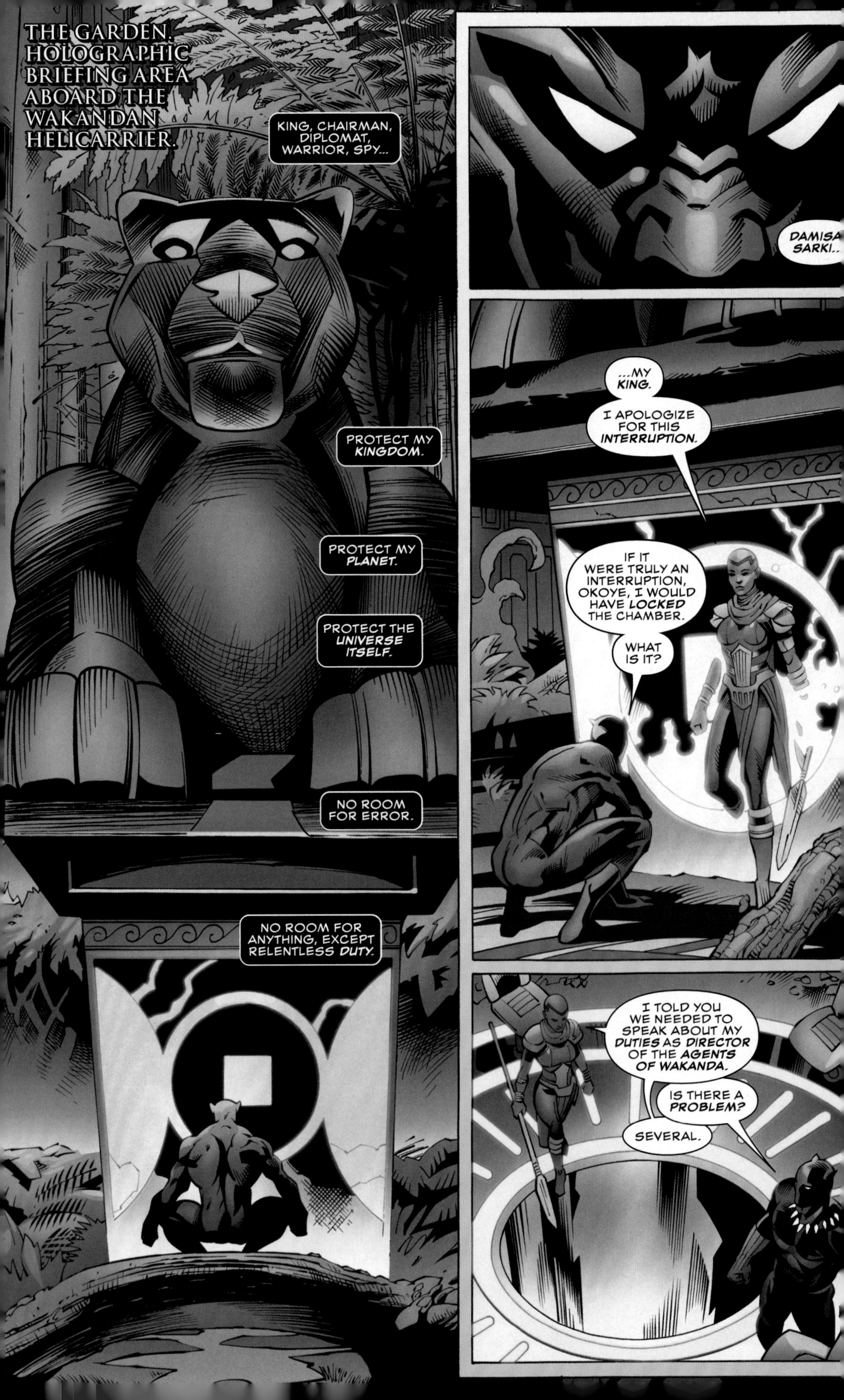
THE GARDEN. HOLOGRAPHIC BRIEFING AREA ABOARD THE WAKANDAN HELICARRIER.
KING, CHAIRMAN, DIPLOMAT, WARRIOR, SPY...
PROTECT MY KINGDOM.
PROTECT MY PLANET.
PROTECT THE UNIVERSE ITSELF.
NO ROOM FOR ERROR.
NO ROOM FOR ANYTHING, EXCEPT RELENTLESS DUTY.
DAMISA SARKI...
...MY KING.
I APOLOGIZE FOR THIS INTERRUPTION.
IF IT WERE TRULY AN INTERRUPTION, OKOYE, I WOULD HAVE LOCKED THE CHAMBER.
WHAT IS IT?
I TOLD YOU WE NEEDED TO SPEAK ABOUT MY DUTIES AS DIRECTOR OF THE AGENTS OF WAKANDA.
IS THERE A PROBLEM?
SEVERAL.

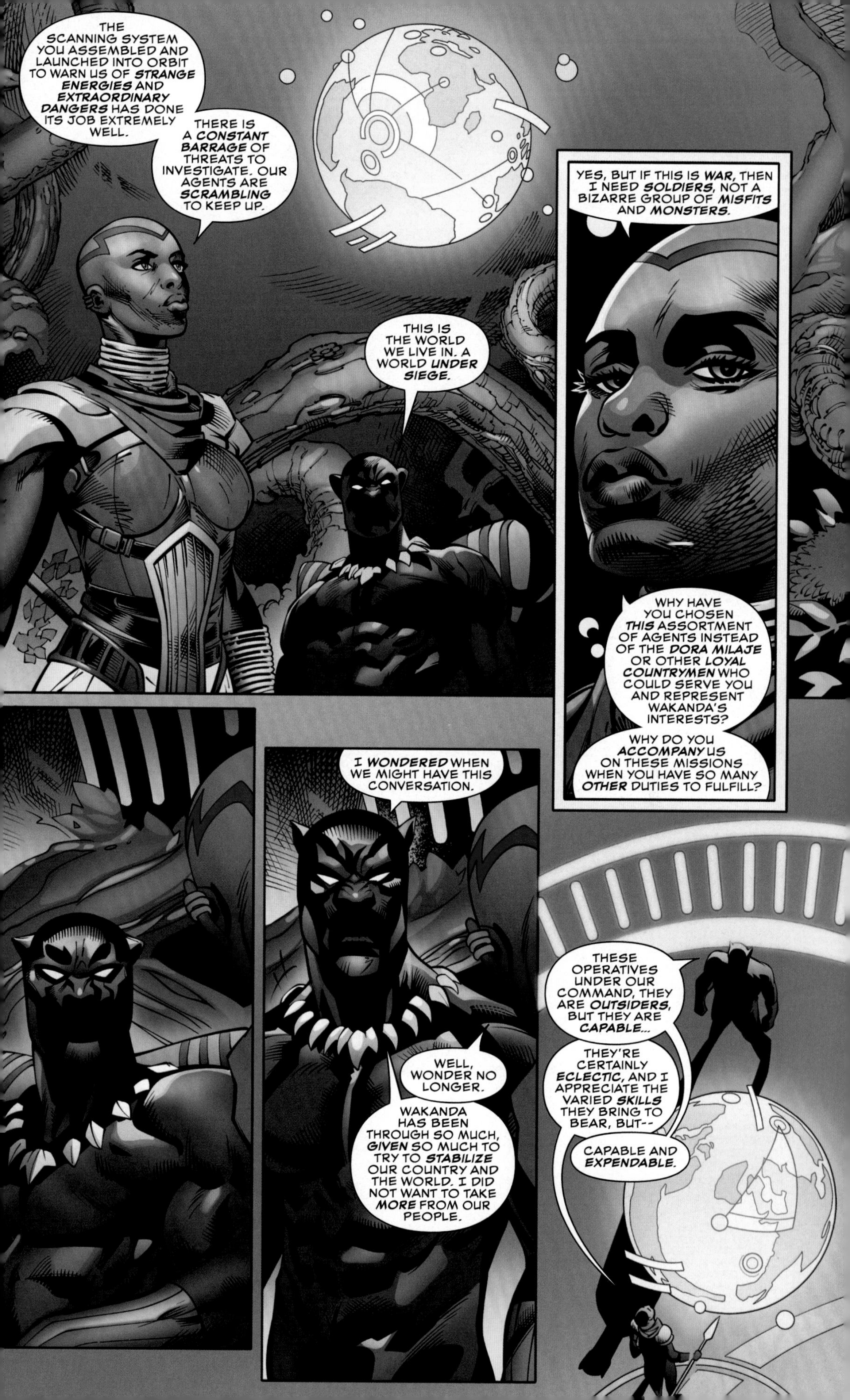
THE SCANNING SYSTEM YOU ASSEMBLED AND LAUNCHED INTO ORBIT TO WARN US OF STRANGE ENERGIES AND EXTRAORDINARY DANGERS HAS DONE ITS JOB EXTREMELY WELL.
THERE IS A CONSTANT BARRAGE OF THREATS TO INVESTIGATE. OUR AGENTS ARE SCRAMBLING TO KEEP UP.
THIS IS THE WORLD WE LIVE IN. A WORLD UNDER SIEGE.
YES, BUT IF THIS IS WAR, THEN I NEED SOLDIERS, NOT A BIZARRE GROUP OF MISFITS AND MONSTERS.
WHY HAVE YOU CHOSEN THIS ASSORTMENT OF AGENTS INSTEAD OF THE DORA MILAJE OR OTHER LOYAL COUNTRYMEN WHO COULD SERVE YOU AND REPRESENT WAKANDA'S INTERESTS?
WHY DO YOU ACCOMPANY US ON THESE MISSIONS WHEN YOU HAVE SO MANY OTHER DUTIES TO FULFILL?
I WONDERED WHEN WE MIGHT HAVE THIS CONVERSATION.
WELL, WONDER NO LONGER.
WAKANDA HAS BEEN THROUGH SO MUCH, GIVEN SO MUCH TO TRY TO STABILIZE OUR COUNTRY AND THE WORLD. I DID NOT WANT TO TAKE MORE FROM OUR PEOPLE.
THESE OPERATIVES UNDER OUR COMMAND, THEY ARE OUTSIDERS, BUT THEY ARE CAPABLE...
THEY'RE CERTAINLY ECLECTIC, AND I APPRECIATE THE VARIED SKILLS THEY BRING TO BEAR, BUT--
CAPABLE AND EXPENDABLE.

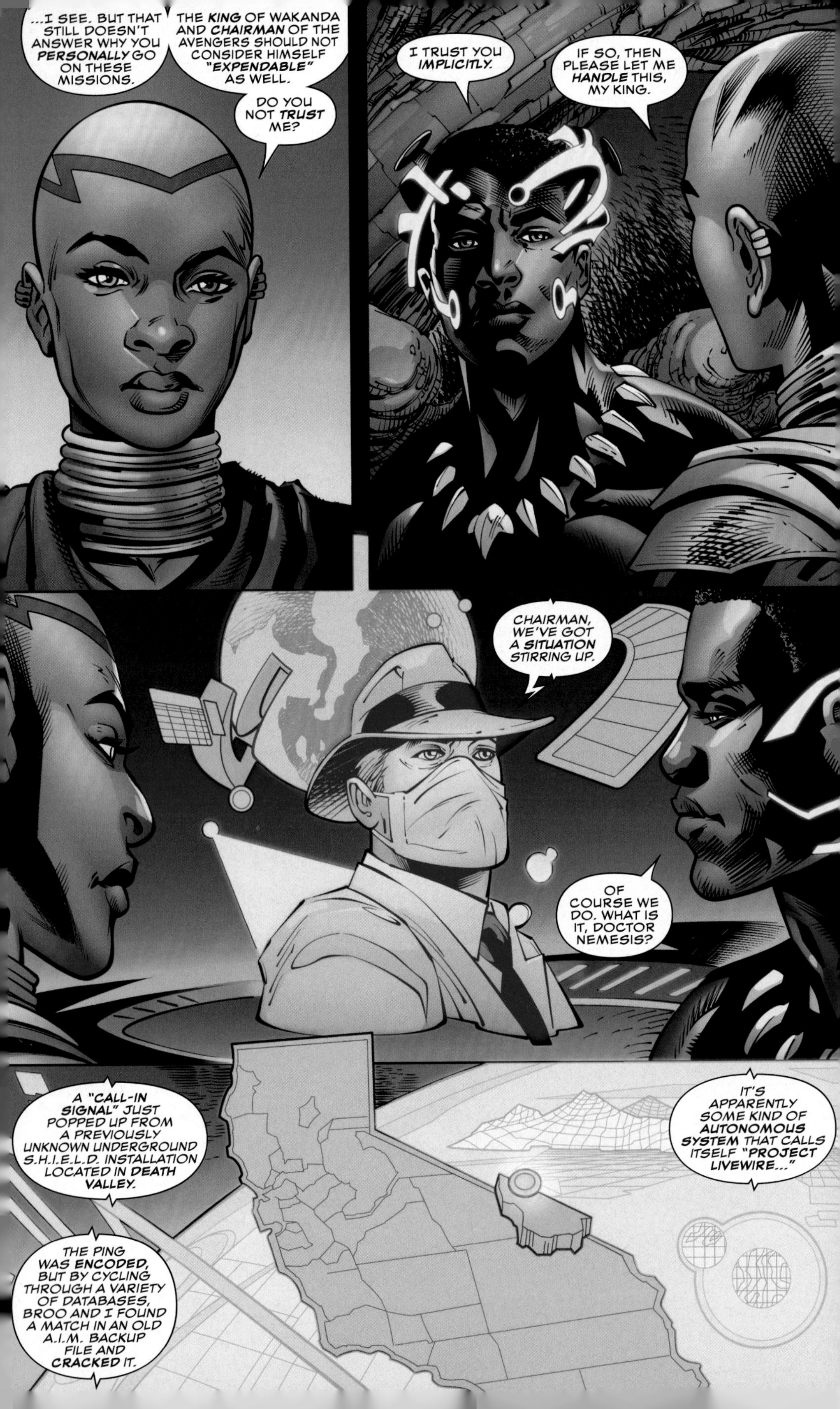
...I SEE. BUT THAT STILL DOESN'T ANSWER WHY YOU PERSONALLY GO ON THESE MISSIONS.
THE KING OF WAKANDA AND CHAIRMAN OF THE AVENGERS SHOULD NOT CONSIDER HIMSELF "EXPENDABLE" AS WELL.
DO YOU NOT TRUST ME?
I TRUST YOU IMPLICITLY.
IF SO, THEN PLEASE LET ME HANDLE THIS, MY KING.
CHAIRMAN, WE'VE GOT A SITUATION STIRRING UP.
OF COURSE WE DO. WHAT IS IT, DOCTOR NEMESIS?
A "CALL-IN SIGNAL" JUST POPPED UP FROM A PREVIOUSLY UNKNOWN UNDERGROUND S.H.I.E.L.D. INSTALLATION LOCATED IN DEATH VALLEY.
THE PING WAS ENCODED, BUT BY CYCLING THROUGH A VARIETY OF DATABASES, BROO AND I FOUND A MATCH IN AN OLD A.I.M. BACKUP FILE AND CRACKED IT.
IT'S APPARENTLY SOME KIND OF AUTONOMOUS SYSTEM THAT CALLS ITSELF "PROJECT LIVEWIRE..."

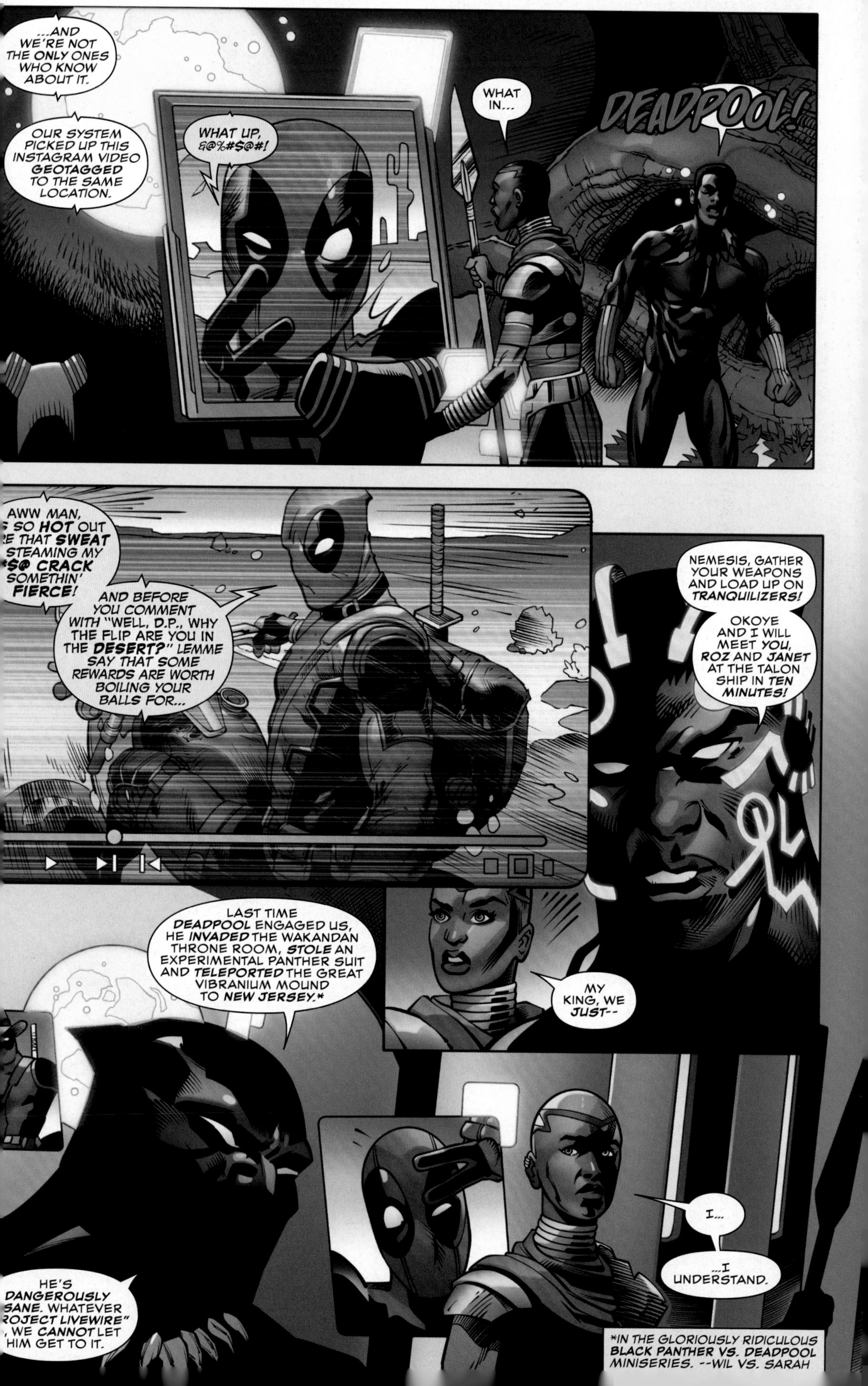
...AND WE'RE NOT THE ONLY ONES WHO KNOW ABOUT IT.
OUR SYSTEM PICKED UP THIS INSTAGRAM VIDEO GEOTAGGED TO THE SAME LOCATION.
WHAT UP, &@%#$@#!
WHAT IN...
DEADPOOL!
AWW MAN, S SO HOT OUT E THAT SWEAT STEAMING MY *$@ CRACK SOMETHIN' FIERCE!
AND BEFORE YOU COMMENT WITH "WELL, D.P., WHY THE FLIP ARE YOU IN THE DESERT?" LEMME SAY THAT SOME REWARDS ARE WORTH BOILING YOUR BALLS FOR...
NEMESIS, GATHER YOUR WEAPONS AND LOAD UP ON TRANQUILIZERS!
OKOYE AND I WILL MEET YOU, ROZ AND JANET AT THE TALON SHIP IN TEN MINUTES!
LAST TIME DEADPOOL ENGAGED US, HE INVADED THE WAKANDAN THRONE ROOM, STOLE AN EXPERIMENTAL PANTHER SUIT AND TELEPORTED THE GREAT VIBRANIUM MOUND TO NEW JERSEY.*
MY KING, WE JUST--
HE'S DANGEROUSLY SANE. WHATEVER ROJECT LIVEWIRE" , WE CANNOT LET HIM GET TO IT.
I...
...I UNDERSTAND.
*IN THE GLORIOUSLY RIDICULOUS BLACK PANTHER VS. DEADPOOL MINISERIES. --WIL VS. SARAH

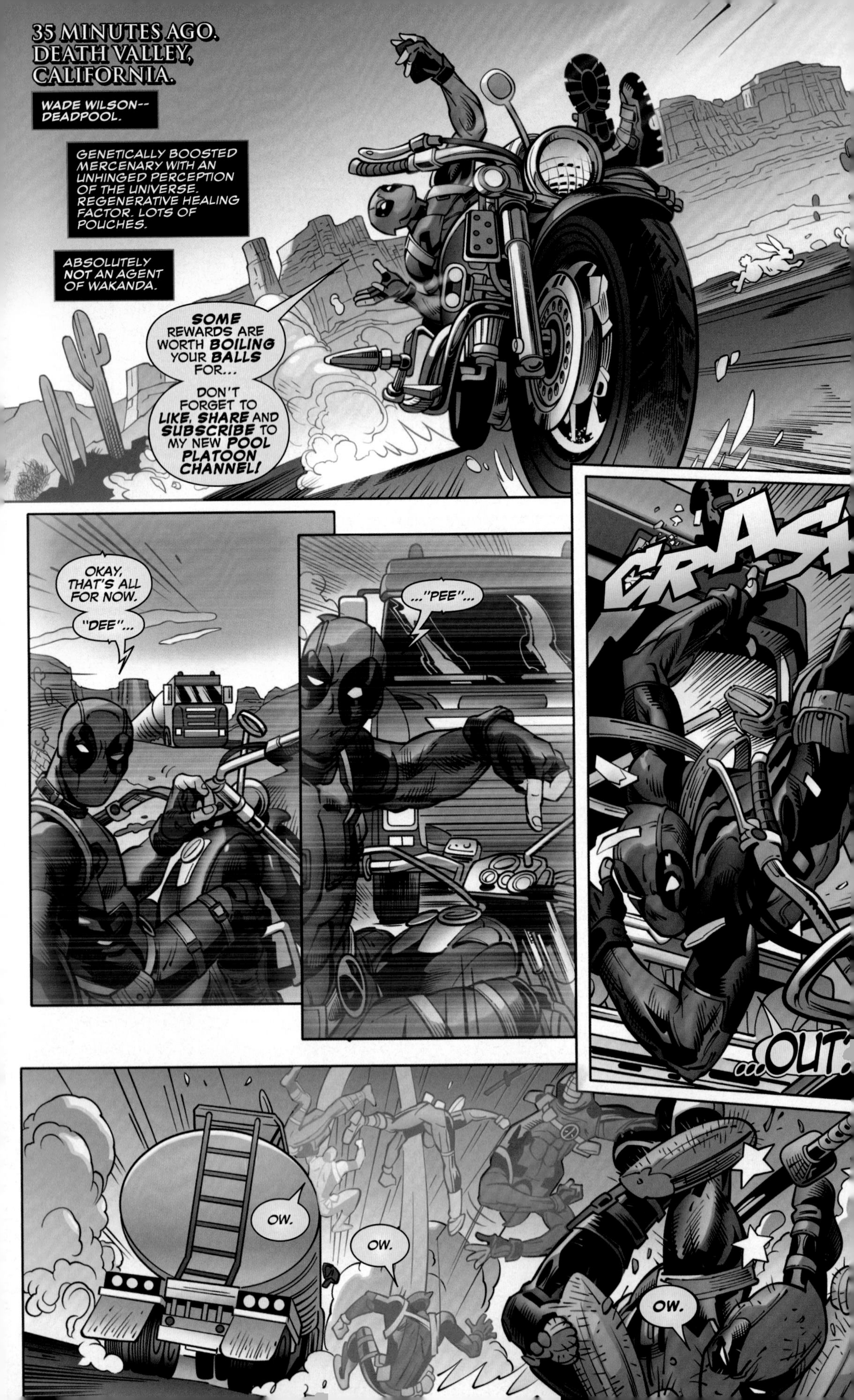
35 MINUTES AGO. DEATH VALLEY, CALIFORNIA.
WADE WILSON-- DEADPOOL.
GENETICALLY BOOSTED MERCENARY WITH AN UNHINGED PERCEPTION OF THE UNIVERSE. REGENERATIVE HEALING FACTOR. LOTS OF POUCHES.
ABSOLUTELY NOT AN AGENT OF WAKANDA.
SOME REWARDS ARE WORTH BOILING YOUR BALLS FOR...
DON'T FORGET TO LIKE, SHARE AND SUBSCRIBE TO MY NEW POOL PLATOON CHANNEL!
OKAY, THAT'S ALL FOR NOW.
"DEE"...
..."PEE"...
CRASH
...OUT!
OW.
OW.
OW.

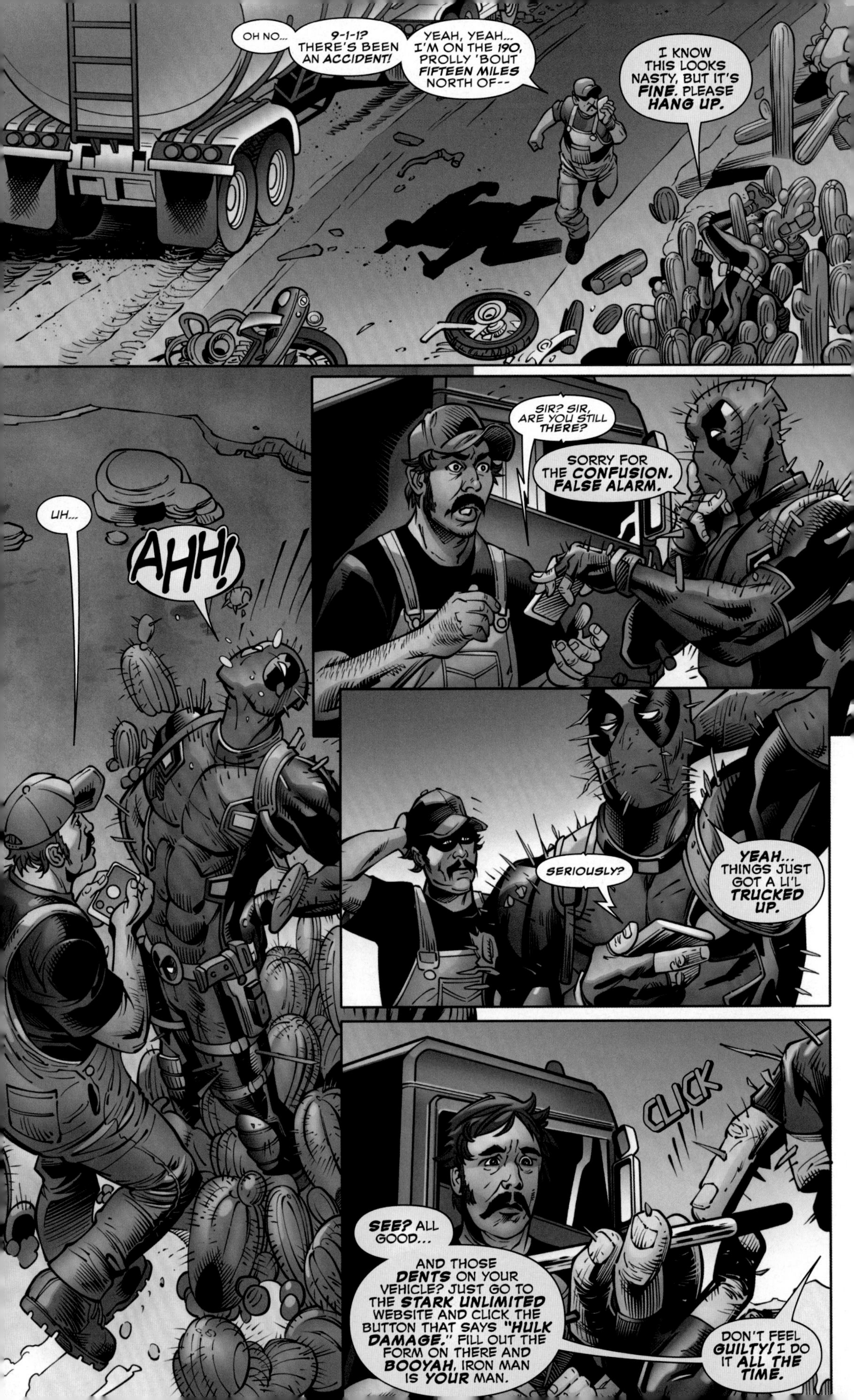
OH NO...
9-1-1? THERE'S BEEN AN ACCIDENT!
YEAH, YEAH... I'M ON THE 190, PROLLY 'BOUT FIFTEEN MILES NORTH OF--
I KNOW THIS LOOKS NASTY, BUT IT'S FINE. PLEASE HANG UP.
UH...
AHH!
SIR? SIR, ARE YOU STILL THERE?
SORRY FOR THE CONFUSION. FALSE ALARM.
SERIOUSLY?
YEAH... THINGS JUST GOT A LI'L TRUCKED UP.
CLICK
SEE? ALL GOOD...
AND THOSE DENTS ON YOUR VEHICLE? JUST GO TO THE STARK UNLIMITED WEBSITE AND CLICK THE BUTTON THAT SAYS "HULK DAMAGE." FILL OUT THE FORM ON THERE AND BOOYAH, IRON MAN IS YOUR MAN.
DON'T FEEL GUILTY! I DO IT ALL THE TIME.

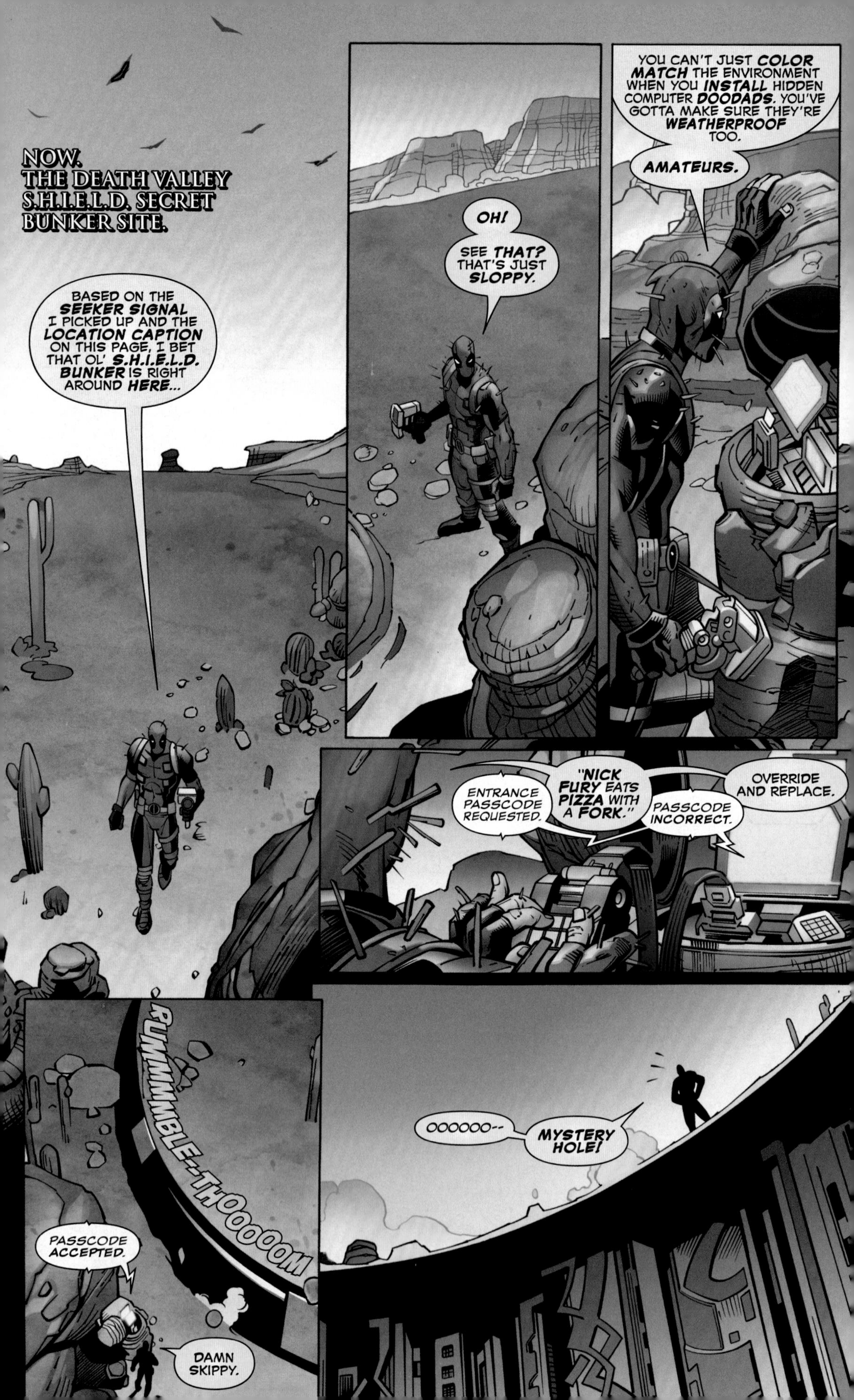
NOW.
THE DEATH VALLEY S.H.I.E.L.D. SECRET BUNKER SITE.
BASED ON THE SEEKER SIGNAL I PICKED UP AND THE LOCATION CAPTION ON THIS PAGE, I BET THAT OL' S.H.I.E.L.D. BUNKER IS RIGHT AROUND HERE...
OH!
SEE THAT? THAT'S JUST SLOPPY.
YOU CAN'T JUST COLOR MATCH THE ENVIRONMENT WHEN YOU INSTALL HIDDEN COMPUTER DOODADS. YOU'VE GOTTA MAKE SURE THEY'RE WEATHERPROOF TOO.
AMATEURS.
ENTRANCE PASSCODE REQUESTED.
"NICK FURY EATS PIZZA WITH A FORK."
PASSCODE INCORRECT.
OVERRIDE AND REPLACE.
RUMMMMBLE-THOOOOOM
PASSCODE ACCEPTED.
DAMN SKIPPY.
OOOOOO--
MYSTERY HOLE!

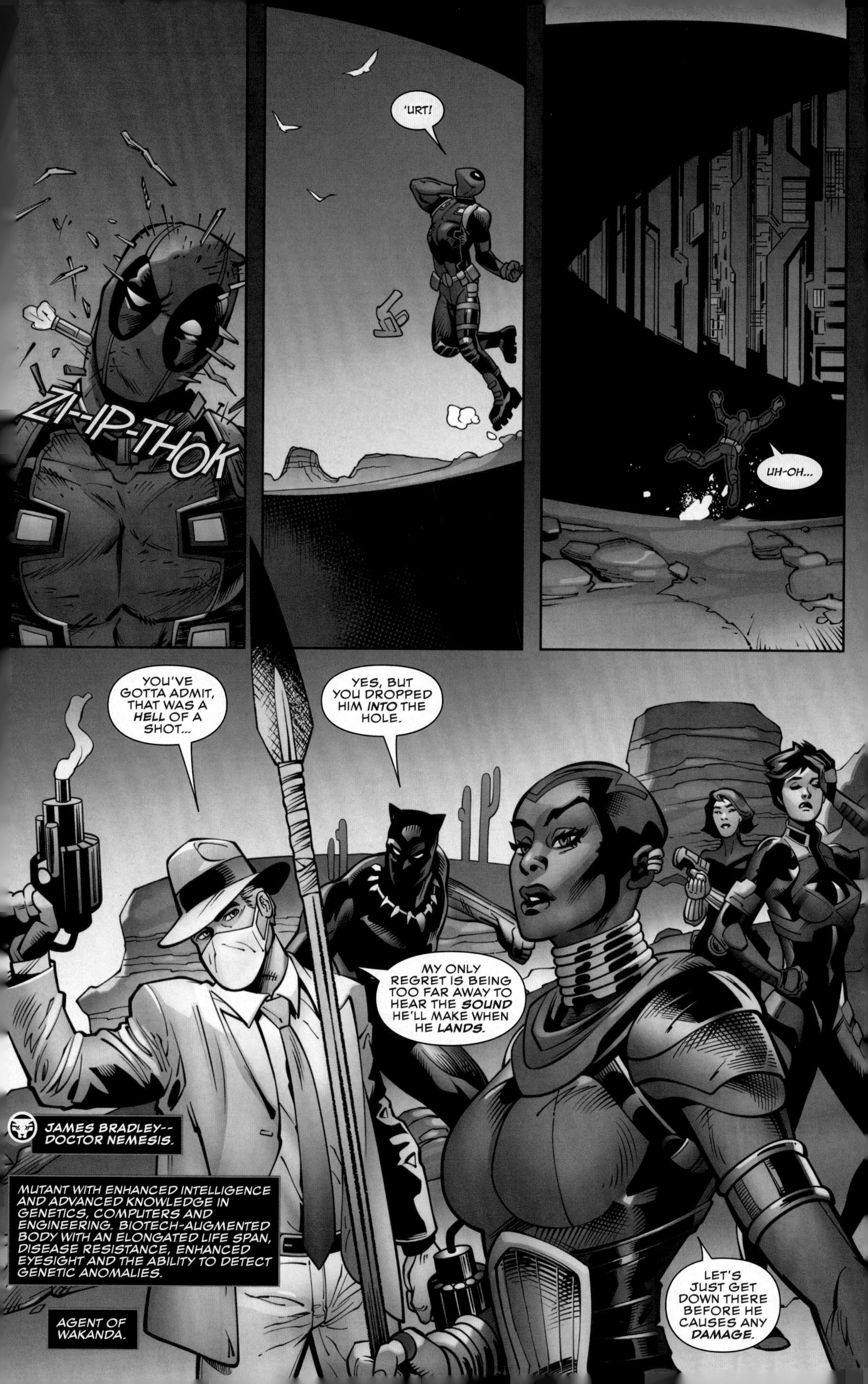
ZI-IP-THOK
'URT!
UH-OH...
YOU'VE GOTTA ADMIT, THAT WAS A HELL OF A SHOT...
YES, BUT YOU DROPPED HIM INTO THE HOLE.
MY ONLY REGRET IS BEING TOO FAR AWAY TO HEAR THE SOUND HE'LL MAKE WHEN HE LANDS.
JAMES BRADLEY-- DOCTOR NEMESIS.
MUTANT WITH ENHANCED INTELLIGENCE AND ADVANCED KNOWLEDGE IN GENETICS, COMPUTERS AND ENGINEERING. BIOTECH-AUGMENTED BODY WITH AN ELONGATED LIFE SPAN, DISEASE RESISTANCE, ENHANCED EYESIGHT AND THE ABILITY TO DETECT GENETIC ANOMALIES.
AGENT OF WAKANDA.
LET'S JUST GET DOWN THERE BEFORE HE CAUSES ANY DAMAGE.

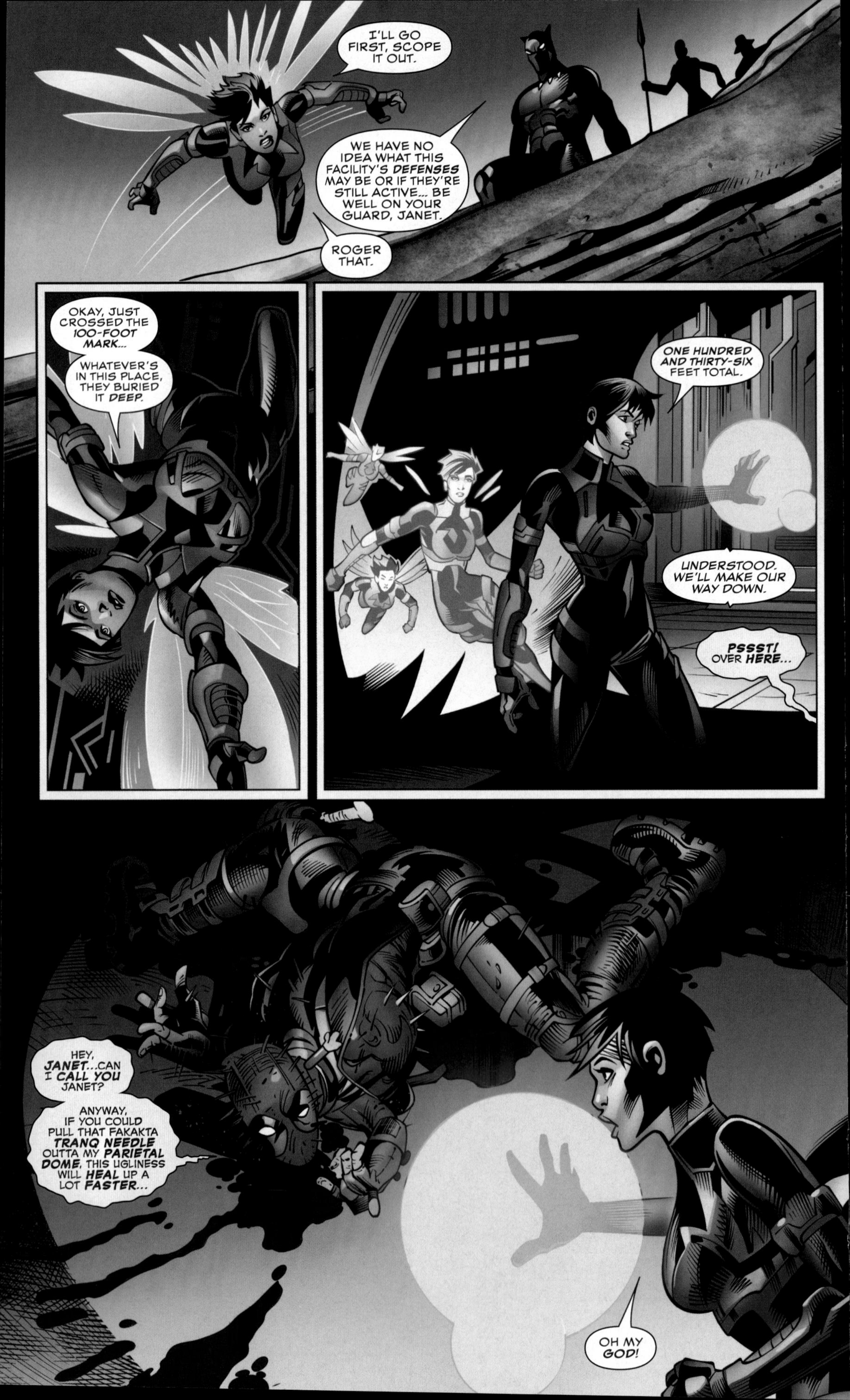

I'LL GO FIRST, SCOPE IT OUT.
WE HAVE NO IDEA WHAT THIS FACILITY'S DEFENSES MAY BE OR IF THEY'RE STILL ACTIVE... BE WELL ON YOUR GUARD, JANET.
ROGER THAT.
OKAY, JUST CROSSED THE 100-FOOT MARK...
WHATEVER'S IN THIS PLACE, THEY BURIED IT DEEP.
ONE HUNDRED AND THIRTY-SIX FEET TOTAL.
UNDERSTOOD. WE'LL MAKE OUR WAY DOWN.
PSSST! OVER HERE...
HEY, JANET...CAN I CALL YOU JANET?
ANYWAY, IF YOU COULD PULL THAT FAKAKTA TRANQ NEEDLE OUTTA MY PARIETAL DOME, THIS UGLINESS WILL HEAL UP A LOT FASTER...
OH MY GOD!

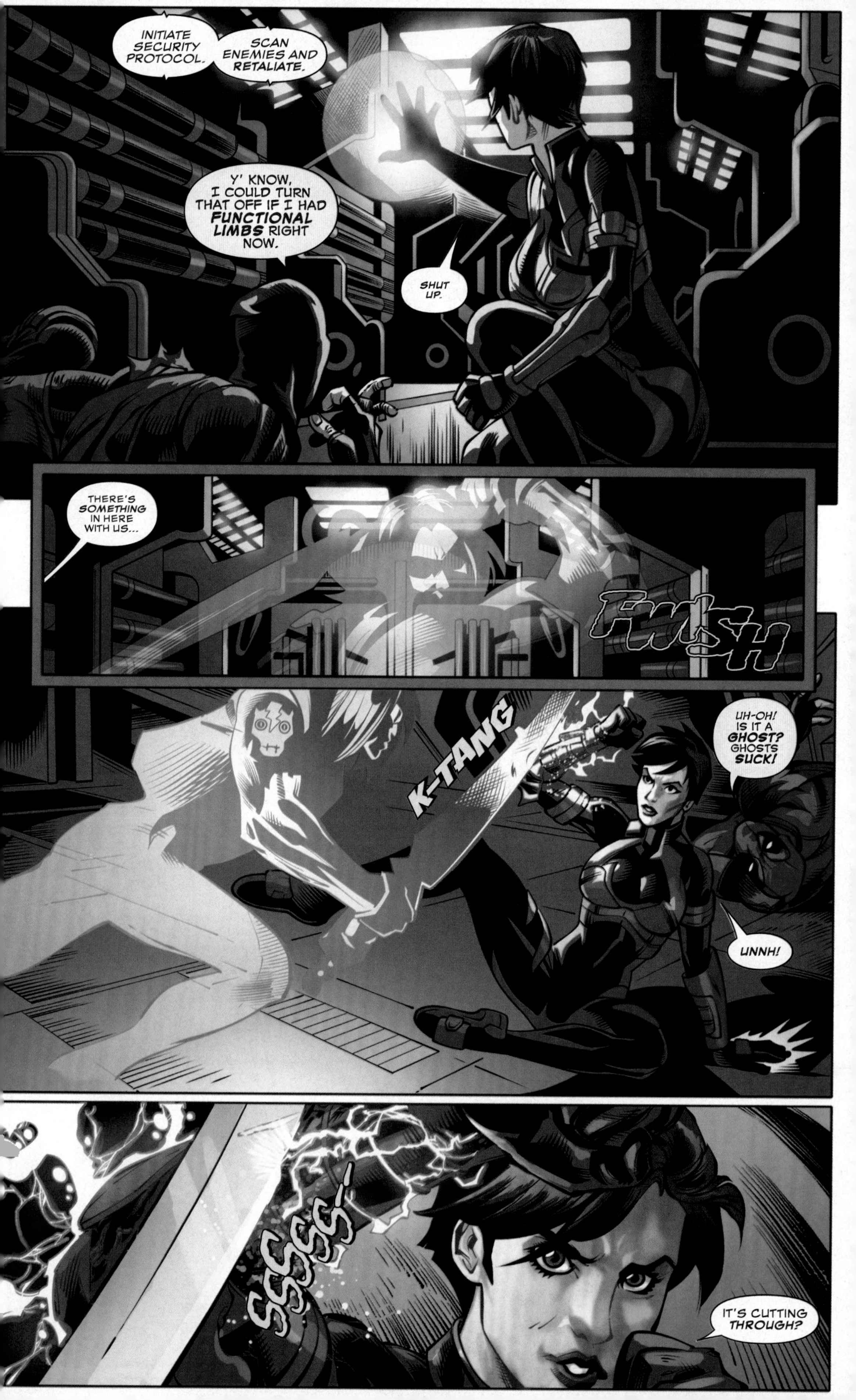
INITIATE SECURITY PROTOCOL.
SCAN ENEMIES AND RETALIATE.
Y' KNOW, I COULD TURN THAT OFF IF I HAD FUNCTIONAL LIMBS RIGHT NOW.
SHUT UP.
THERE'S SOMETHING IN HERE WITH US...
FWISH
K-TANG
UH-OH! IS IT A GHOST? GHOSTS SUCK!
UNNH!
SSSSS-
IT'S CUTTING THROUGH?

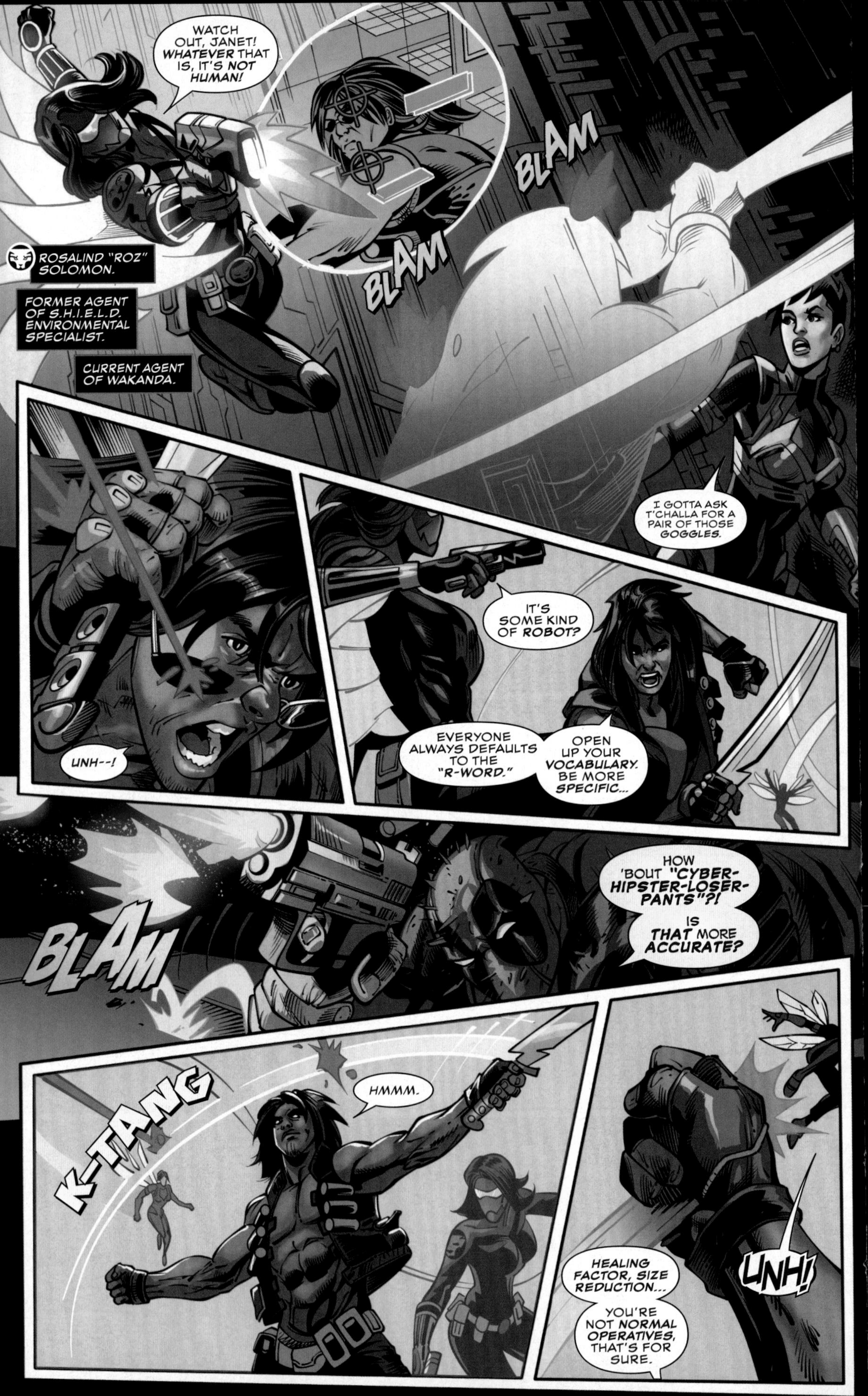
WATCH OUT, JANET! WHATEVER THAT IS, IT'S NOT HUMAN!
BLAM
BLAM
ROSALIND "ROZ" SOLOMON.
FORMER AGENT OF S.H.I.E.L.D. ENVIRONMENTAL SPECIALIST.
CURRENT AGENT OF WAKANDA.
I GOTTA ASK T'CHALLA FOR A PAIR OF THOSE GOGGLES.
UNH--!
IT'S SOME KIND OF ROBOT?
EVERYONE ALWAYS DEFAULTS TO THE "R-WORD."
OPEN UP YOUR VOCABULARY. BE MORE SPECIFIC...
BLAM
HOW 'BOUT "CYBER-HIPSTER-LOSER-PANTS"?!
IS THAT MORE ACCURATE?
K-TANG
HMMM.
UNH!
HEALING FACTOR, SIZE REDUCTION...
YOU'RE NOT NORMAL OPERATIVES, THAT'S FOR SURE.

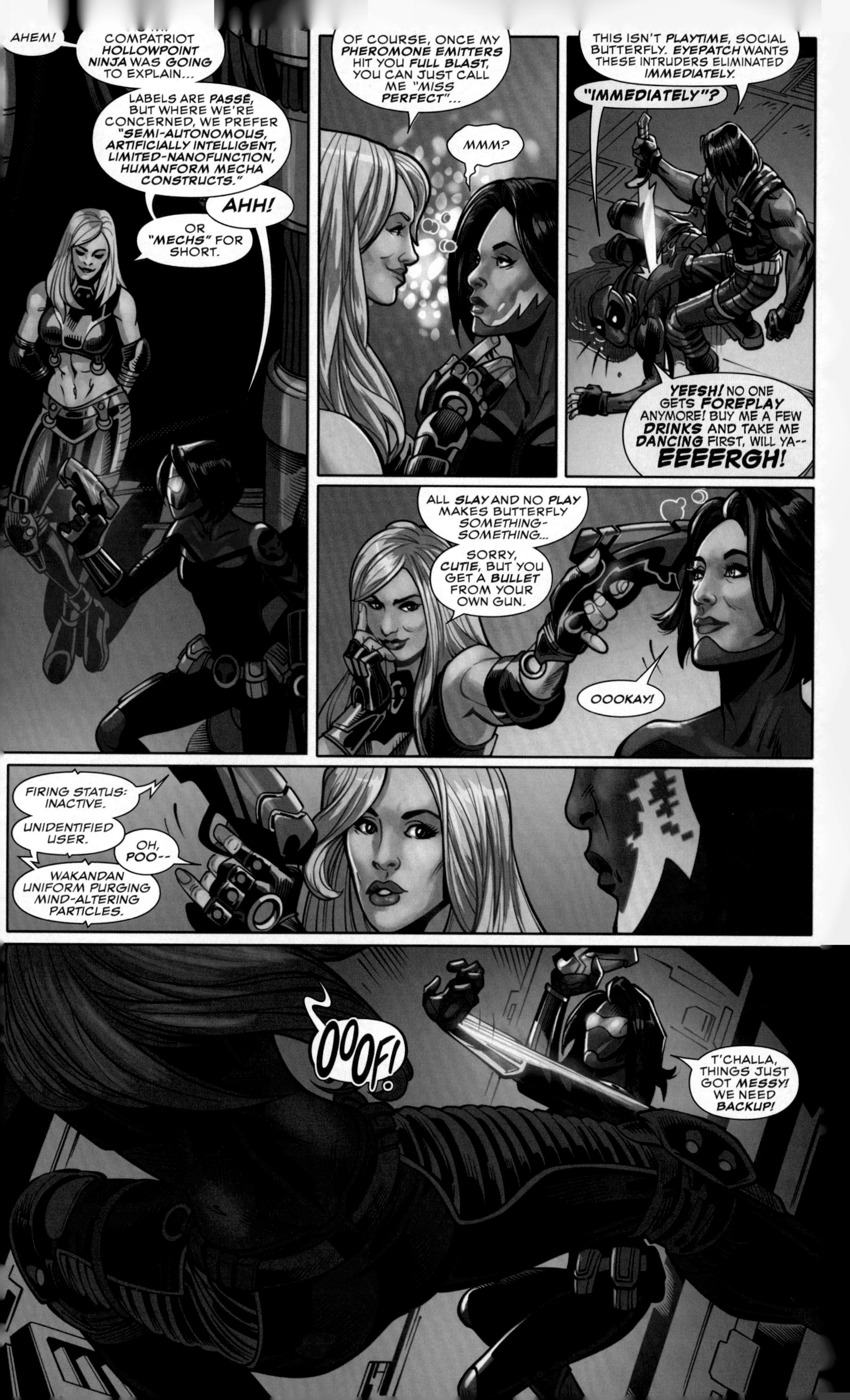

AHEM!
COMPATRIOT HOLLOWPOINT NINJA WAS GOING TO EXPLAIN...
LABELS ARE PASSÉ, BUT WHERE WE'RE CONCERNED, WE PREFER "SEMI-AUTONOMOUS, ARTIFICIALLY INTELLIGENT, LIMITED-NANOFUNCTION, HUMANFORM MECHA CONSTRUCTS."
AHH!
OR "MECHS" FOR SHORT.
OF COURSE, ONCE MY PHEROMONE EMITTERS HIT YOU FULL BLAST, YOU CAN JUST CALL ME "MISS PERFECT"...
MMM?
THIS ISN'T PLAYTIME, SOCIAL BUTTERFLY. EYEPATCH WANTS THESE INTRUDERS ELIMINATED IMMEDIATELY.
"IMMEDIATELY"?
YEESH! NO ONE GETS FOREPLAY ANYMORE! BUY ME A FEW DRINKS AND TAKE ME DANCING FIRST, WILL YA-- EEEERGH!
ALL SLAY AND NO PLAY MAKES BUTTERFLY SOMETHING-SOMETHING...
SORRY, CUTIE, BUT YOU GET A BULLET FROM YOUR OWN GUN.
OOOKAY!
FIRING STATUS: INACTIVE.
UNIDENTIFIED USER.
OH, POO--
WAKANDAN UNIFORM PURGING MIND-ALTERING PARTICLES.
OOOF!
T'CHALLA, THINGS JUST GOT MESSY! WE NEED BACKUP!

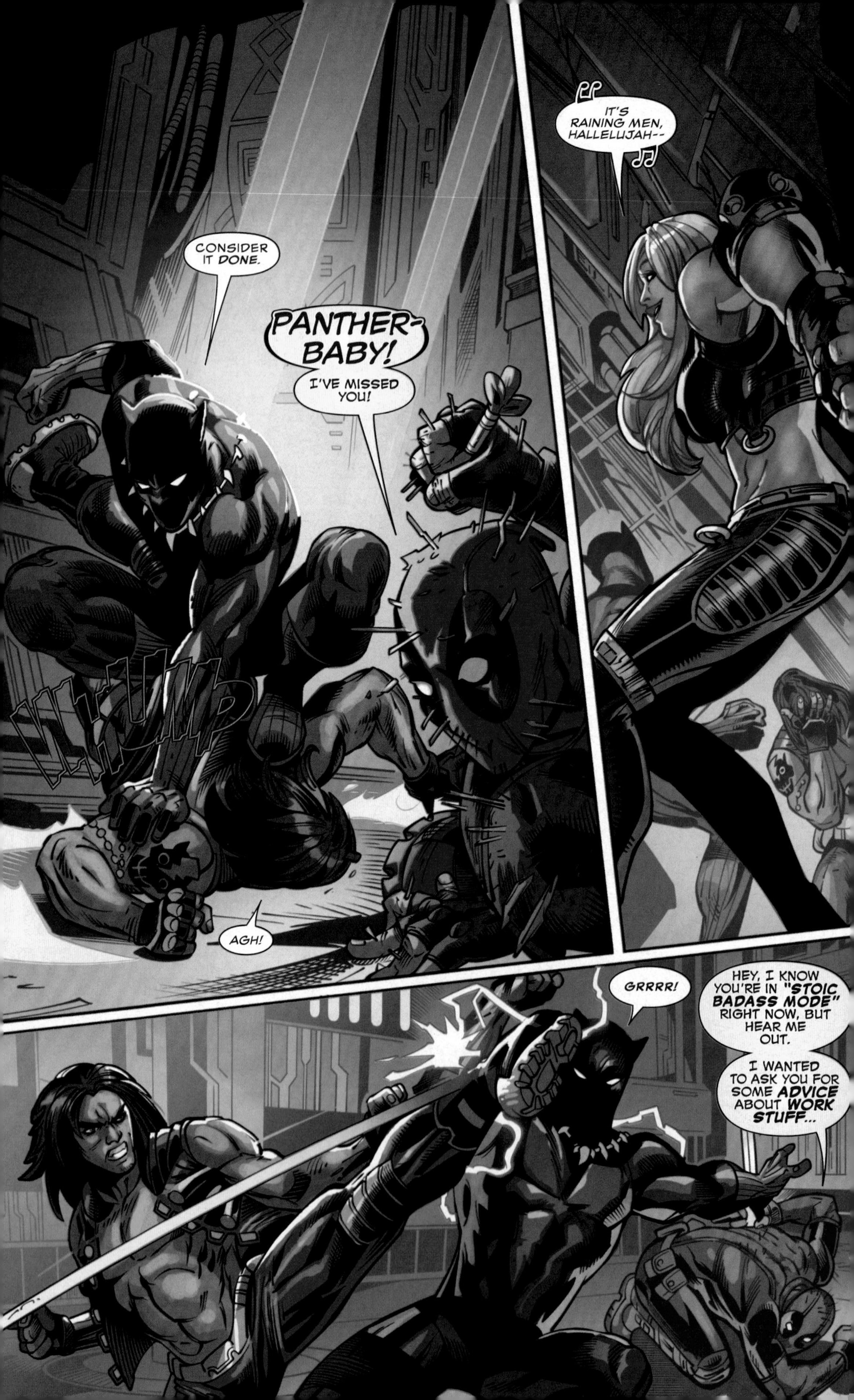
CONSIDER IT DONE.
PANTHER-BABY!
I'VE MISSED YOU!
IT'S RAINING MEN, HALLELUJAH--
AGH!
GRRRR!
HEY, I KNOW YOU'RE IN "STOIC BADASS MODE" RIGHT NOW, BUT HEAR ME OUT.
I WANTED TO ASK YOU FOR SOME ADVICE ABOUT WORK STUFF...

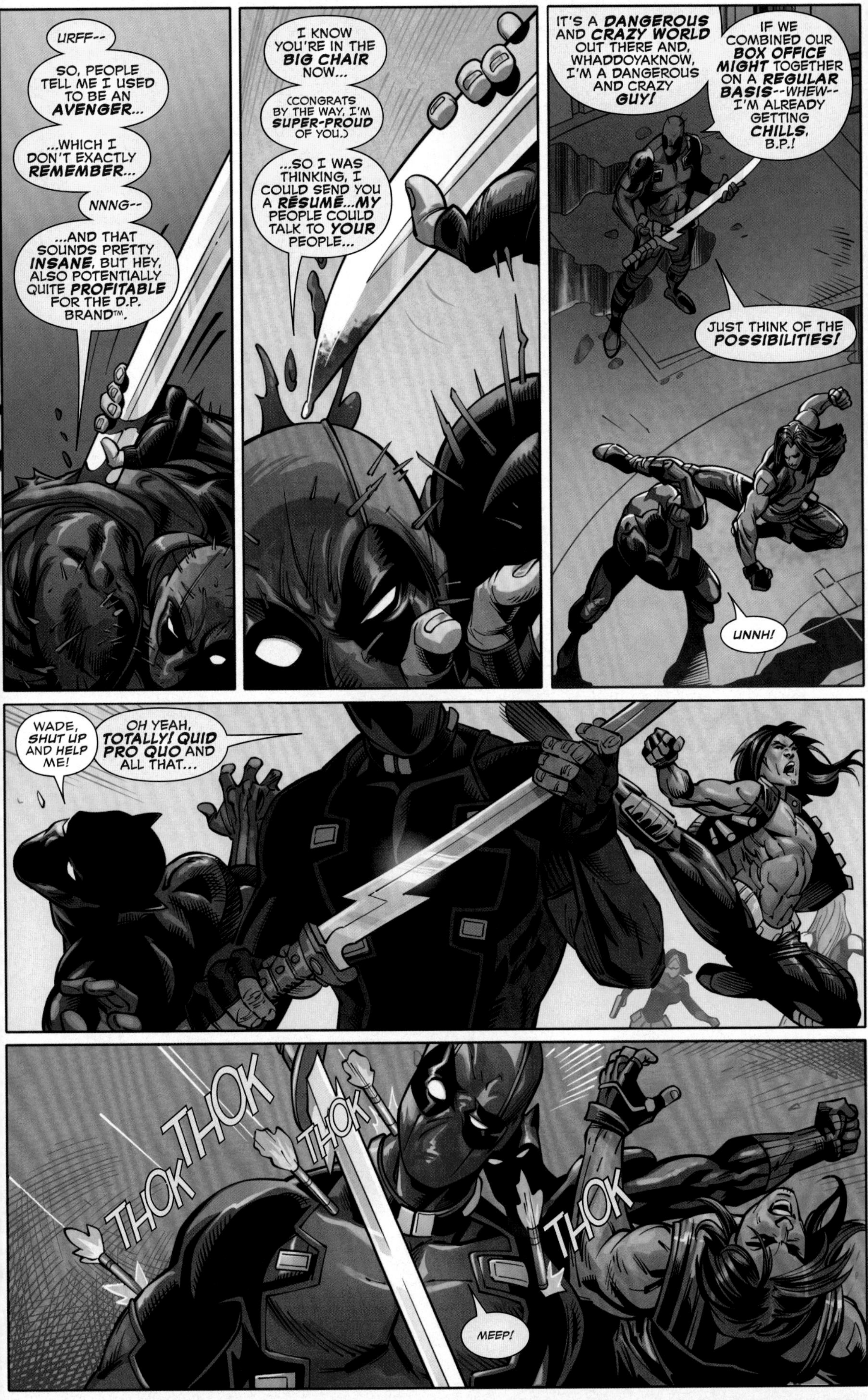

URFF--
SO, PEOPLE TELL ME I USED TO BE AN AVENGER...
...WHICH I DON'T EXACTLY REMEMBER...
NNNG--
...AND THAT SOUNDS PRETTY INSANE, BUT HEY, ALSO POTENTIALLY QUITE PROFITABLE FOR THE D.P. BRAND™.
I KNOW YOU'RE IN THE BIG CHAIR NOW...
(CONGRATS BY THE WAY, I'M SUPER-PROUD OF YOU.)
...SO I WAS THINKING, I COULD SEND YOU A RESUME...MY PEOPLE COULD TALK TO YOUR PEOPLE...
IT'S A DANGEROUS AND CRAZY WORLD OUT THERE AND, WHADDOYAKNOW, I'M A DANGEROUS AND CRAZY GUY!
IF WE COMBINED OUR BOX OFFICE MIGHT TOGETHER ON A REGULAR BASIS--WHEW--I'M ALREADY GETTING CHILLS, B.P.!
JUST THINK OF THE POSSIBILITIES!
UNNH!
WADE, SHUT UP AND HELP ME!
OH YEAH, TOTALLY! QUID PRO QUO AND ALL THAT...
THOK
THOK
THOK
THOK
MEEP!

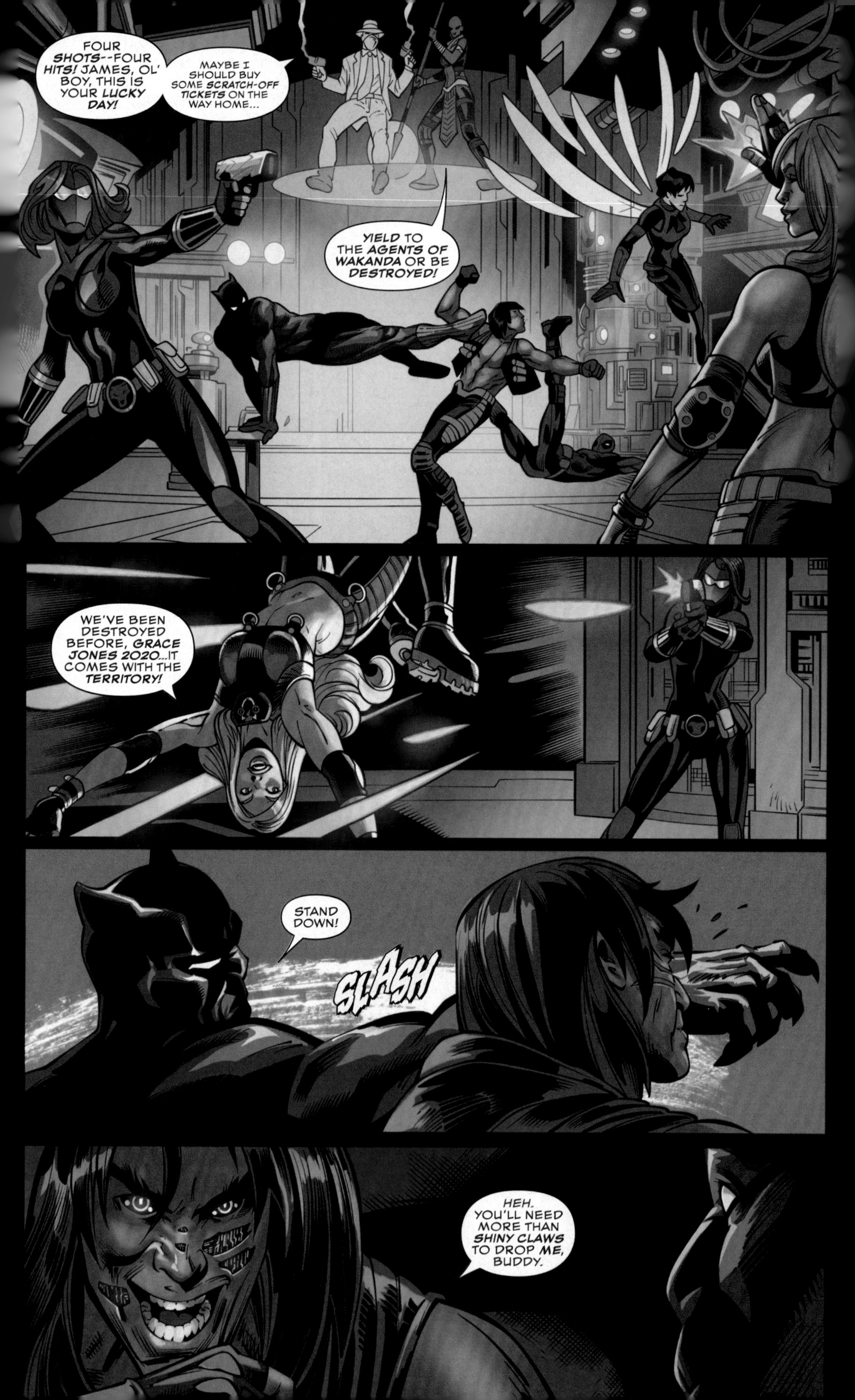

FOUR SHOTS--FOUR HITS! JAMES, OL' BOY, THIS IS YOUR LUCKY DAY!
MAYBE I SHOULD BUY SOME SCRATCH-OFF TICKETS ON THE WAY HOME...
YIELD TO THE AGENTS OF WAKANDA OR BE DESTROYED!
WE'VE BEEN DESTROYED BEFORE, GRACE JONES 2020...IT COMES WITH THE TERRITORY!
STAND DOWN!
SLASH
HEH. YOU'LL NEED MORE THAN SHINY CLAWS TO DROP ME, BUDDY.

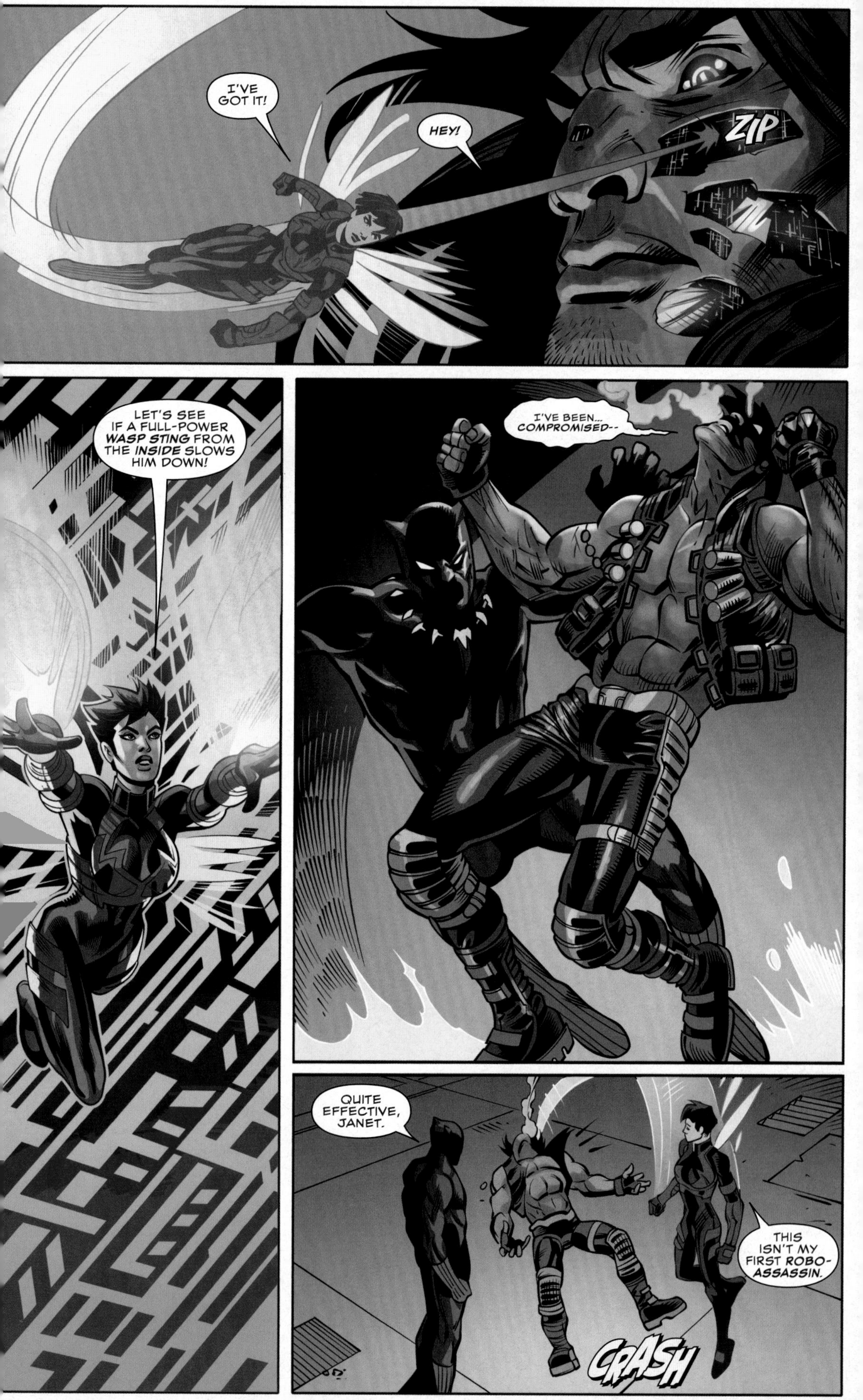
I'VE GOT IT!
HEY!
ZIP
LET'S SEE IF A FULL-POWER WASP STING FROM THE INSIDE SLOWS HIM DOWN!
I'VE BEEN... COMPROMISED--
QUITE EFFECTIVE, JANET.
THIS ISN'T MY FIRST ROBO-ASSASSIN.
CRASH

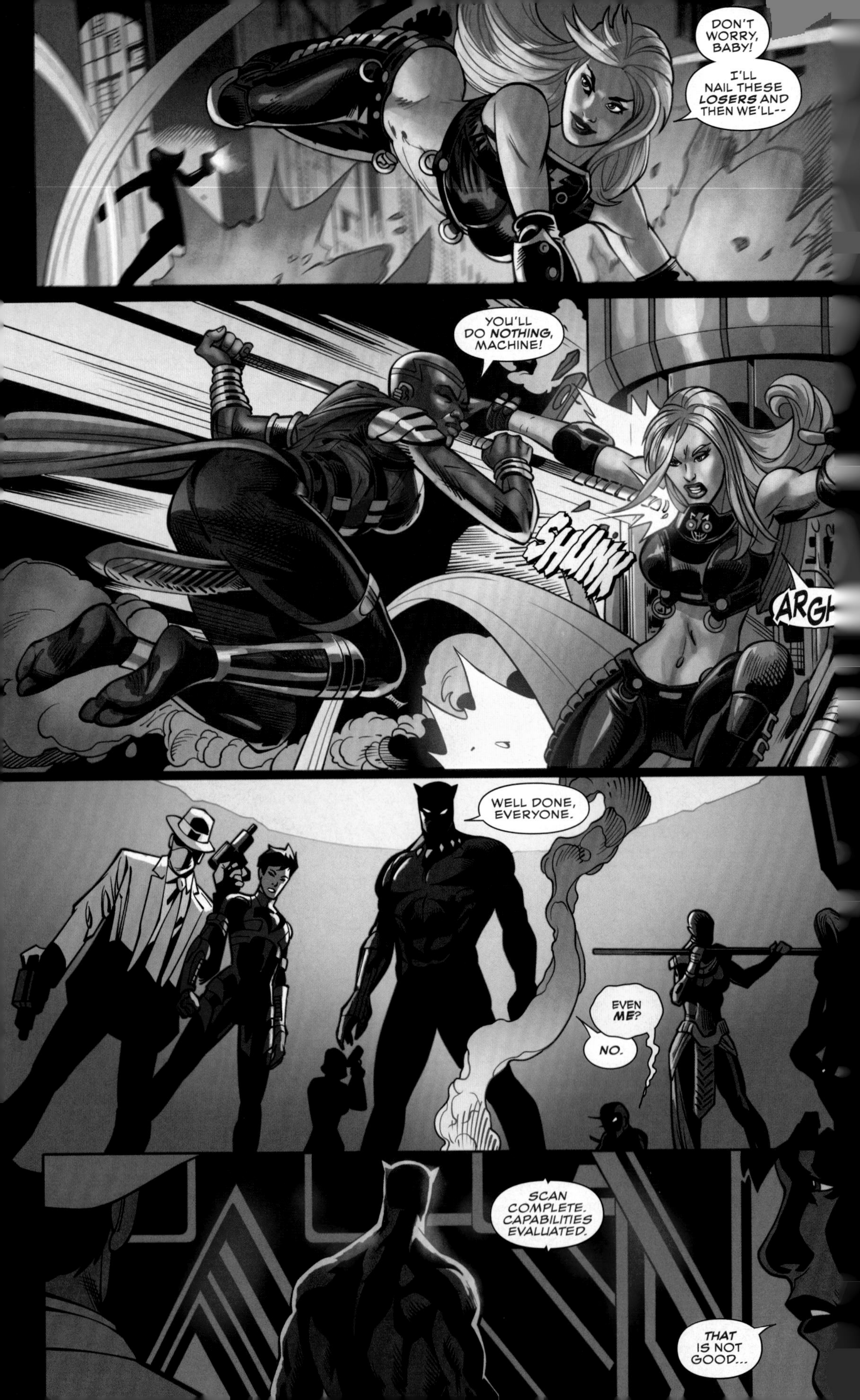
DON'T WORRY, BABY!
I'LL NAIL THESE LOSERS AND THEN WE'LL--
YOU'LL DO NOTHING, MACHINE!
SHUNK
ARGH
WELL DONE, EVERYONE.
EVEN ME?
NO.
SCAN COMPLETE. CAPABILITIES EVALUATED.
THAT IS NOT GOOD...

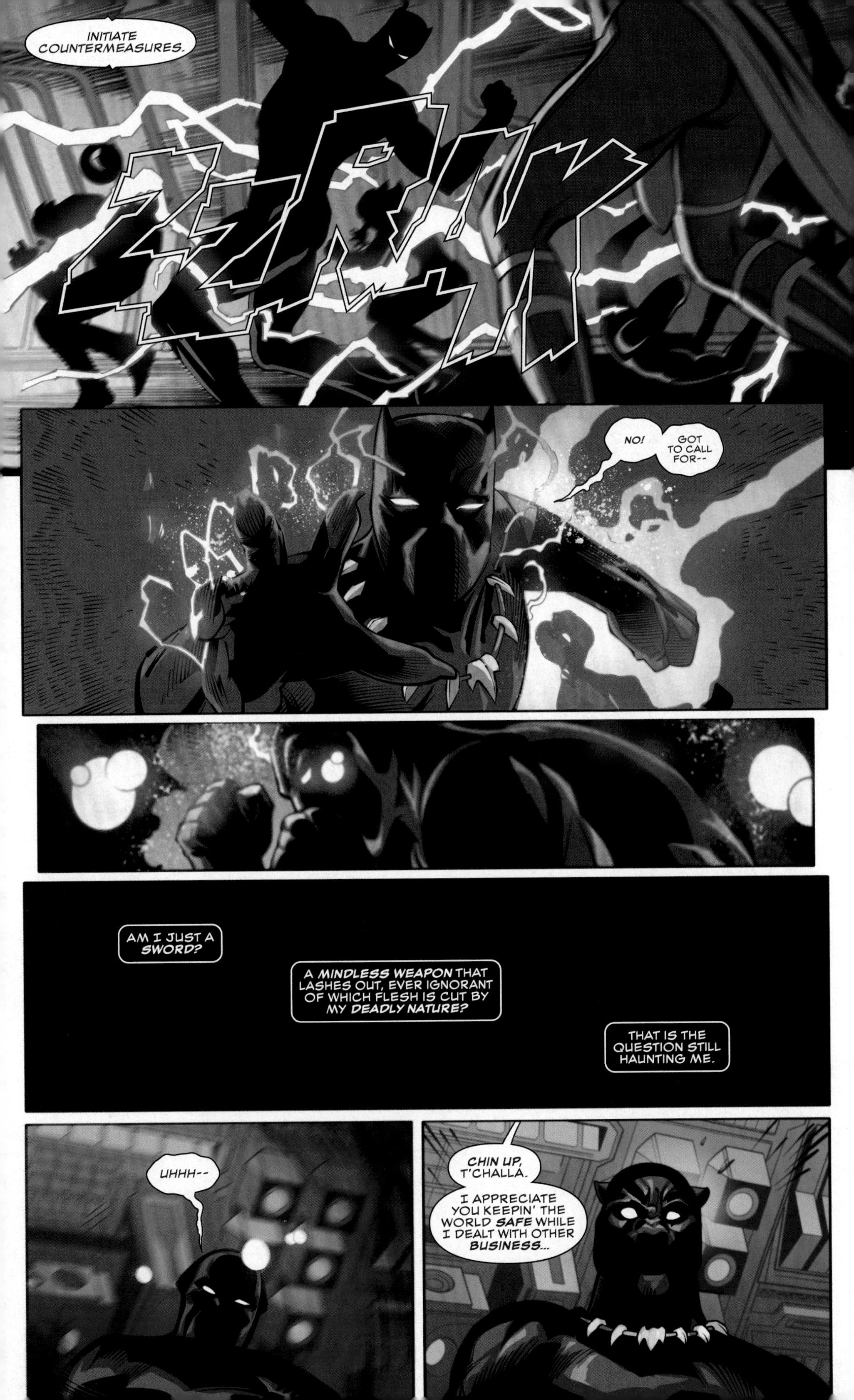
INITIATE COUNTERMEASURES.
ZZRAK
NO!
GOT TO CALL FOR--
AM I JUST A SWORD?
A MINDLESS WEAPON THAT LASHES OUT, EVER IGNORANT OF WHICH FLESH IS CUT BY MY DEADLY NATURE?
THAT IS THE QUESTION STILL HAUNTING ME.
UHHH--
CHIN UP, T'CHALLA.
I APPRECIATE YOU KEEPIN' THE WORLD SAFE WHILE I DEALT WITH OTHER BUSINESS...

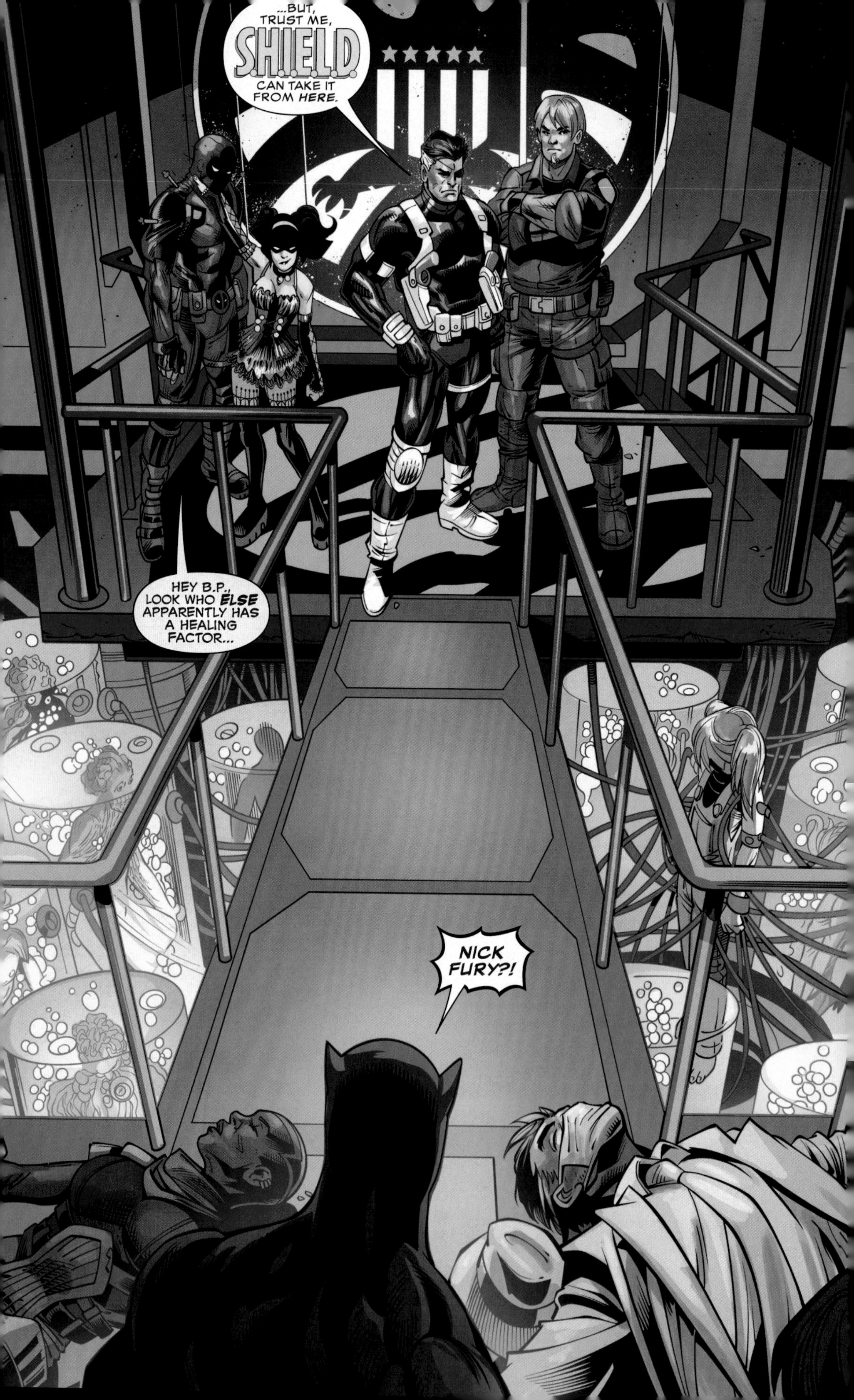
...BUT, TRUST ME, S.H.I.E.L.D. CAN TAKE IT FROM HERE.
HEY B.P., LOOK WHO ELSE APPARENTLY HAS A HEALING FACTOR...
NICK FURY?!

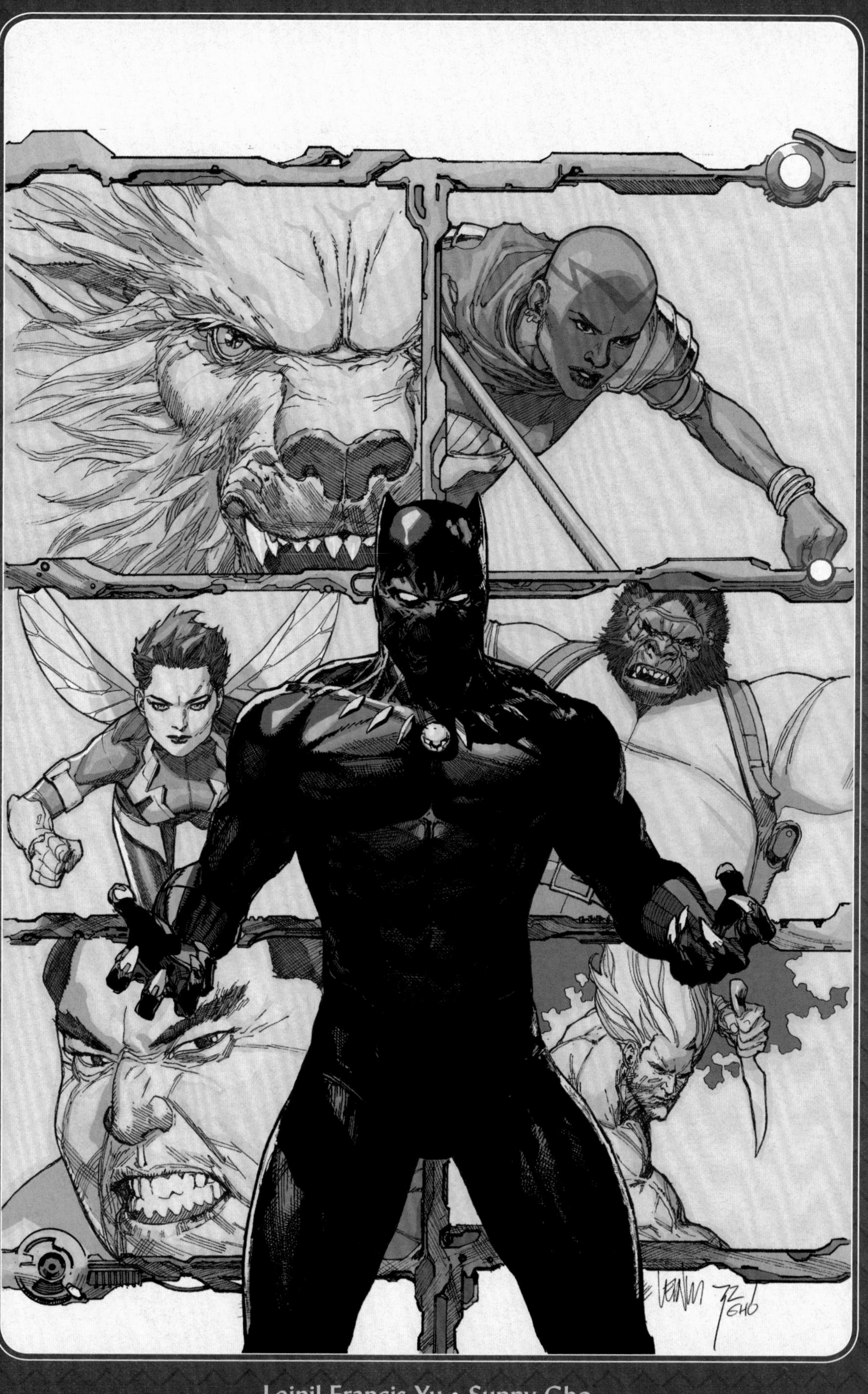

Leinil Francis Yu & Sunny Gho
1 VARIANT

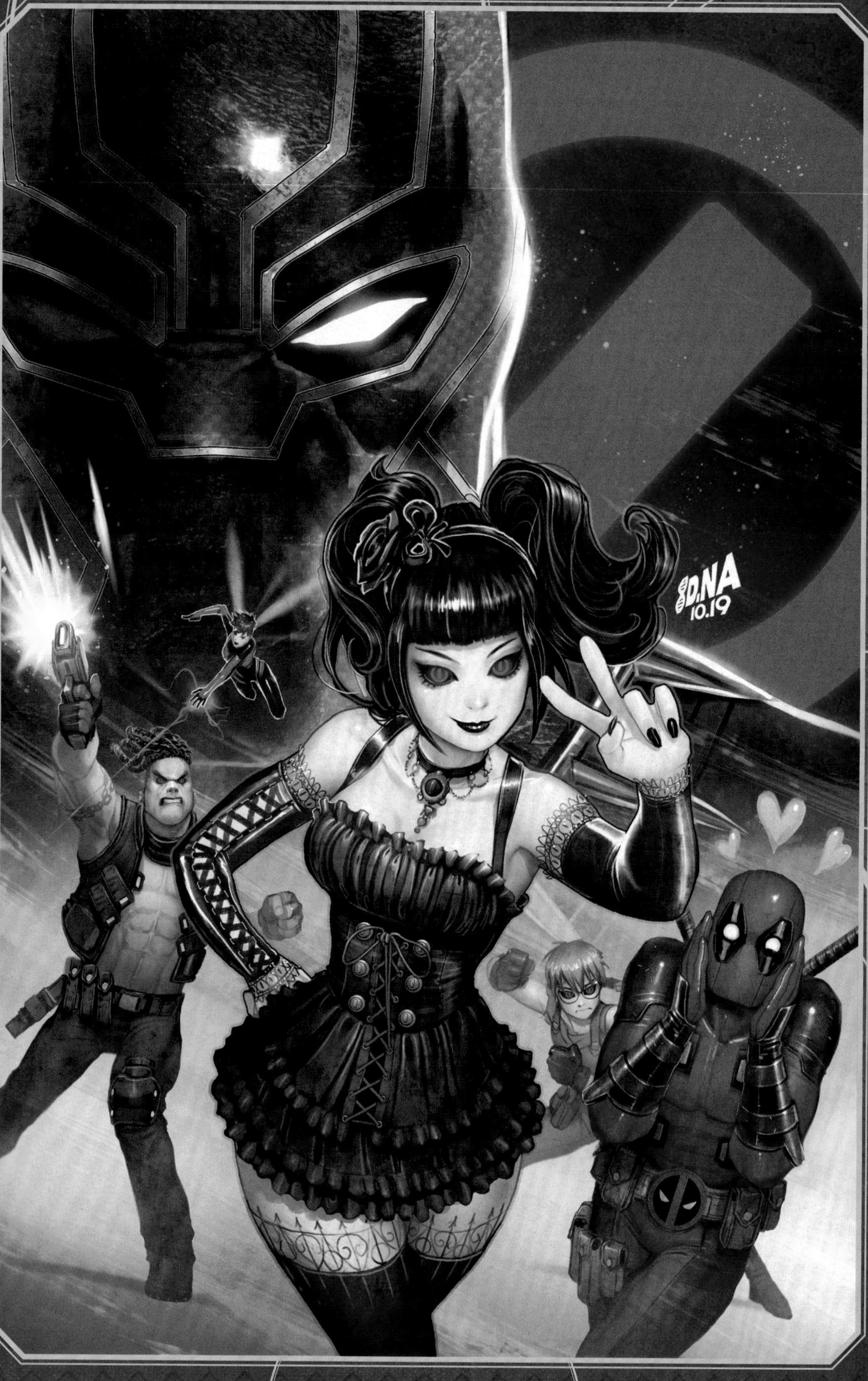
D.NA
10.19

6

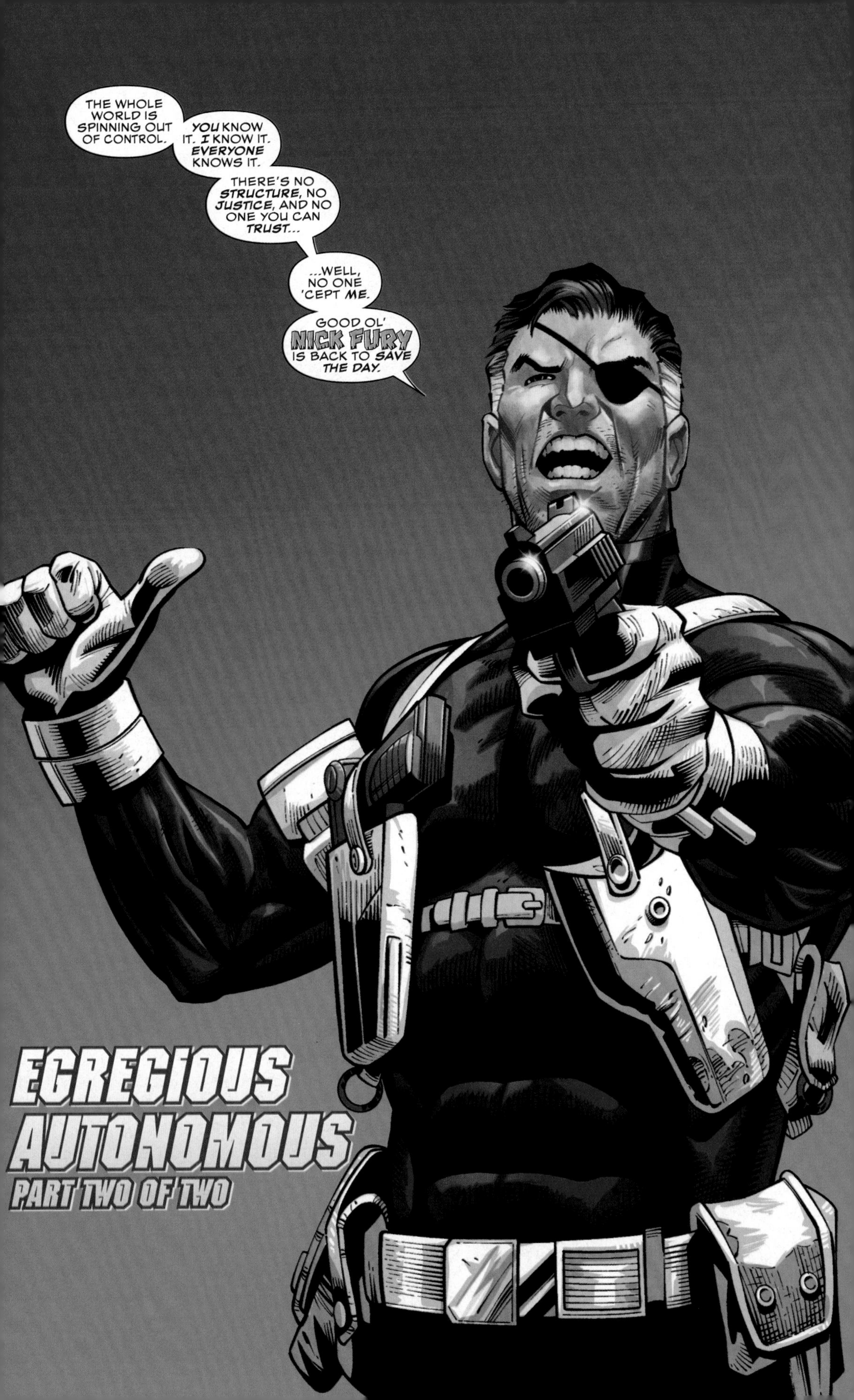
THE WHOLE WORLD IS SPINNING OUT OF CONTROL.
YOU KNOW IT. I KNOW IT. EVERYONE KNOWS IT.
THERE'S NO STRUCTURE, NO JUSTICE, AND NO ONE YOU CAN TRUST...
...WELL, NO ONE 'CEPT ME.
GOOD OL' NICK FURY IS BACK TO SAVE THE DAY.
EGRECIOUS AUTONOMOUS
PART TWO OF TWO

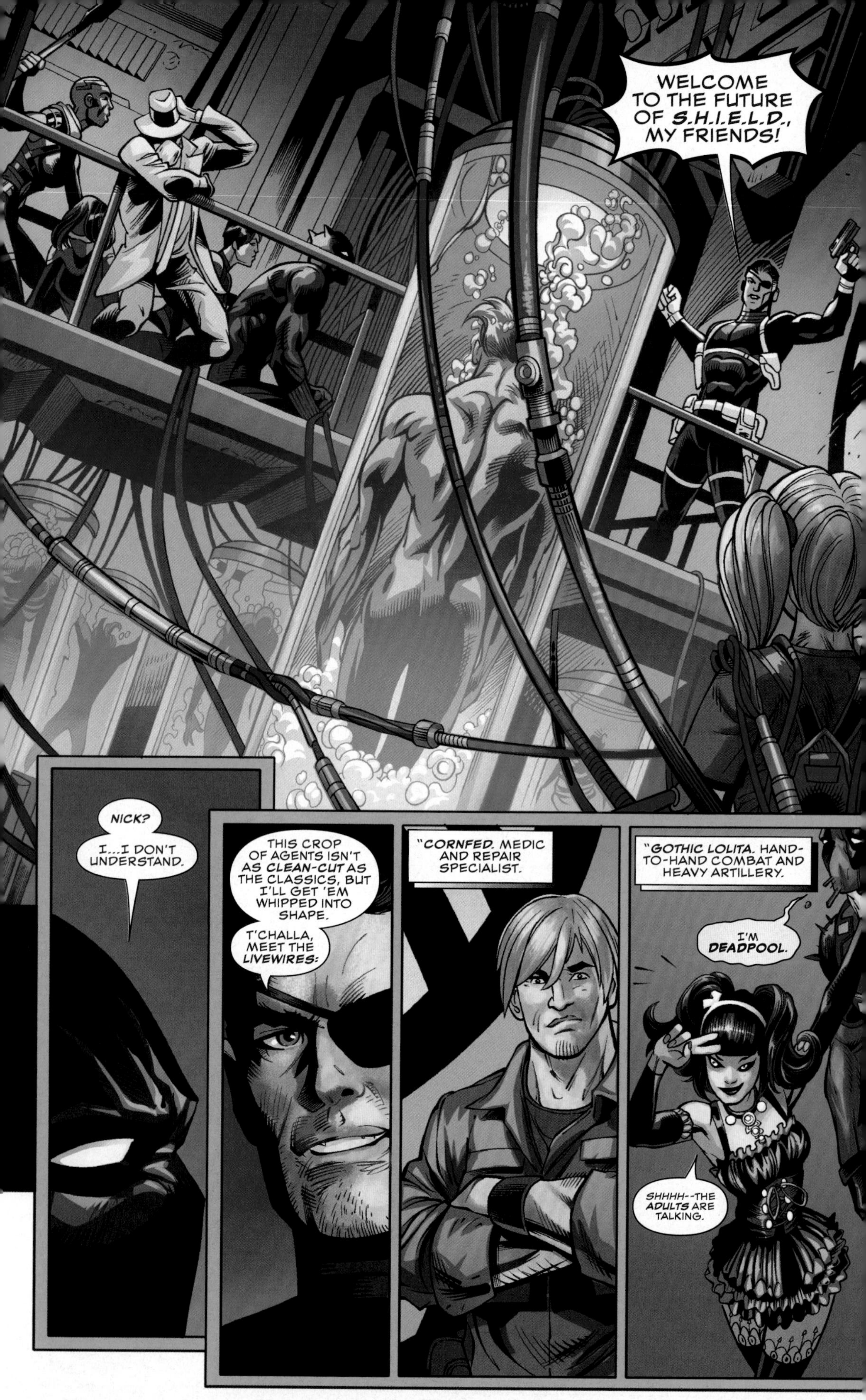
WELCOME TO THE FUTURE OF S.H.I.E.L.D., MY FRIENDS!
NICK?
I...I DON'T UNDERSTAND.
THIS CROP OF AGENTS ISN'T AS CLEAN-CUT AS THE CLASSICS, BUT I'LL GET 'EM WHIPPED INTO SHAPE.
T'CHALLA, MEET THE LIVEWIRES:
"CORNFED. MEDIC AND REPAIR SPECIALIST.
"GOTHIC LOLITA. HAND-TO-HAND COMBAT AND HEAVY ARTILLERY.
I'M DEADPOOL.
SHHHH--THE ADULTS ARE TALKING.

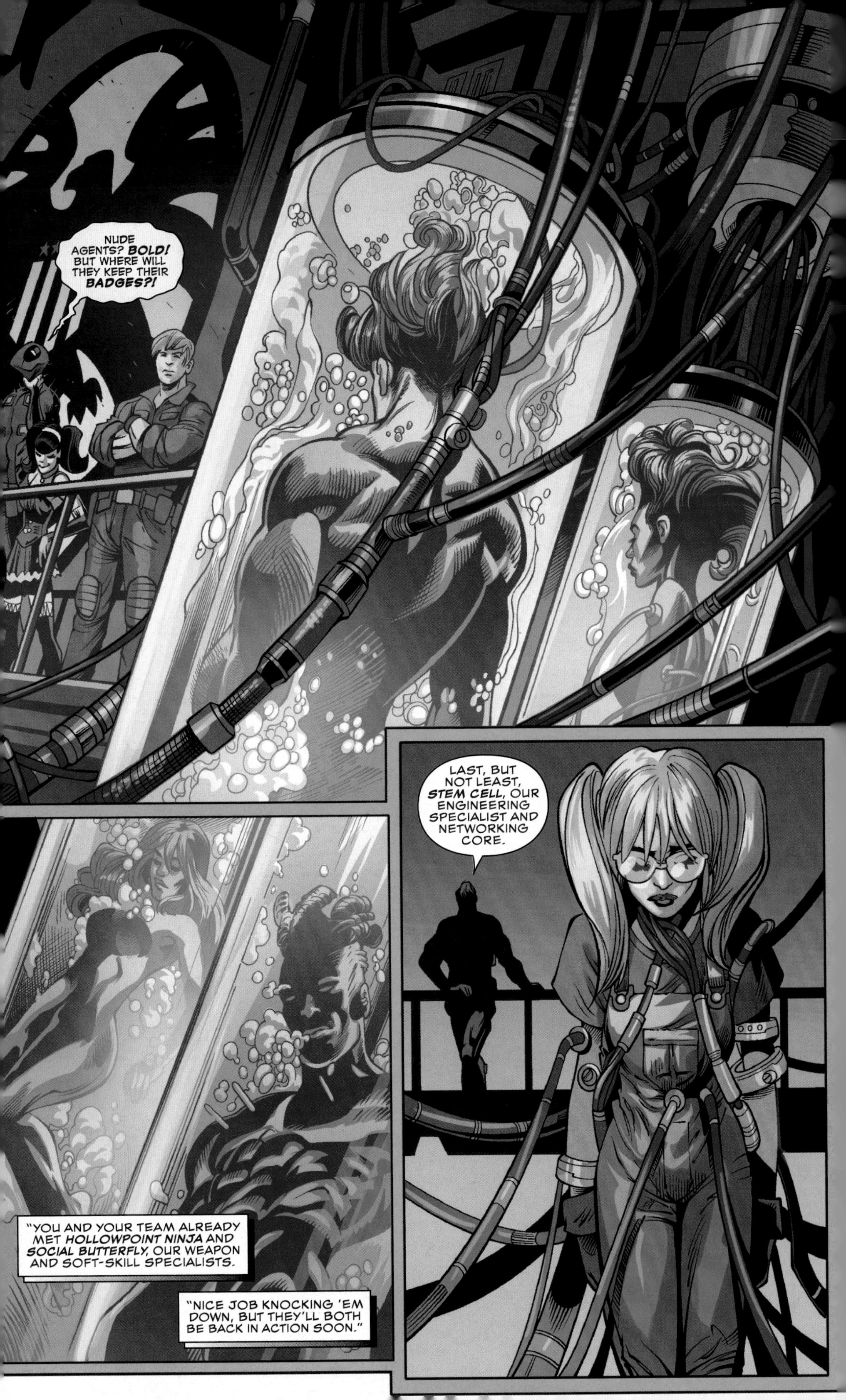
NUDE AGENTS? BOLD! BUT WHERE WILL THEY KEEP THEIR BADGES?!
LAST, BUT NOT LEAST, STEM CELL, OUR ENGINEERING SPECIALIST AND NETWORKING CORE.
"YOU AND YOUR TEAM ALREADY MET HOLLOWPOINT NINJA AND SOCIAL BUTTERFLY, OUR WEAPON AND SOFT-SKILL SPECIALISTS.
"NICE JOB KNOCKING 'EM DOWN, BUT THEY'LL BOTH BE BACK IN ACTION SOON."

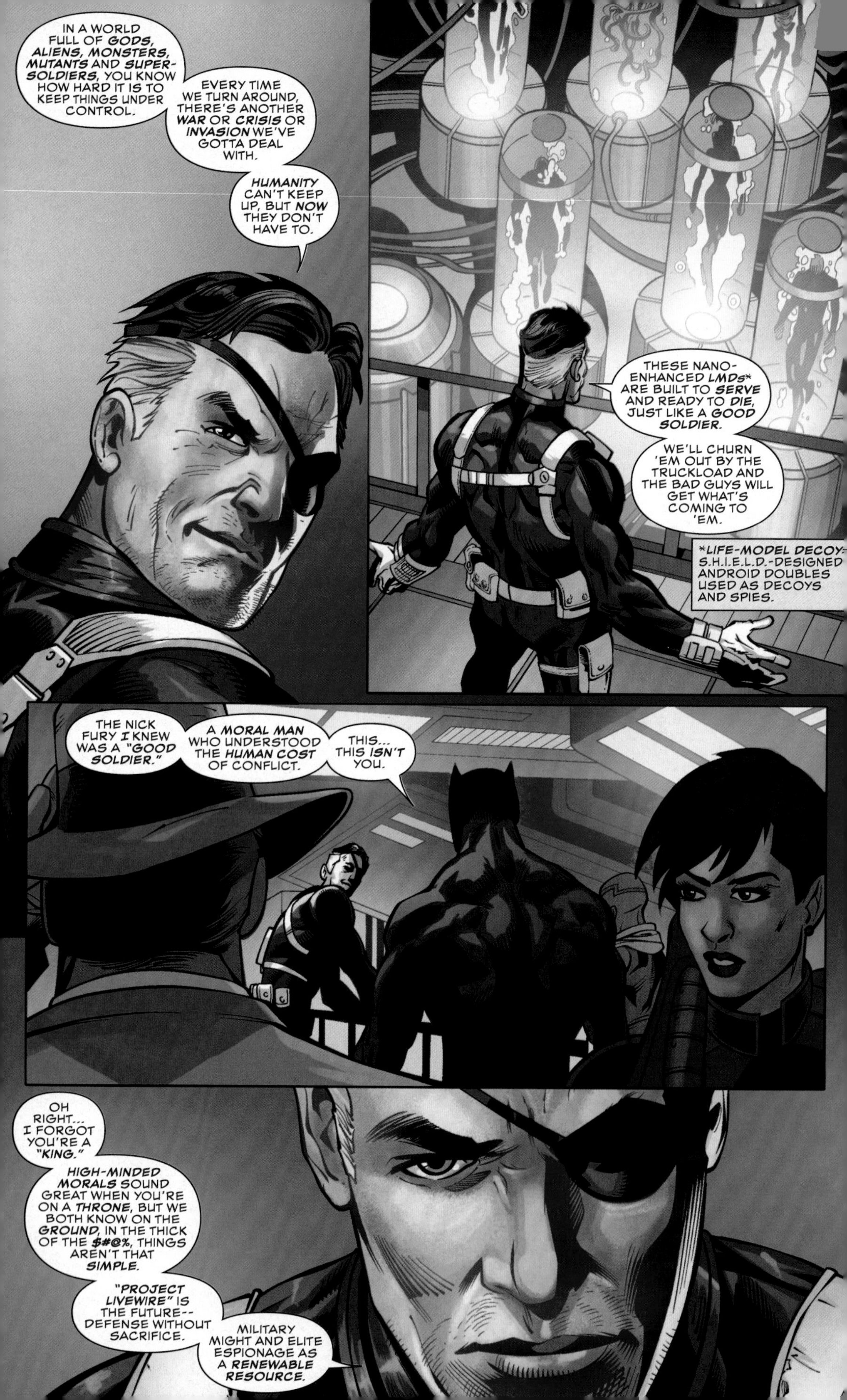

IN A WORLD FULL OF GODS, ALIENS, MONSTERS, MUTANTS AND SUPER-SOLDIERS, YOU KNOW HOW HARD IT IS TO KEEP THINGS UNDER CONTROL.
EVERY TIME WE TURN AROUND, THERE'S ANOTHER WAR OR CRISIS OR INVASION WE'VE GOTTA DEAL WITH.
HUMANITY CAN'T KEEP UP, BUT NOW THEY DON'T HAVE TO.
THESE NANO-ENHANCED LMDs* ARE BUILT TO SERVE AND READY TO DIE, JUST LIKE A GOOD SOLDIER.
WE'LL CHURN 'EM OUT BY THE TRUCKLOAD AND THE BAD GUYS WILL GET WHAT'S COMING TO 'EM.
*LIFE-MODEL DECOY: S.H.I.E.L.D.-DESIGNED ANDROID DOUBLES USED AS DECOYS AND SPIES.
THE NICK FURY I KNEW WAS A "GOOD SOLDIER."
A MORAL MAN WHO UNDERSTOOD THE HUMAN COST OF CONFLICT.
THIS... THIS ISN'T YOU.
OH RIGHT... I FORGOT YOU'RE A "KING."
HIGH-MINDED MORALS SOUND GREAT WHEN YOU'RE ON A THRONE, BUT WE BOTH KNOW ON THE GROUND, IN THE THICK OF THE $#@%, THINGS AREN'T THAT SIMPLE.
"PROJECT LIVEWIRE" IS THE FUTURE-- DEFENSE WITHOUT SACRIFICE.
MILITARY MIGHT AND ELITE ESPIONAGE AS A RENEWABLE RESOURCE.

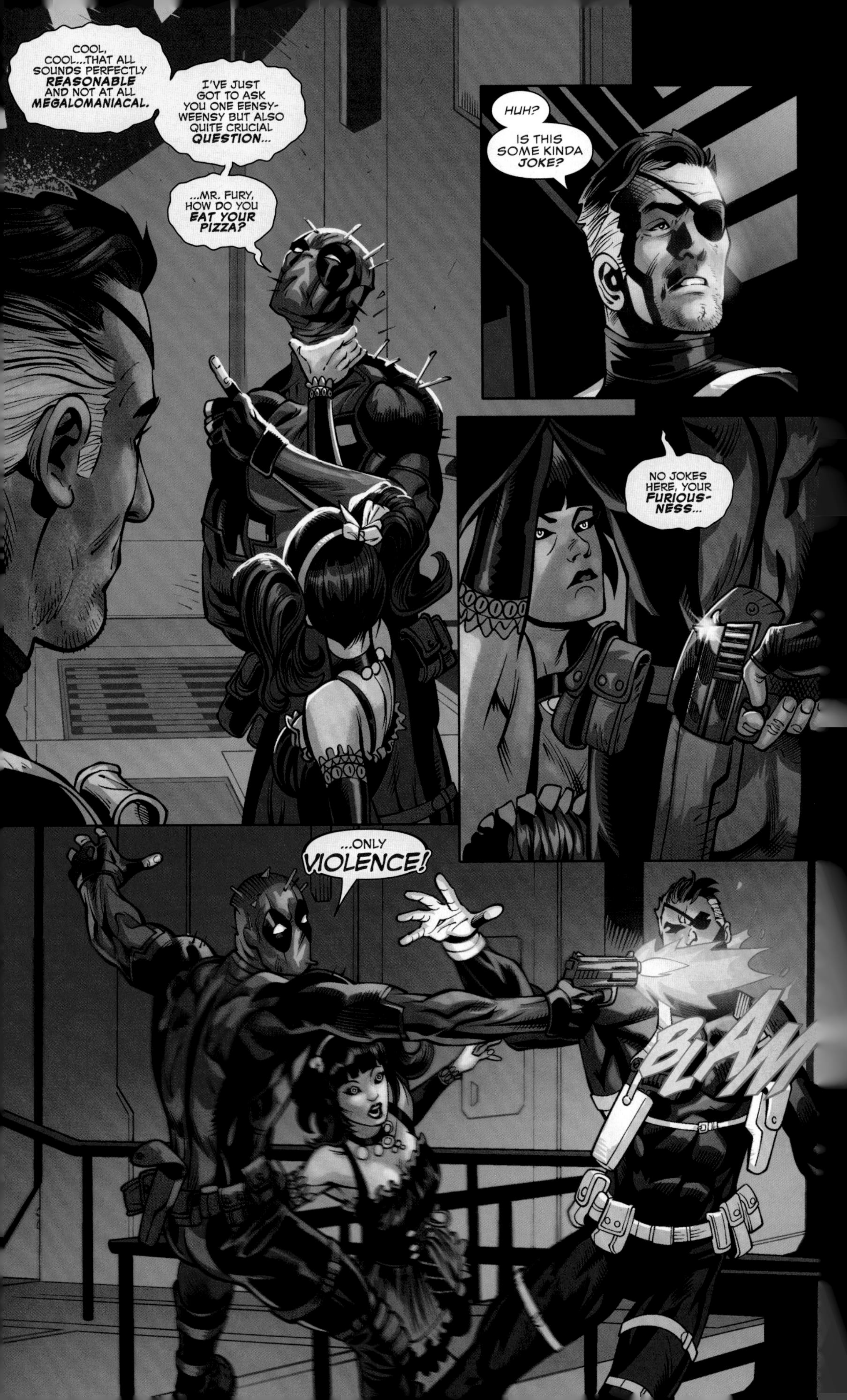

COOL, COOL...THAT ALL SOUNDS PERFECTLY REASONABLE AND NOT AT ALL MEGALOMANIACAL.
I'VE JUST GOT TO ASK YOU ONE EENSY-WEENSY BUT ALSO QUITE CRUCIAL QUESTION...
...MR. FURY, HOW DO YOU EAT YOUR PIZZA?
HUH?
IS THIS SOME KINDA JOKE?
NO JOKES HERE, YOUR FURIOUS-NESS...
...ONLY VIOLENCE!
BLAM

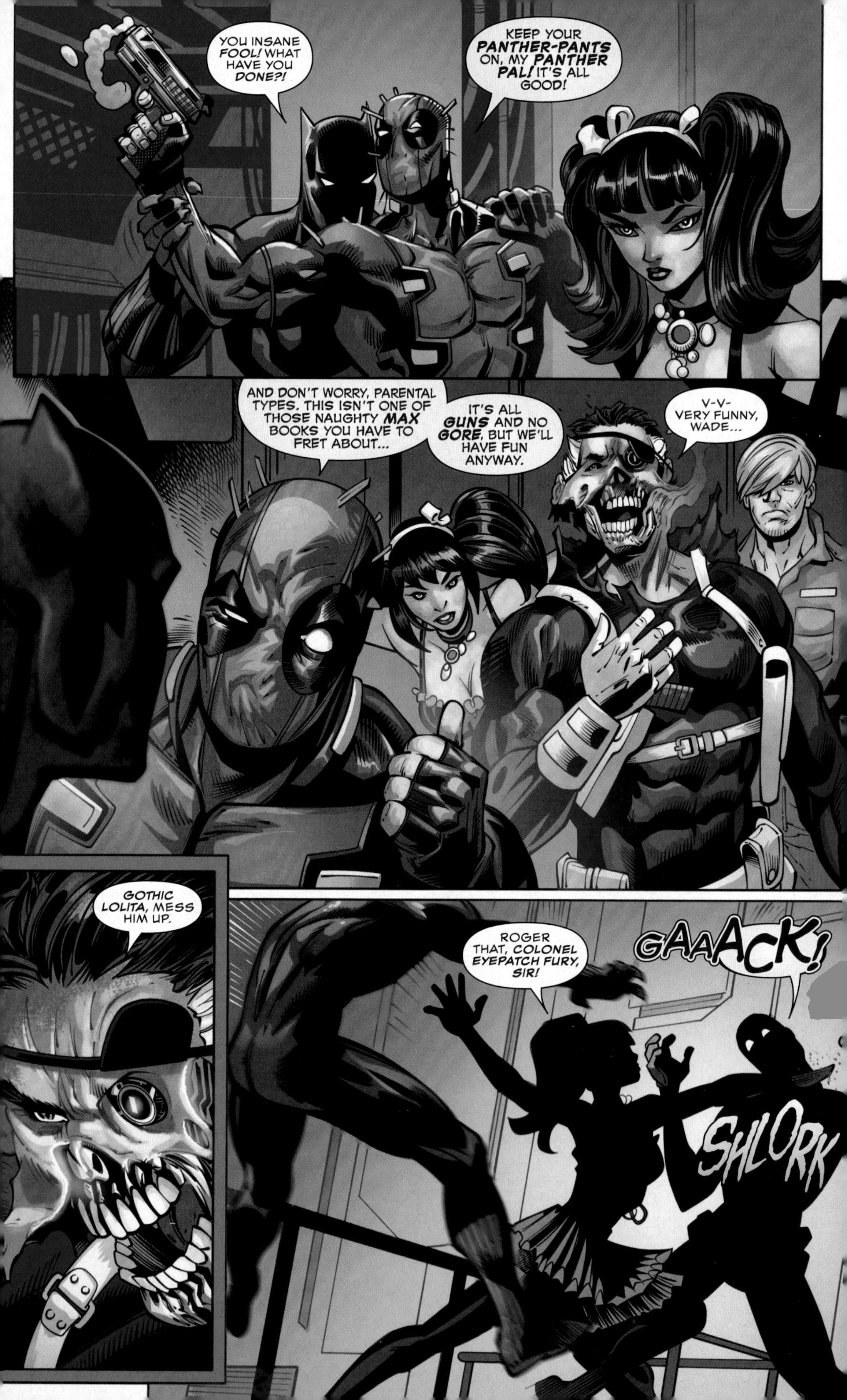
YOU INSANE FOOL! WHAT HAVE YOU DONE?!
KEEP YOUR PANTHER-PANTS ON, MY PANTHER PAL! IT'S ALL GOOD!
AND DON'T WORRY, PARENTAL TYPES. THIS ISN'T ONE OF THOSE NAUGHTY MAX BOOKS YOU HAVE TO FRET ABOUT...
IT'S ALL GUNS AND NO GORE, BUT WE'LL HAVE FUN ANYWAY.
V-V-VERY FUNNY, WADE...
GOTHIC LOLITA, MESS HIM UP.
ROGER THAT, COLONEL EYEPATCH FURY, SIR!
GAAACK!
SHLORK

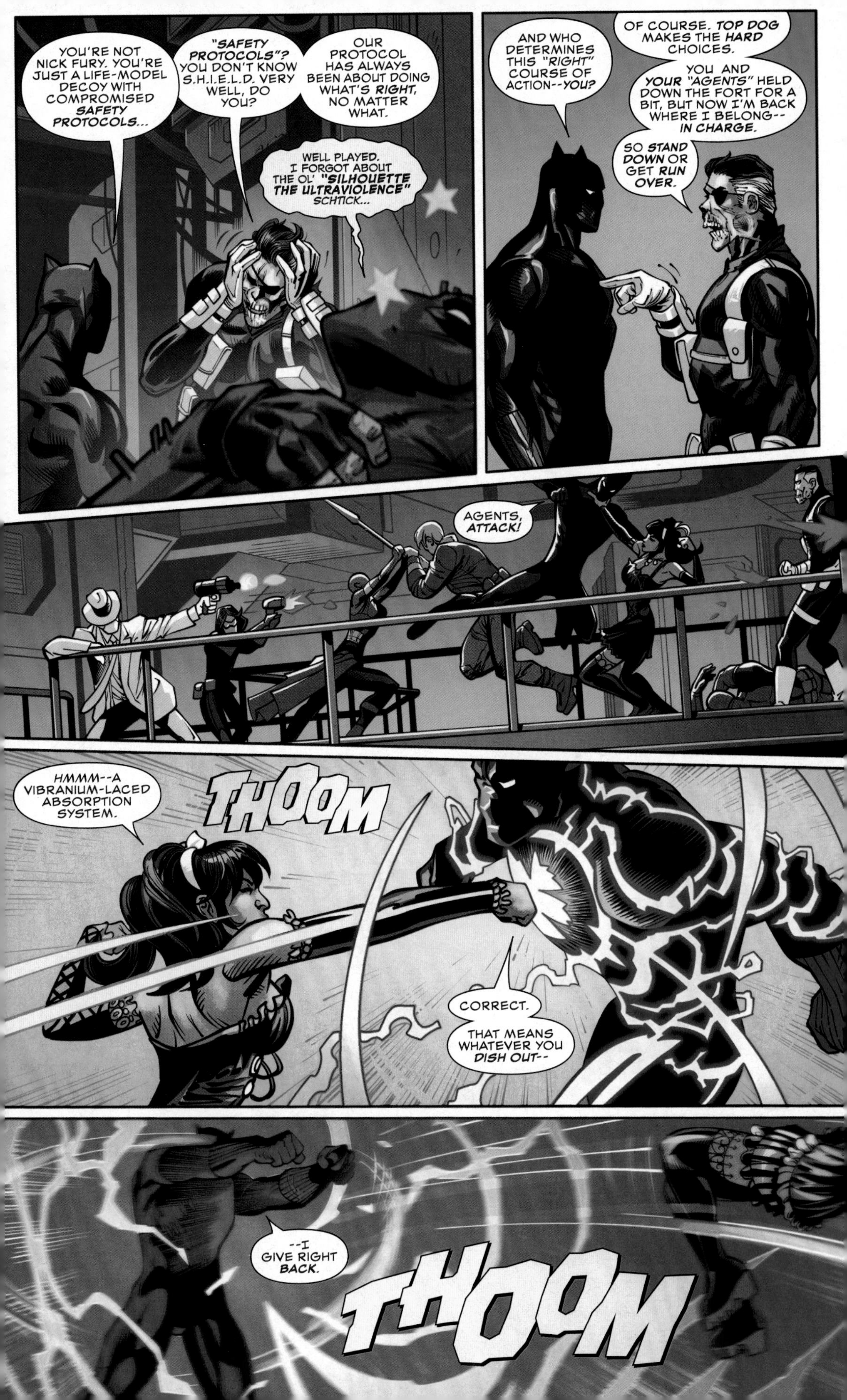
YOU'RE NOT NICK FURY. YOU'RE JUST A LIFE-MODEL DECOY WITH COMPROMISED SAFETY PROTOCOLS...
"SAFETY PROTOCOLS"? YOU DON'T KNOW S.H.I.E.L.D. VERY WELL, DO YOU?
OUR PROTOCOL HAS ALWAYS BEEN ABOUT DOING WHAT'S RIGHT, NO MATTER WHAT.
WELL PLAYED. I FORGOT ABOUT THE OL' "SILHOUETTE THE ULTRAVIOLENCE" SCHTICK...
AND WHO DETERMINES THIS "RIGHT" COURSE OF ACTION--YOU?
OF COURSE. TOP DOG MAKES THE HARD CHOICES.
YOU AND YOUR "AGENTS" HELD DOWN THE FORT FOR A BIT, BUT NOW I'M BACK WHERE I BELONG--IN CHARGE.
SO STAND DOWN OR GET RUN OVER.
AGENTS, ATTACK!
HMMM--A VIBRANIUM-LACED ABSORPTION SYSTEM.
THOOM
CORRECT.
THAT MEANS WHATEVER YOU DISH OUT--
--I GIVE RIGHT BACK.
THOOM

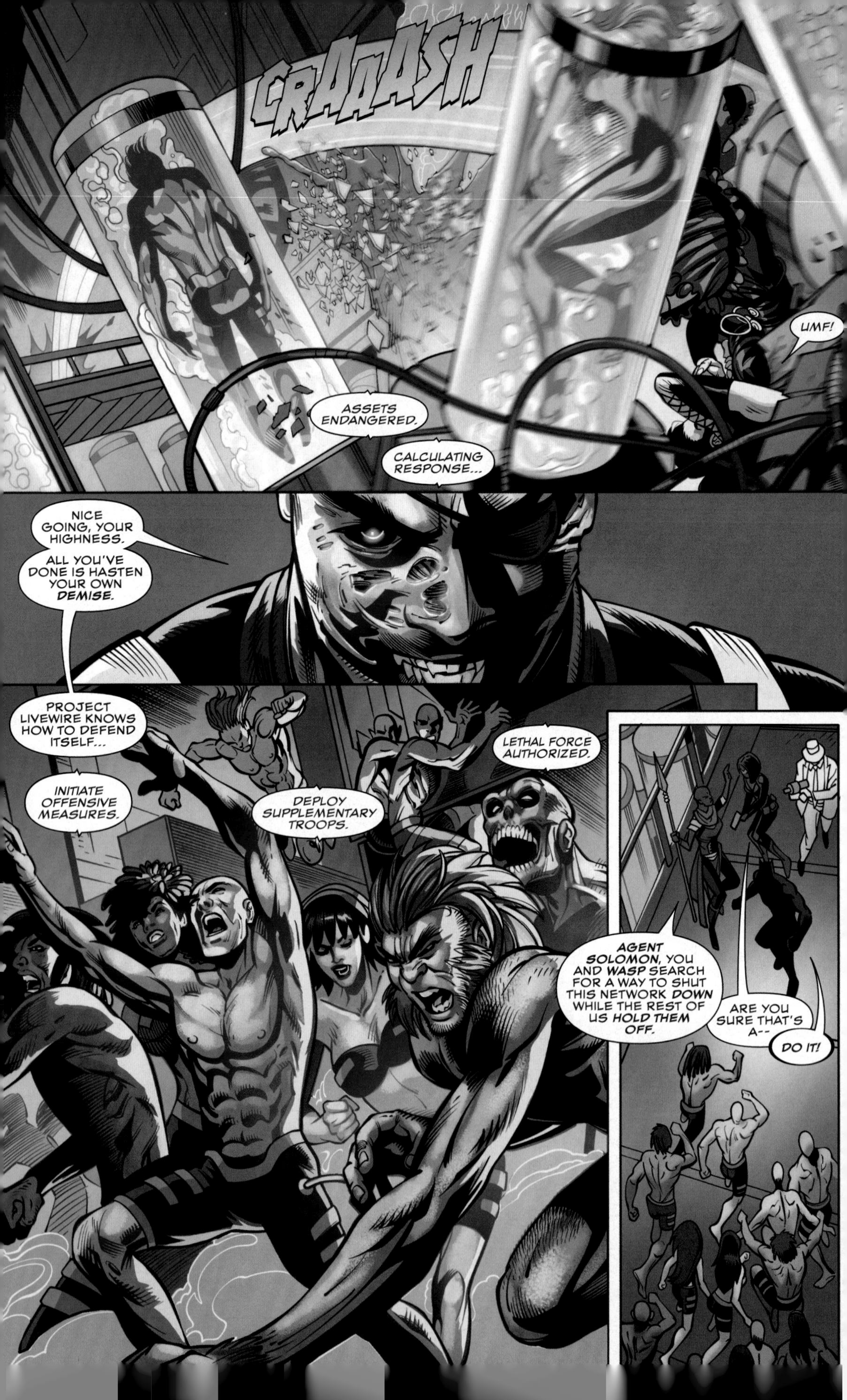
CRAAASH
UMF!
ASSETS ENDANGERED.
CALCULATING RESPONSE...
NICE GOING, YOUR HIGHNESS.
ALL YOU'VE DONE IS HASTEN YOUR OWN DEMISE.
PROJECT LIVEWIRE KNOWS HOW TO DEFEND ITSELF...
INITIATE OFFENSIVE MEASURES.
DEPLOY SUPPLEMENTARY TROOPS.
LETHAL FORCE AUTHORIZED.
AGENT SOLOMON, YOU AND WASP SEARCH FOR A WAY TO SHUT THIS NETWORK DOWN WHILE THE REST OF US HOLD THEM OFF.
ARE YOU SURE THAT'S A--
DO IT!

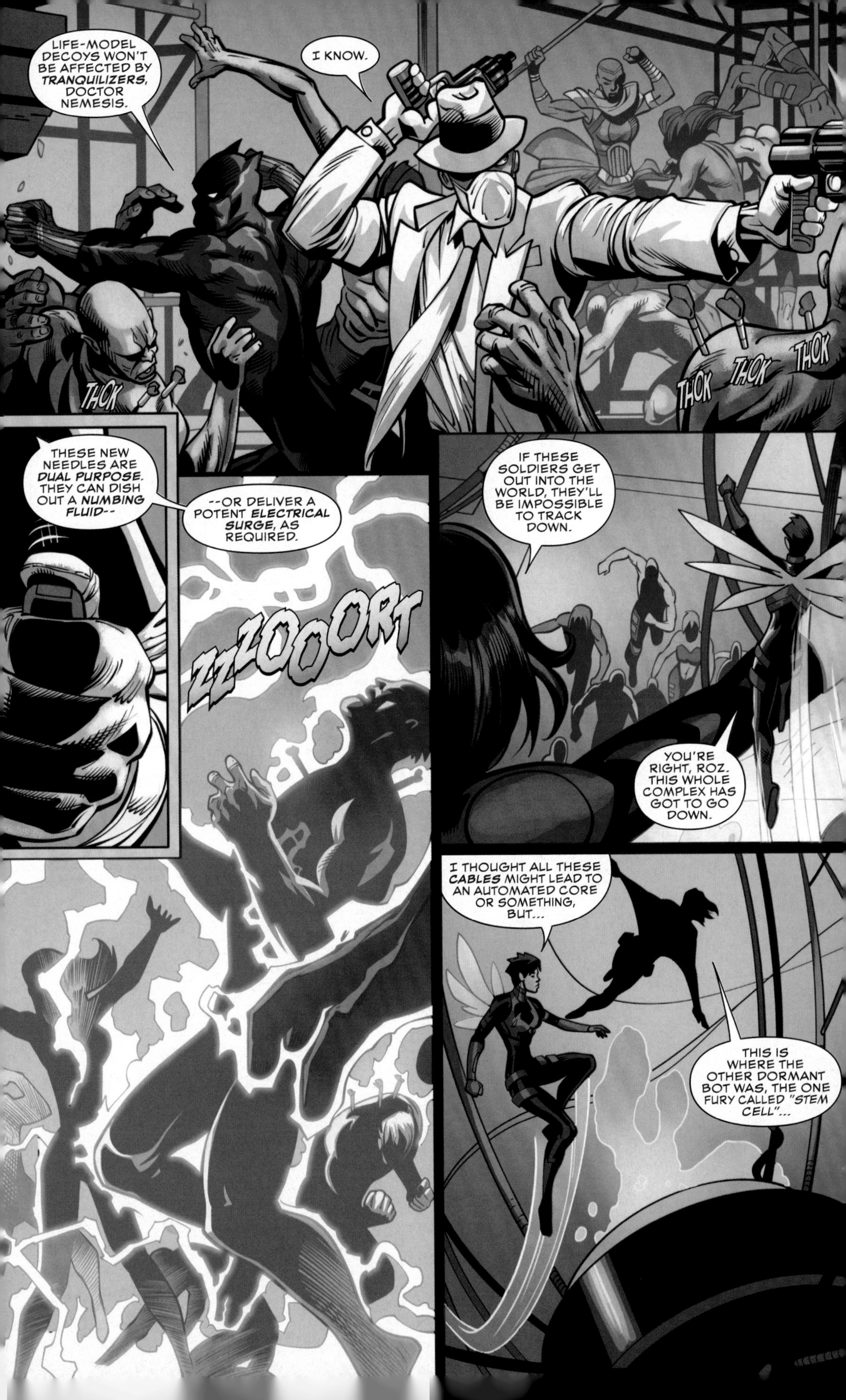

LIFE-MODEL DECOYS WON'T BE AFFECTED BY TRANQUILIZERS, DOCTOR NEMESIS.
I KNOW.
THOK
THOK THOK THOK
THESE NEW NEEDLES ARE DUAL PURPOSE. THEY CAN DISH OUT A NUMBING FLUID--
--OR DELIVER A POTENT ELECTRICAL SURGE, AS REQUIRED.
ZZZOOOORT
IF THESE SOLDIERS GET OUT INTO THE WORLD, THEY'LL BE IMPOSSIBLE TO TRACK DOWN.
YOU'RE RIGHT, ROZ. THIS WHOLE COMPLEX HAS GOT TO GO DOWN.
I THOUGHT ALL THESE CABLES MIGHT LEAD TO AN AUTOMATED CORE OR SOMETHING, BUT...
THIS IS WHERE THE OTHER DORMANT BOT WAS, THE ONE FURY CALLED "STEM CELL"...

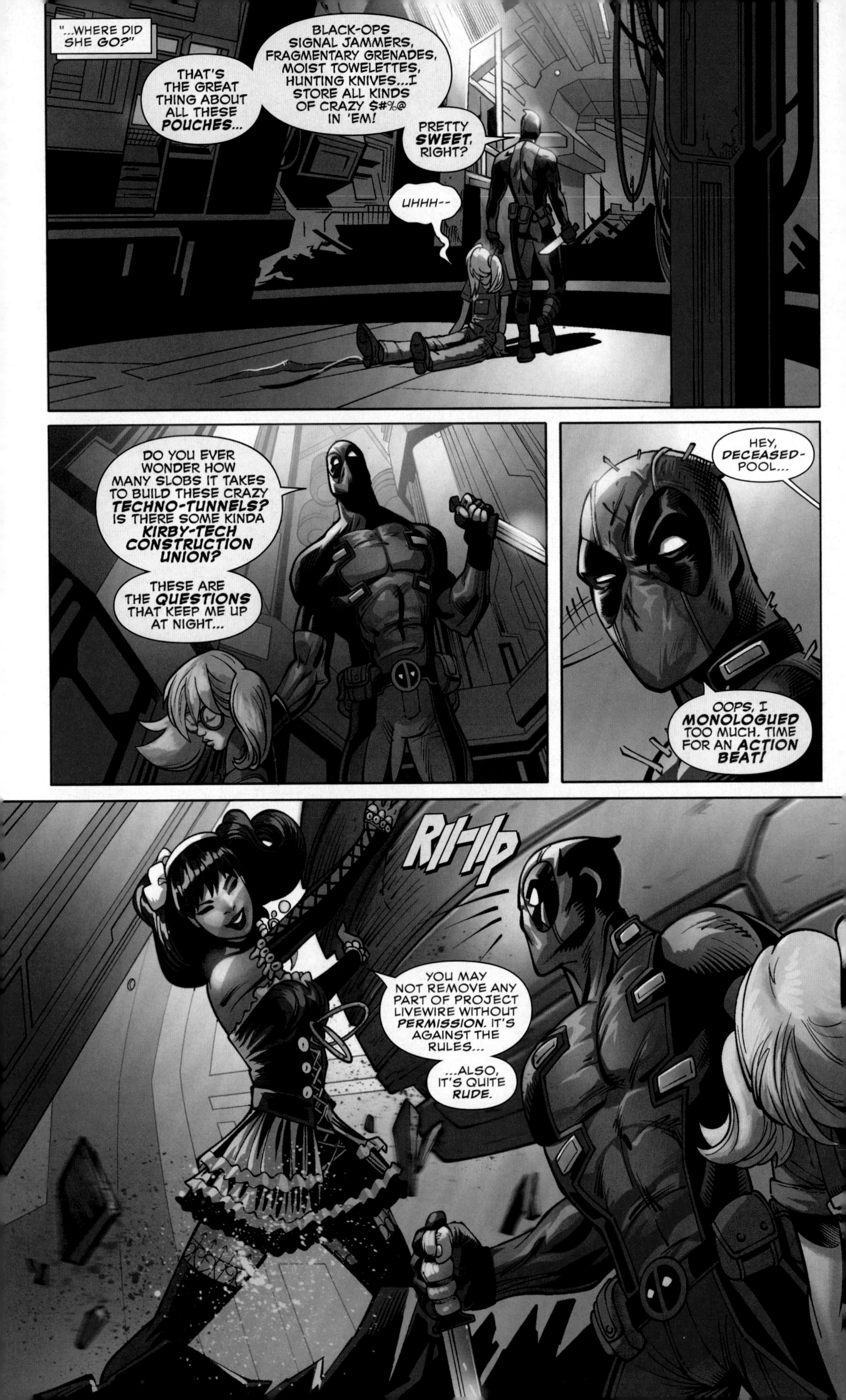
"...WHERE DID SHE GO?"
THAT'S THE GREAT THING ABOUT ALL THESE POUCHES...
BLACK-OPS SIGNAL JAMMERS, FRAGMENTARY GRENADES, MOIST TOWELETTES, HUNTING KNIVES...I STORE ALL KINDS OF CRAZY $#%@ IN 'EM!
PRETTY SWEET, RIGHT?
UHHH--
DO YOU EVER WONDER HOW MANY SLOBS IT TAKES TO BUILD THESE CRAZY TECHNO-TUNNELS? IS THERE SOME KINDA KIRBY-TECH CONSTRUCTION UNION?
THESE ARE THE QUESTIONS THAT KEEP ME UP AT NIGHT...
HEY, DECEASED-POOL...
OOPS, I MONOLOGUED TOO MUCH. TIME FOR AN ACTION BEAT!
RIIIIP
YOU MAY NOT REMOVE ANY PART OF PROJECT LIVEWIRE WITHOUT PERMISSION. IT'S AGAINST THE RULES...
...ALSO, IT'S QUITE RUDE.

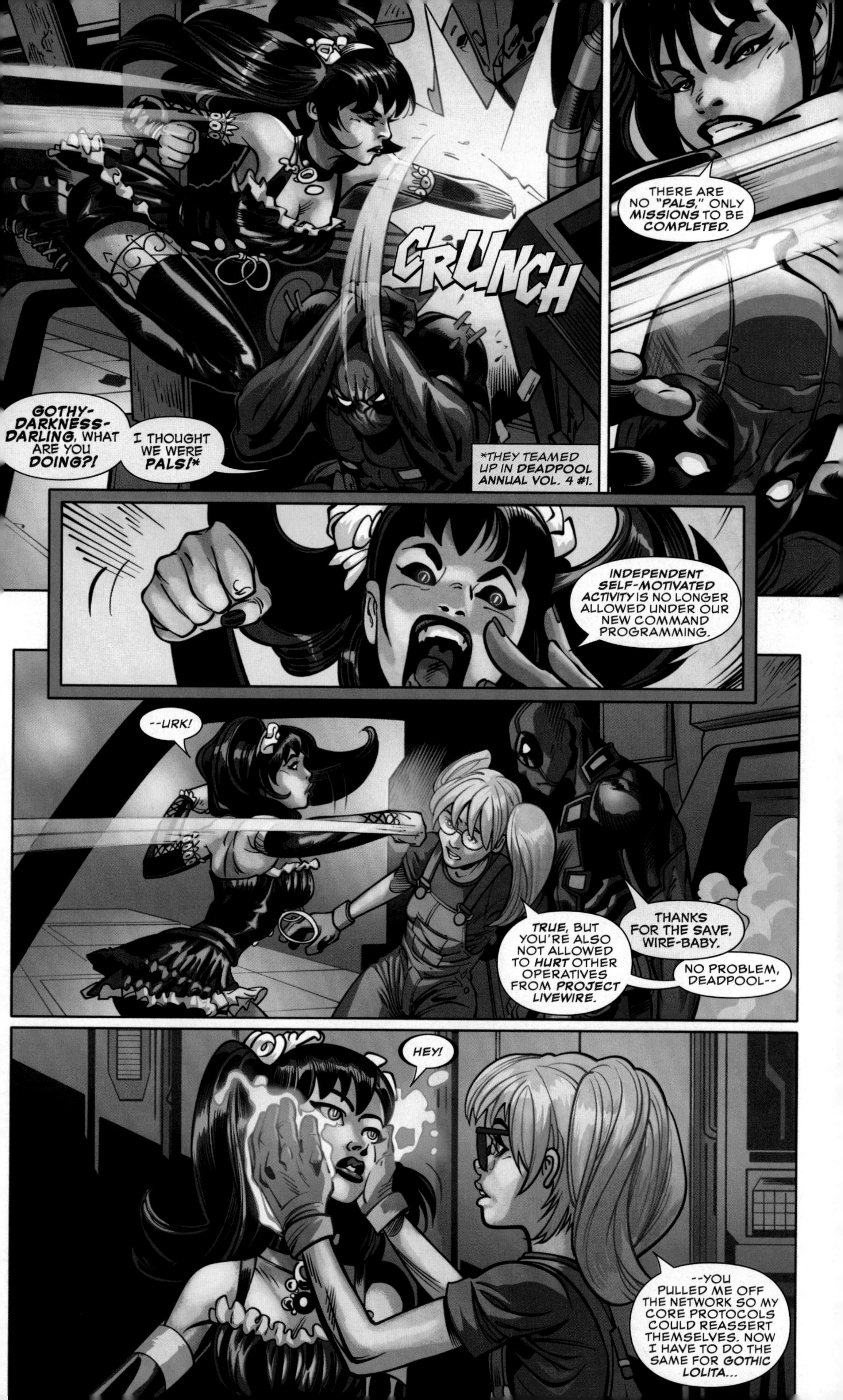
CRUNCH
THERE ARE NO "PALS," ONLY MISSIONS TO BE COMPLETED.
GOTHY-DARKNESS-DARLING, WHAT ARE YOU DOING?!
I THOUGHT WE WERE PALS!*
*THEY TEAMED UP IN DEADPOOL ANNUAL VOL. 4 #1.
INDEPENDENT SELF-MOTIVATED ACTIVITY IS NO LONGER ALLOWED UNDER OUR NEW COMMAND PROGRAMMING.
--URK!
TRUE, BUT YOU'RE ALSO NOT ALLOWED TO HURT OTHER OPERATIVES FROM PROJECT LIVEWIRE.
THANKS FOR THE SAVE, WIRE-BABY.
NO PROBLEM, DEADPOOL--
HEY!
--YOU PULLED ME OFF THE NETWORK SO MY CORE PROTOCOLS COULD REASSERT THEMSELVES. NOW I HAVE TO DO THE SAME FOR GOTHIC LOLITA...

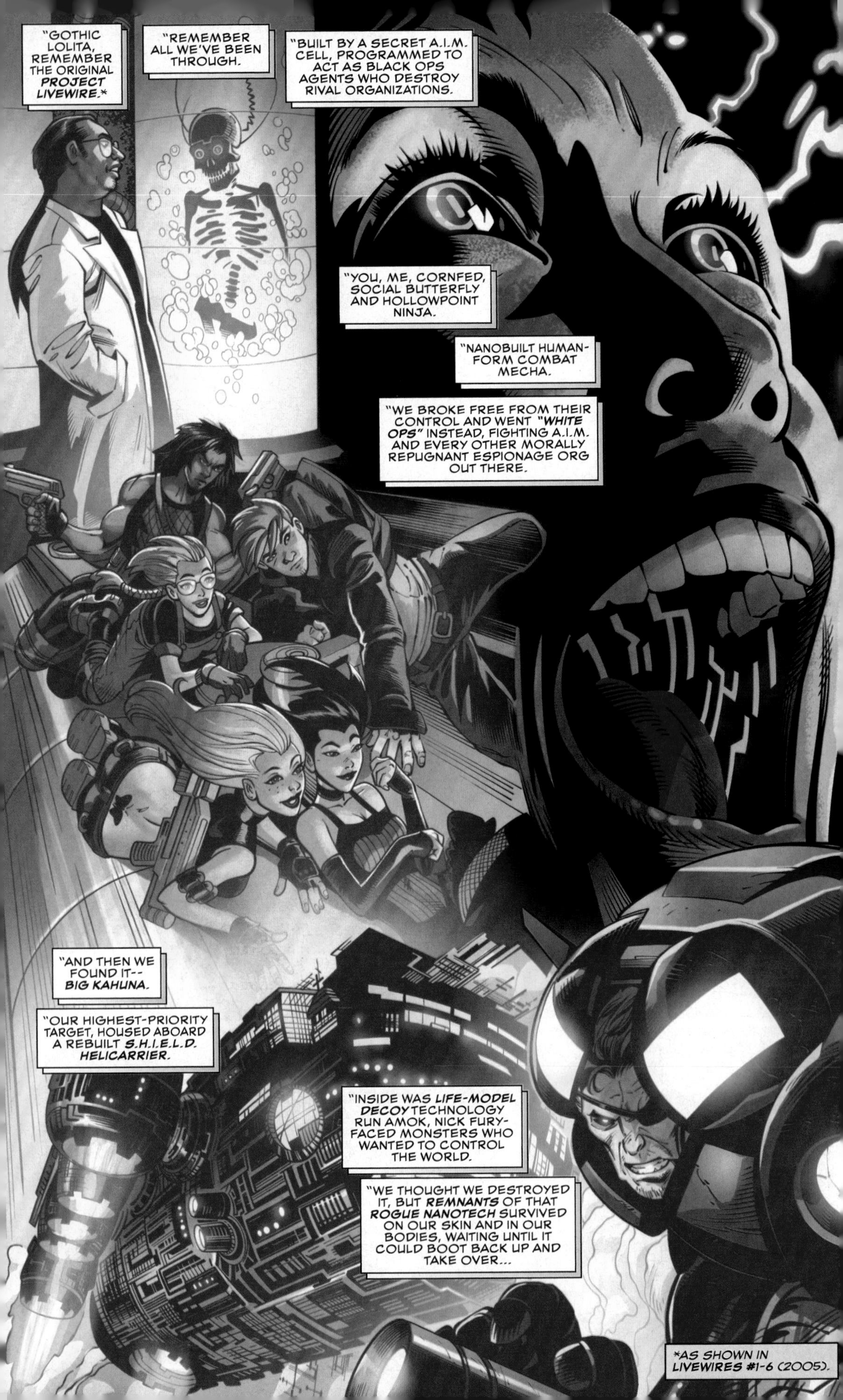
"GOTHIC LOLITA, REMEMBER THE ORIGINAL PROJECT LIVEWIRE.*
"REMEMBER ALL WE'VE BEEN THROUGH.
"BUILT BY A SECRET A.I.M. CELL, PROGRAMMED TO ACT AS BLACK OPS AGENTS WHO DESTROY RIVAL ORGANIZATIONS.
"YOU, ME, CORNFED, SOCIAL BUTTERFLY AND HOLLOWPOINT NINJA.
"NANOBUILT HUMAN-FORM COMBAT MECHA.
"WE BROKE FREE FROM THEIR CONTROL AND WENT "WHITE OPS" INSTEAD, FIGHTING A.I.M. AND EVERY OTHER MORALLY REPUGNANT ESPIONAGE ORG OUT THERE.
"AND THEN WE FOUND IT--BIG KAHUNA.
"OUR HIGHEST-PRIORITY TARGET, HOUSED ABOARD A REBUILT S.H.I.E.L.D. HELICARRIER.
"INSIDE WAS LIFE-MODEL DECOY TECHNOLOGY RUN AMOK, NICK FURY-FACED MONSTERS WHO WANTED TO CONTROL THE WORLD.
"WE THOUGHT WE DESTROYED IT, BUT REMNANTS OF THAT ROGUE NANOTECH SURVIVED ON OUR SKIN AND IN OUR BODIES, WAITING UNTIL IT COULD BOOT BACK UP AND TAKE OVER...
*AS SHOWN IN LIVEWIRES #1-6 (2005).

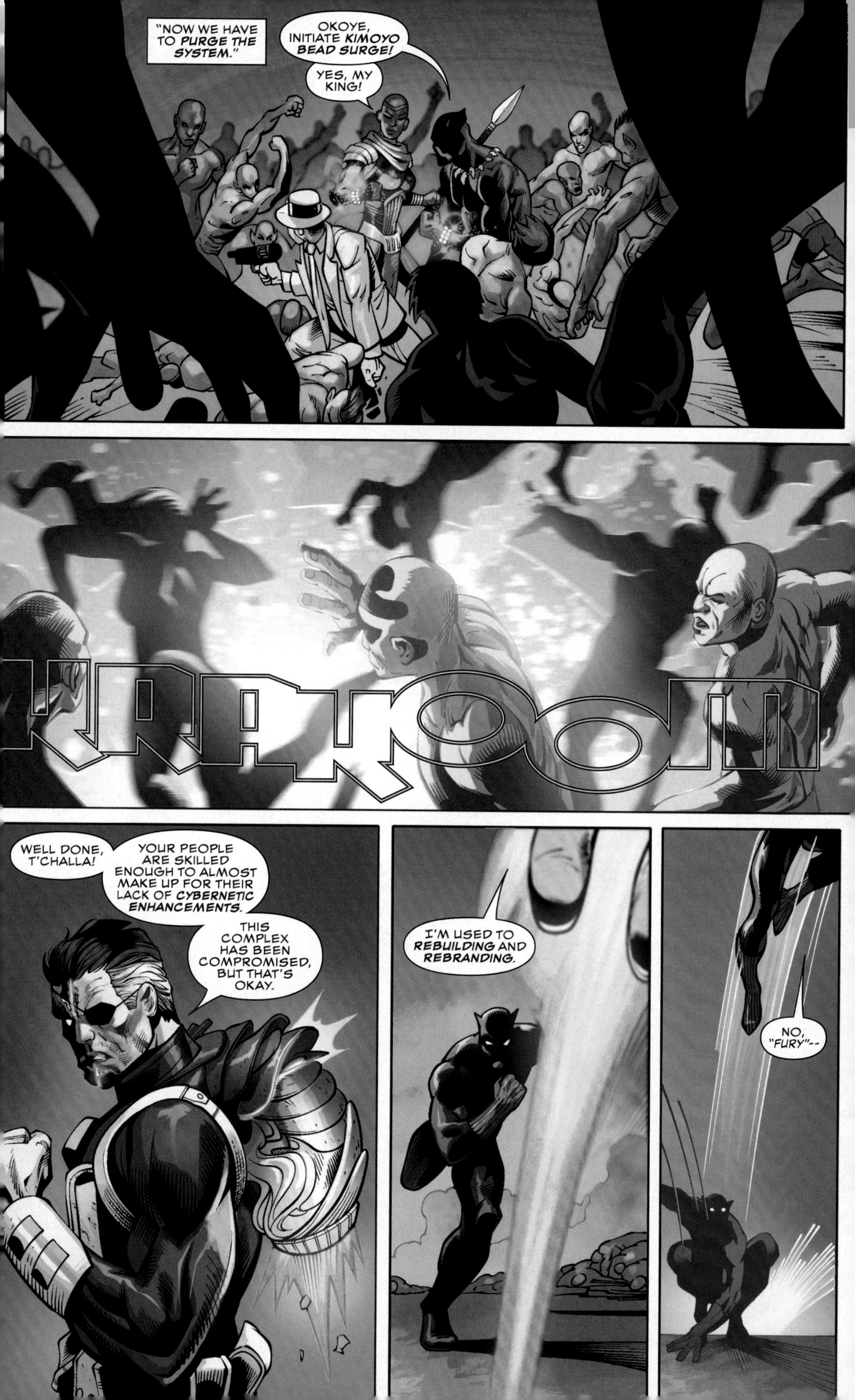
"NOW WE HAVE TO PURGE THE SYSTEM."
OKOYE, INITIATE KIMOYO BEAD SURGE!
YES, MY KING!
KRAKOOM
WELL DONE, T'CHALLA!
YOUR PEOPLE ARE SKILLED ENOUGH TO ALMOST MAKE UP FOR THEIR LACK OF CYBERNETIC ENHANCEMENTS.
THIS COMPLEX HAS BEEN COMPROMISED, BUT THAT'S OKAY.
I'M USED TO REBUILDING AND REBRANDING.
NO, "FURY"--

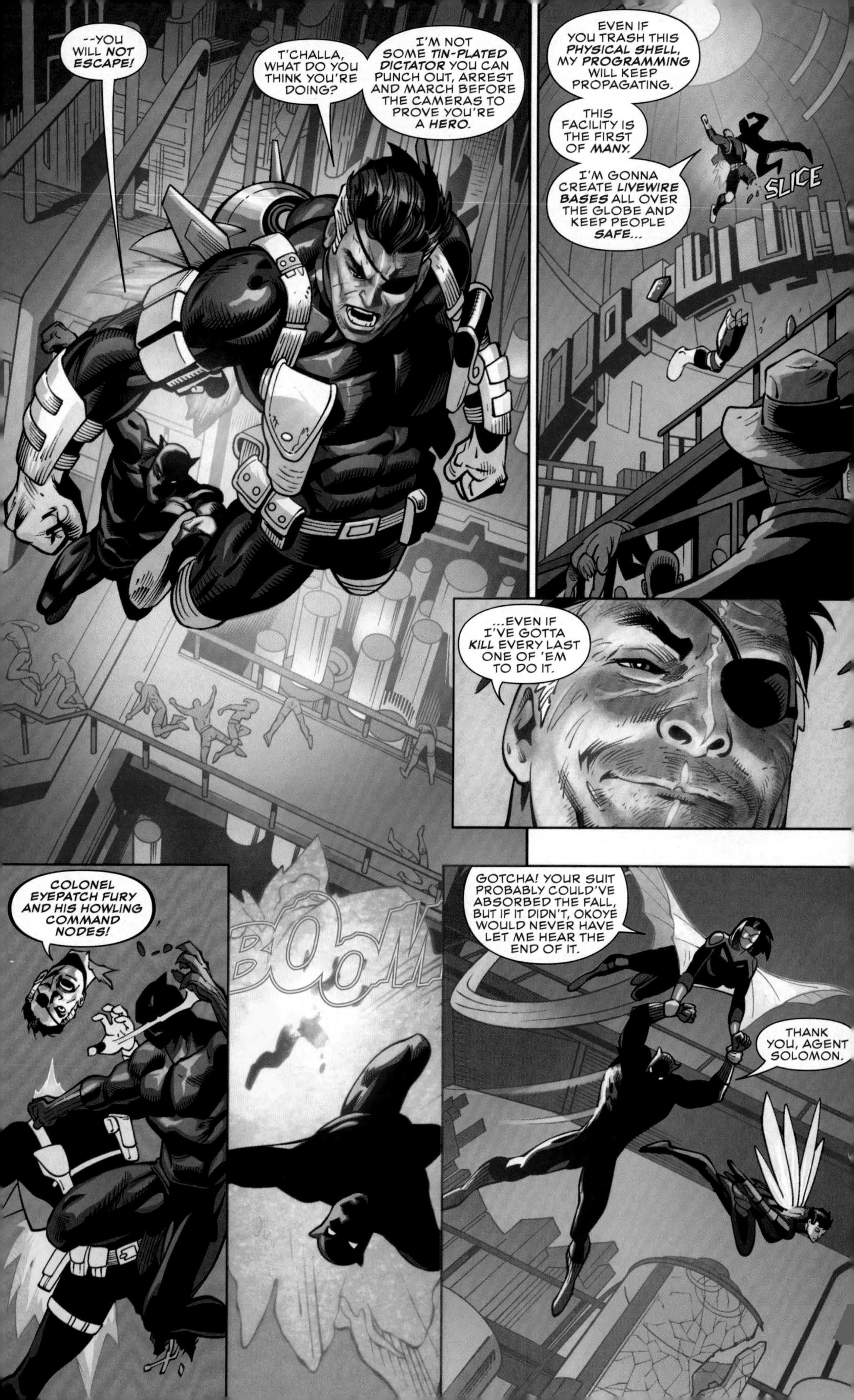
--YOU WILL NOT ESCAPE!
T'CHALLA, WHAT DO YOU THINK YOU'RE DOING?
I'M NOT SOME TIN-PLATED DICTATOR YOU CAN PUNCH OUT, ARREST AND MARCH BEFORE THE CAMERAS TO PROVE YOU'RE A HERO.
EVEN IF YOU TRASH THIS PHYSICAL SHELL, MY PROGRAMMING WILL KEEP PROPAGATING.
THIS FACILITY IS THE FIRST OF MANY.
I'M GONNA CREATE LIVEWIRE BASES ALL OVER THE GLOBE AND KEEP PEOPLE SAFE...
SLICE
...EVEN IF I'VE GOTTA KILL EVERY LAST ONE OF 'EM TO DO IT.
COLONEL EYEPATCH FURY AND HIS HOWLING COMMAND NODES!
BOOM
GOTCHA! YOUR SUIT PROBABLY COULD'VE ABSORBED THE FALL, BUT IF IT DIDN'T, OKOYE WOULD NEVER HAVE LET ME HEAR THE END OF IT.
THANK YOU, AGENT SOLOMON.

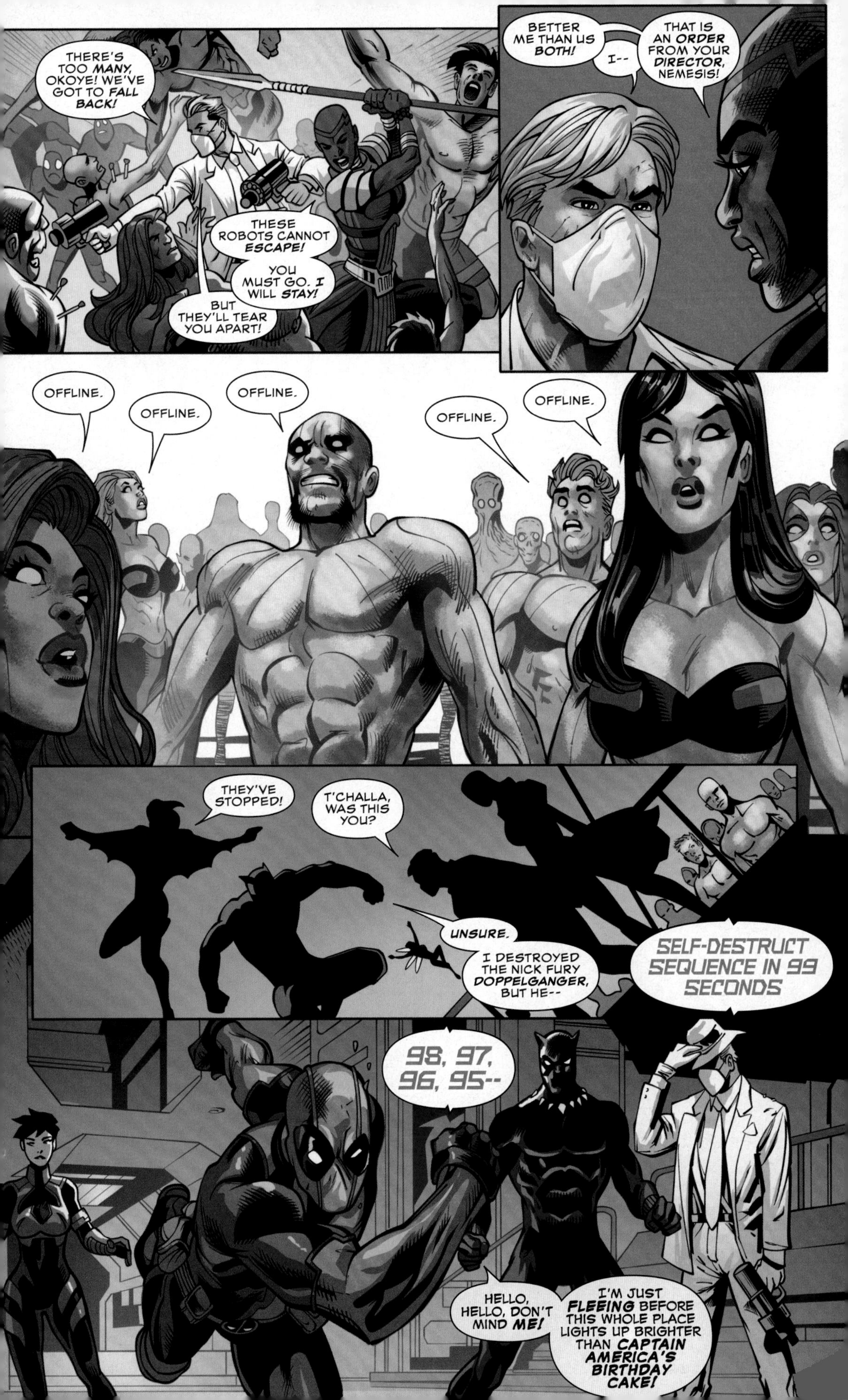
THERE'S TOO MANY, OKOYE! WE'VE GOT TO FALL BACK!
THESE ROBOTS CANNOT ESCAPE!
YOU MUST GO. I WILL STAY!
BUT THEY'LL TEAR YOU APART!
BETTER ME THAN US BOTH!
I--
THAT IS AN ORDER FROM YOUR DIRECTOR, NEMESIS!
OFFLINE.
OFFLINE.
OFFLINE.
OFFLINE.
OFFLINE.
THEY'VE STOPPED!
T'CHALLA, WAS THIS YOU?
UNSURE.
I DESTROYED THE NICK FURY DOPPELGANGER, BUT HE--
SELF-DESTRUCT SEQUENCE IN 99 SECONDS
98, 97, 96, 95--
HELLO, HELLO, DON'T MIND ME!
I'M JUST FLEEING BEFORE THIS WHOLE PLACE LIGHTS UP BRIGHTER THAN CAPTAIN AMERICA'S BIRTHDAY CAKE!

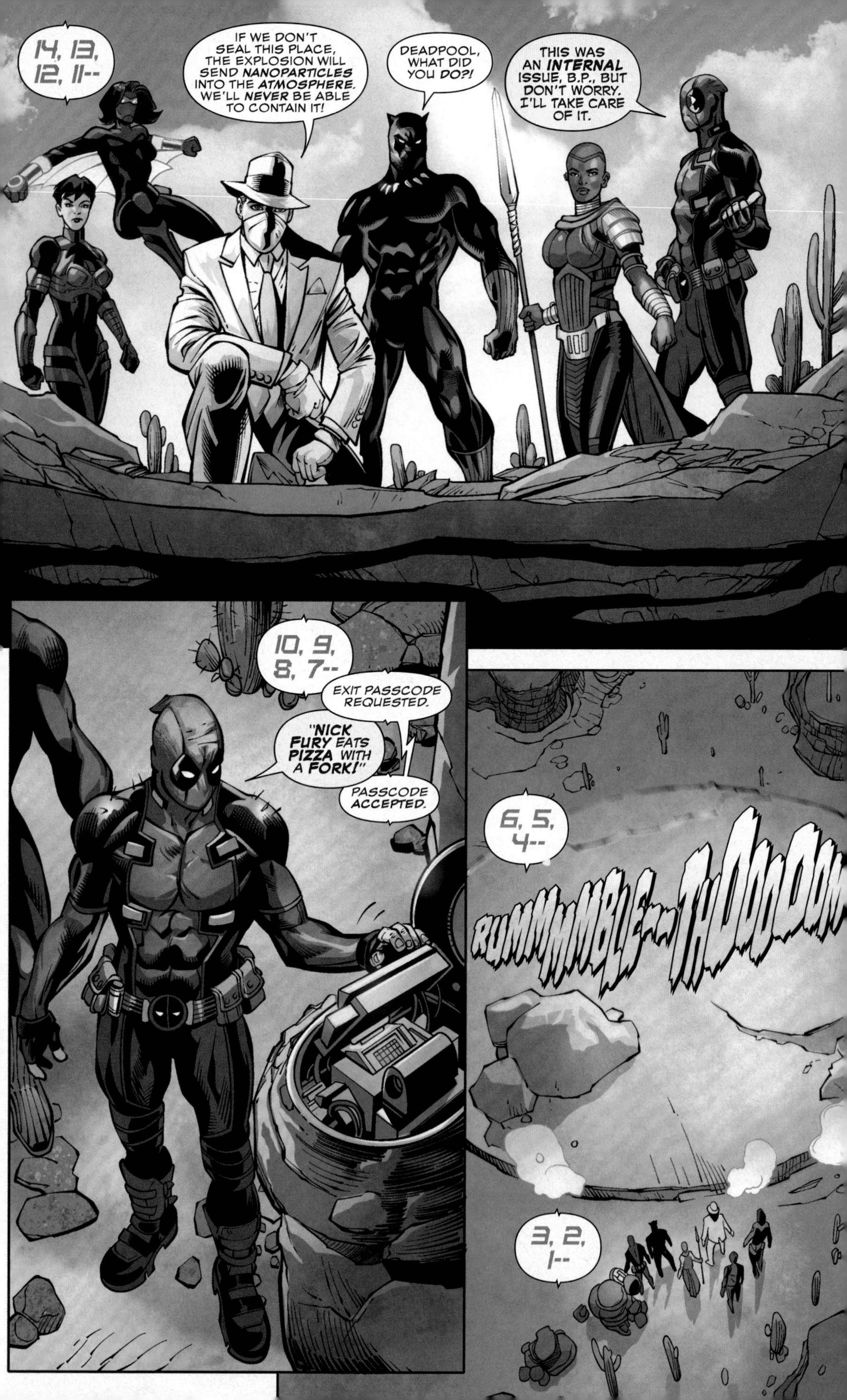
14, 13, 12, 11--
IF WE DON'T SEAL THIS PLACE, THE EXPLOSION WILL SEND NANOPARTICLES INTO THE ATMOSPHERE. WE'LL NEVER BE ABLE TO CONTAIN IT!
DEADPOOL, WHAT DID YOU DO?!
THIS WAS AN INTERNAL ISSUE, B.P., BUT DON'T WORRY. I'LL TAKE CARE OF IT.
10, 9, 8, 7--
EXIT PASSCODE REQUESTED.
"NICK FURY EATS PIZZA WITH A FORK!"
PASSCODE ACCEPTED.
6, 5, 4--
RUMMMMBLE--THOOOOOM
3, 2, 1--

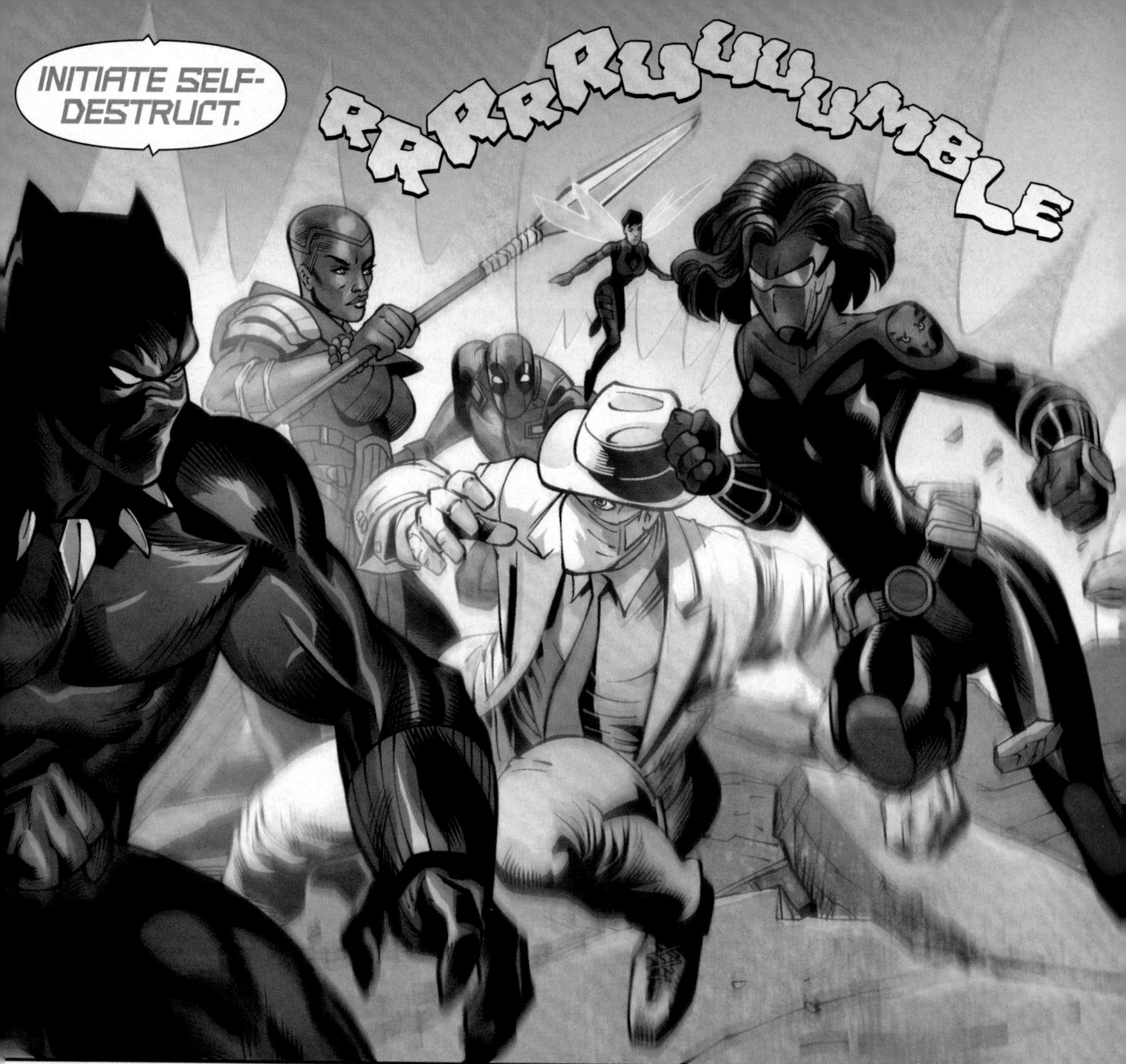
INITIATE SELF-DESTRUCT.
RRRRRUUUUMBLE

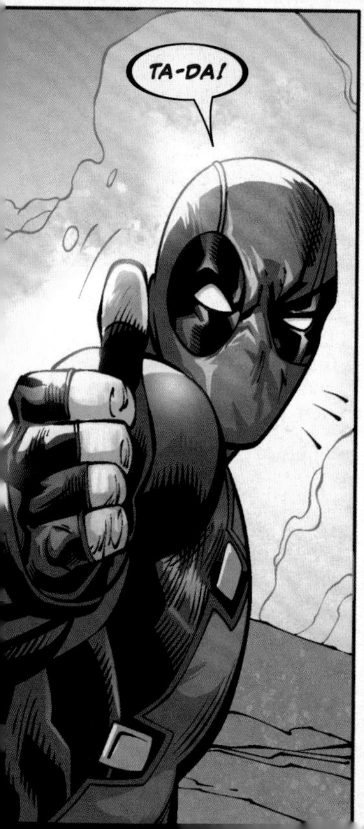
TA-DA!

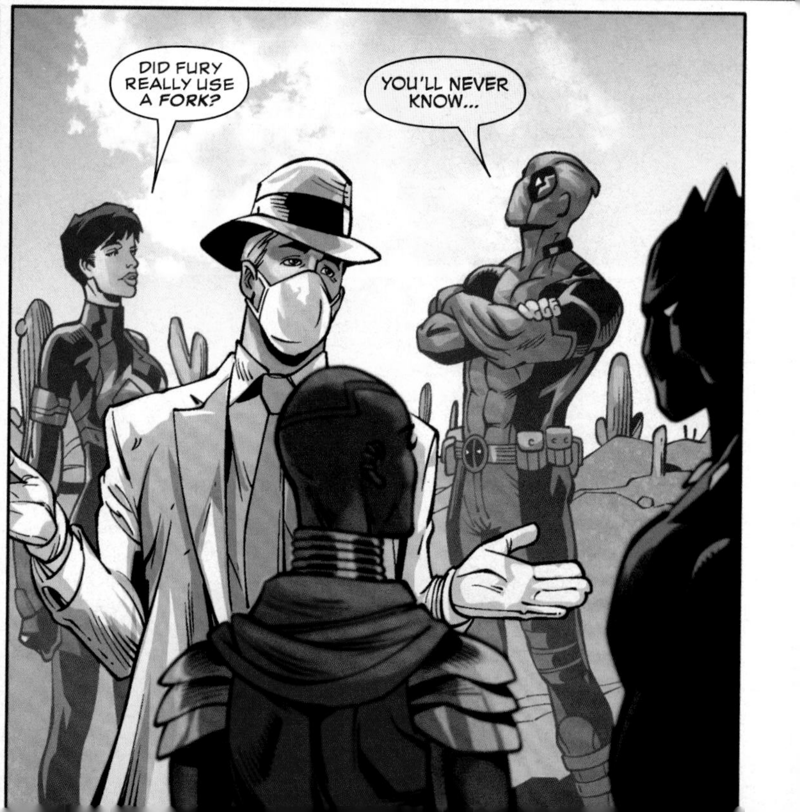
DID FURY REALLY USE A FORK?
YOU'LL NEVER KNOW...

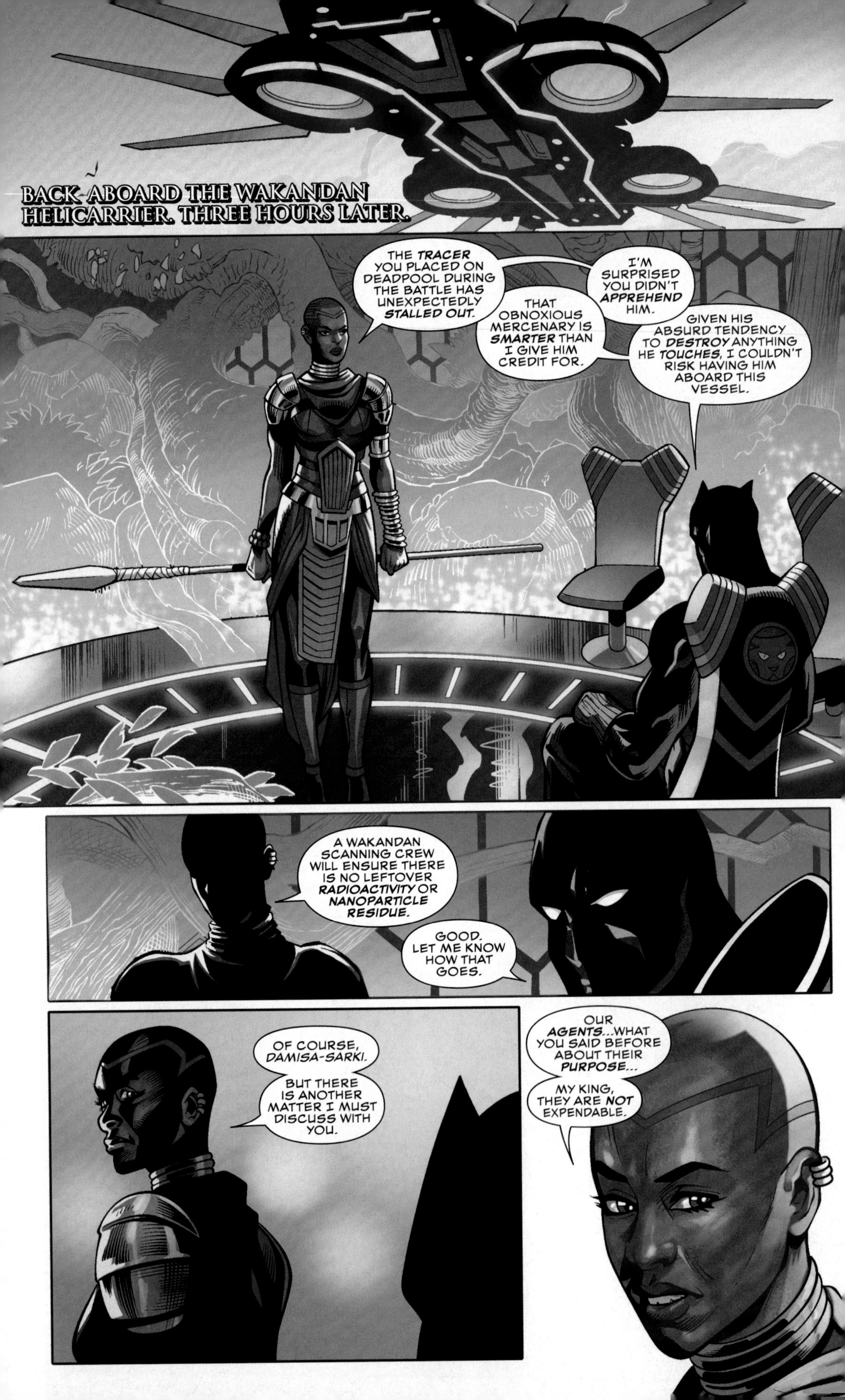

BACK ABOARD THE WAKANDAN HELICARRIER. THREE HOURS LATER.
THE TRACER YOU PLACED ON DEADPOOL DURING THE BATTLE HAS UNEXPECTEDLY STALLED OUT.
THAT OBNOXIOUS MERCENARY IS SMARTER THAN I GIVE HIM CREDIT FOR.
I'M SURPRISED YOU DIDN'T APPREHEND HIM.
GIVEN HIS ABSURD TENDENCY TO DESTROY ANYTHING HE TOUCHES, I COULDN'T RISK HAVING HIM ABOARD THIS VESSEL.
A WAKANDAN SCANNING CREW WILL ENSURE THERE IS NO LEFTOVER RADIOACTIVITY OR NANOPARTICLE RESIDUE.
GOOD. LET ME KNOW HOW THAT GOES.
OF COURSE, DAMISA-SARKI.
BUT THERE IS ANOTHER MATTER I MUST DISCUSS WITH YOU.
OUR AGENTS...WHAT YOU SAID BEFORE ABOUT THEIR PURPOSE...
MY KING, THEY ARE NOT EXPENDABLE.

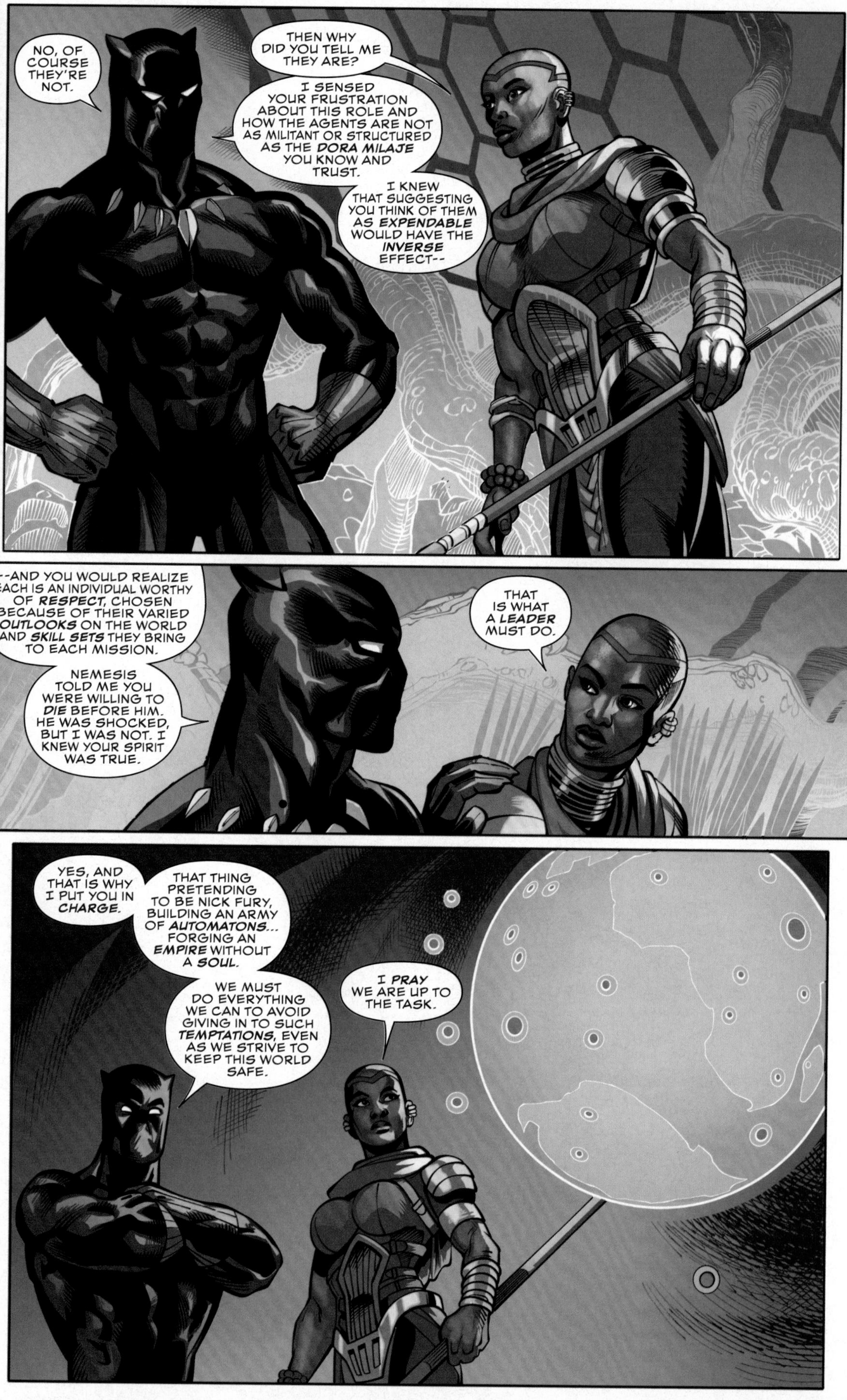
NO, OF COURSE THEY'RE NOT.
THEN WHY DID YOU TELL ME THEY ARE?
I SENSED YOUR FRUSTRATION ABOUT THIS ROLE AND HOW THE AGENTS ARE NOT AS MILITANT OR STRUCTURED AS THE DORA MILAJE YOU KNOW AND TRUST.
I KNEW THAT SUGGESTING YOU THINK OF THEM AS EXPENDABLE WOULD HAVE THE INVERSE EFFECT--
--AND YOU WOULD REALIZE EACH IS AN INDIVIDUAL WORTHY OF RESPECT, CHOSEN BECAUSE OF THEIR VARIED OUTLOOKS ON THE WORLD AND SKILL SETS THEY BRING TO EACH MISSION.
NEMESIS TOLD ME YOU WERE WILLING TO DIE BEFORE HIM. HE WAS SHOCKED, BUT I WAS NOT. I KNEW YOUR SPIRIT WAS TRUE.
THAT IS WHAT A LEADER MUST DO.
YES, AND THAT IS WHY I PUT YOU IN CHARGE.
THAT THING PRETENDING TO BE NICK FURY, BUILDING AN ARMY OF AUTOMATONS... FORGING AN EMPIRE WITHOUT A SOUL.
WE MUST DO EVERYTHING WE CAN TO AVOID GIVING IN TO SUCH TEMPTATIONS, EVEN AS WE STRIVE TO KEEP THIS WORLD SAFE.
I PRAY WE ARE UP TO THE TASK.

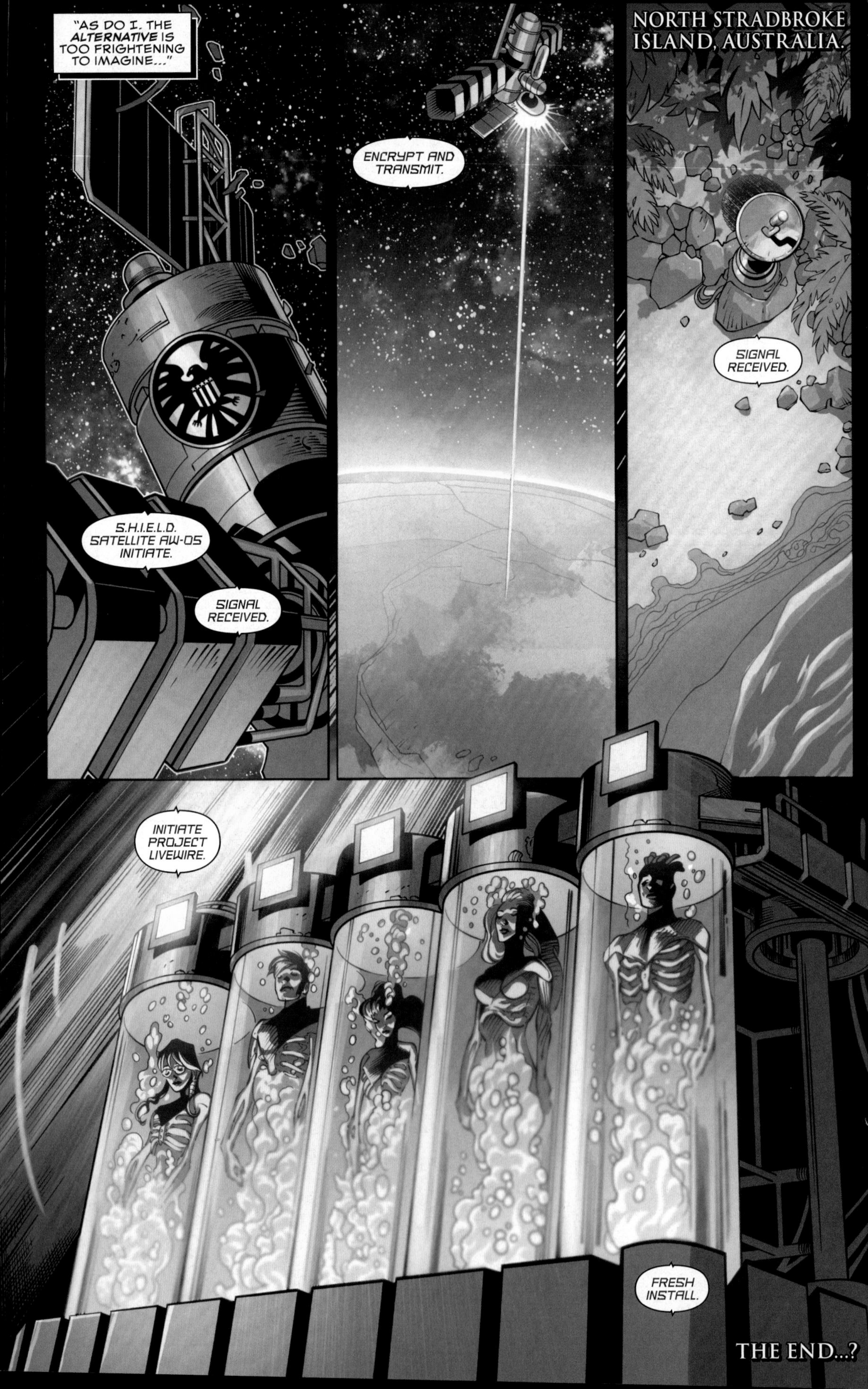
"AS DO I. THE ALTERNATIVE IS TOO FRIGHTENING TO IMAGINE..."
S.H.I.E.L.D. SATELLITE AW-05 INITIATE.
SIGNAL RECEIVED.
ENCRYPT AND TRANSMIT.
NORTH STRADBROKE ISLAND, AUSTRALIA.
SIGNAL RECEIVED.
INITIATE PROJECT LIVEWIRE.
FRESH INSTALL.
THE END...?

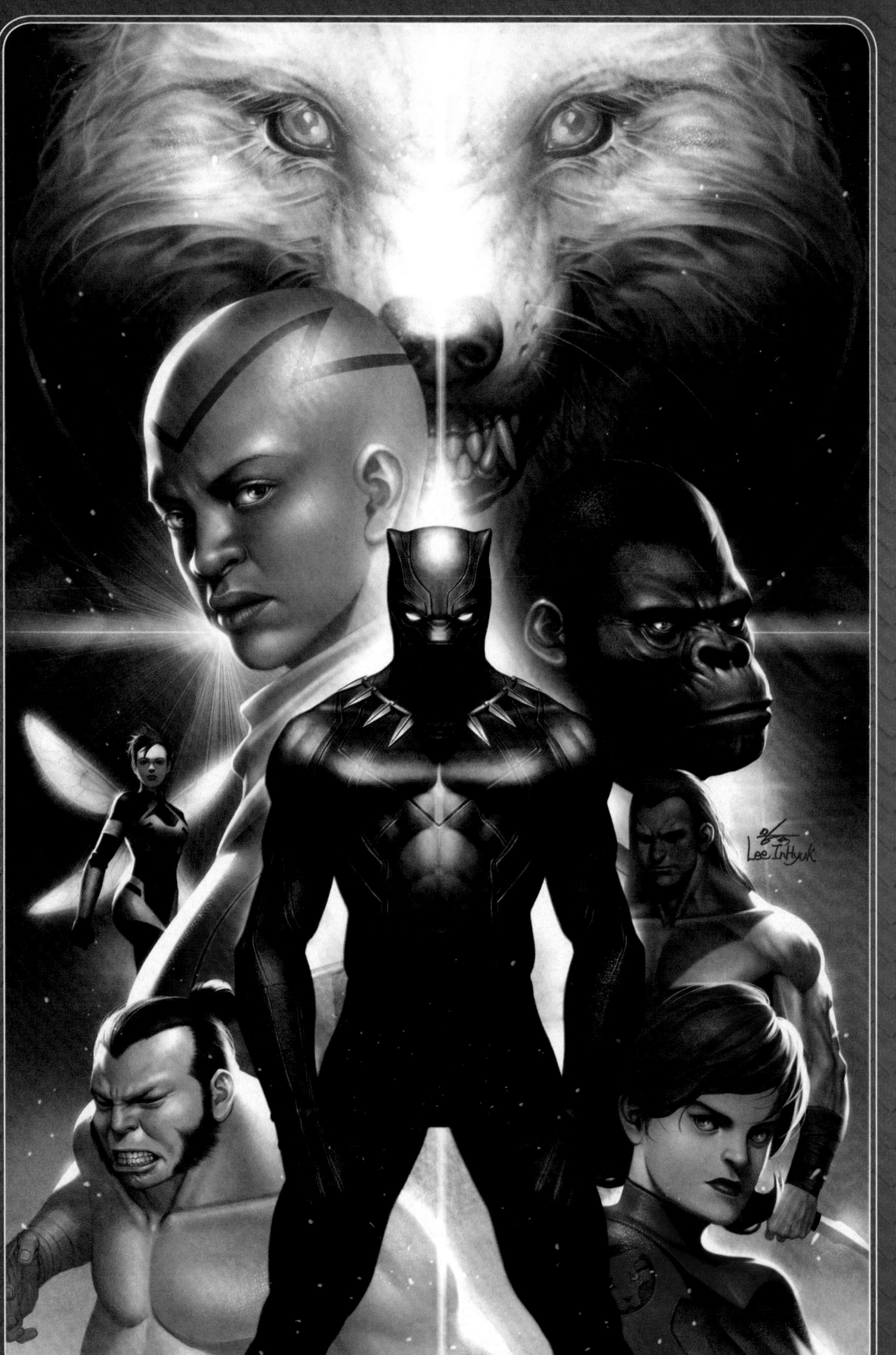
Lee InHyuk

InHyuk Lee
1 VARIANT

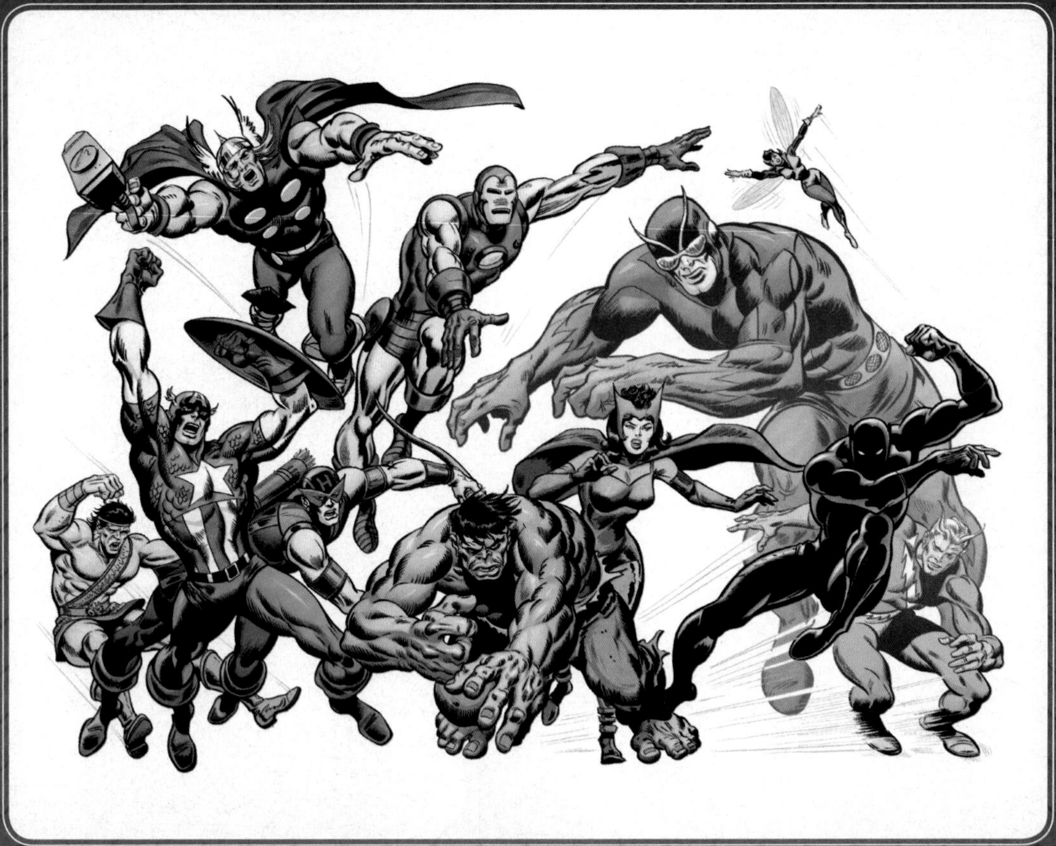

John Buscema & Dave McCaig
1 HIDDEN GEM VARIANT

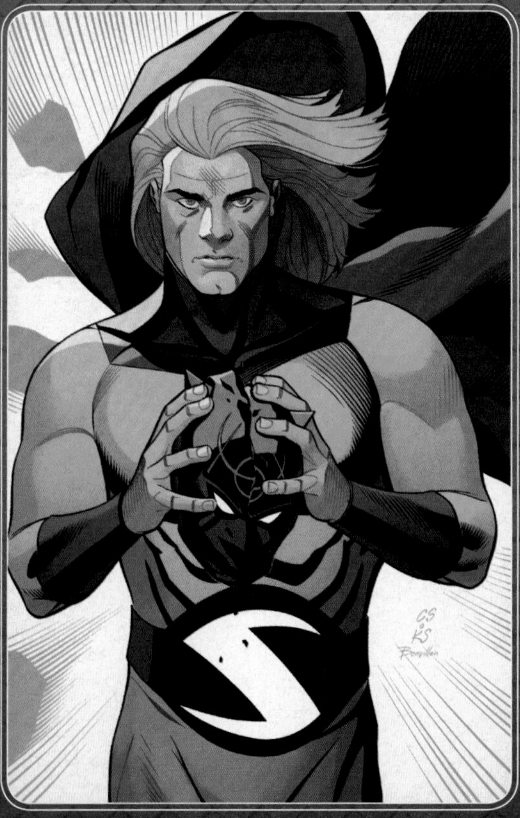

Chris Sprouse, Karl Story & Tamra Bonvillain
2 VARIANT

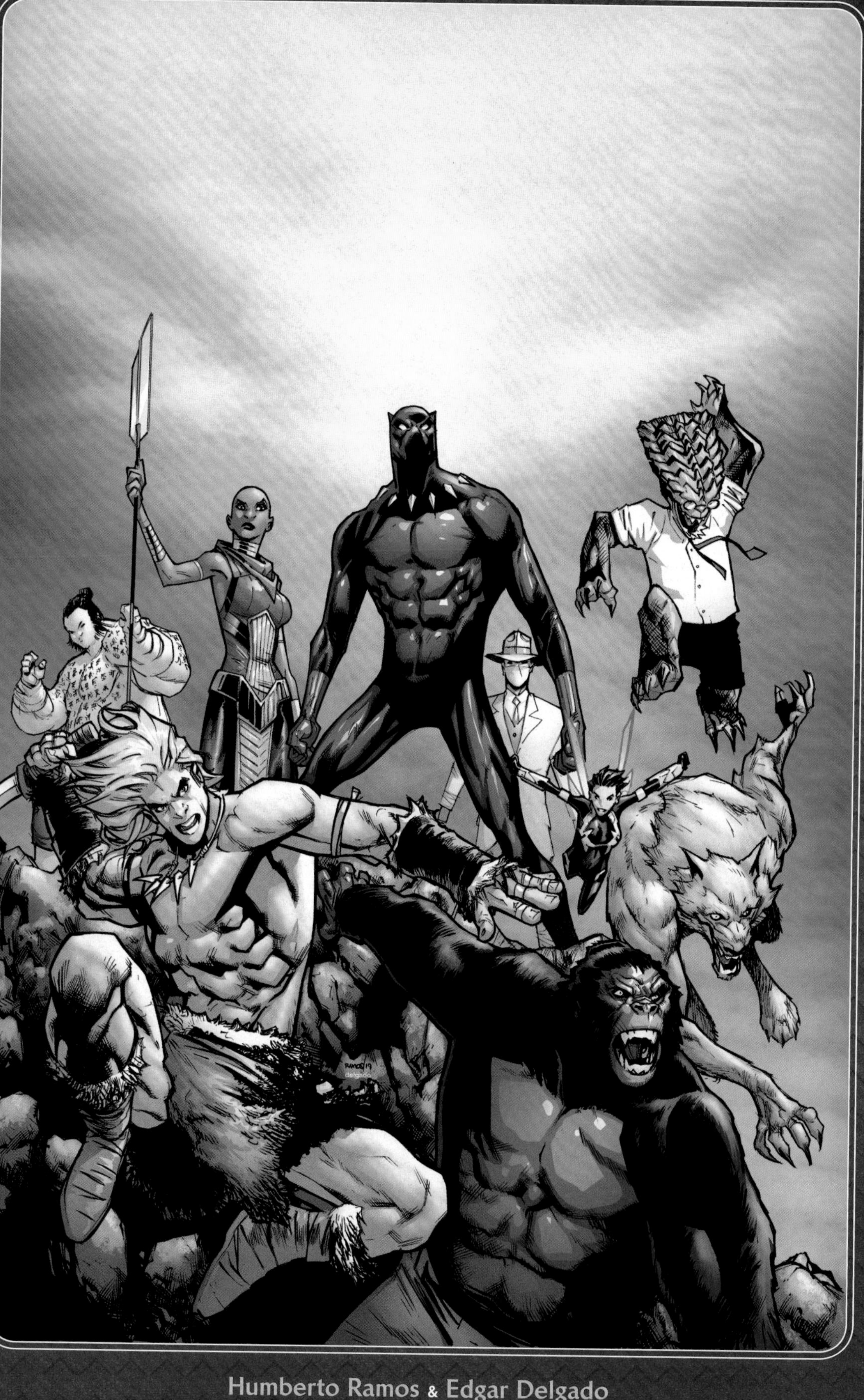

Humberto Ramos & Edgar Delgado
3 VARIANT

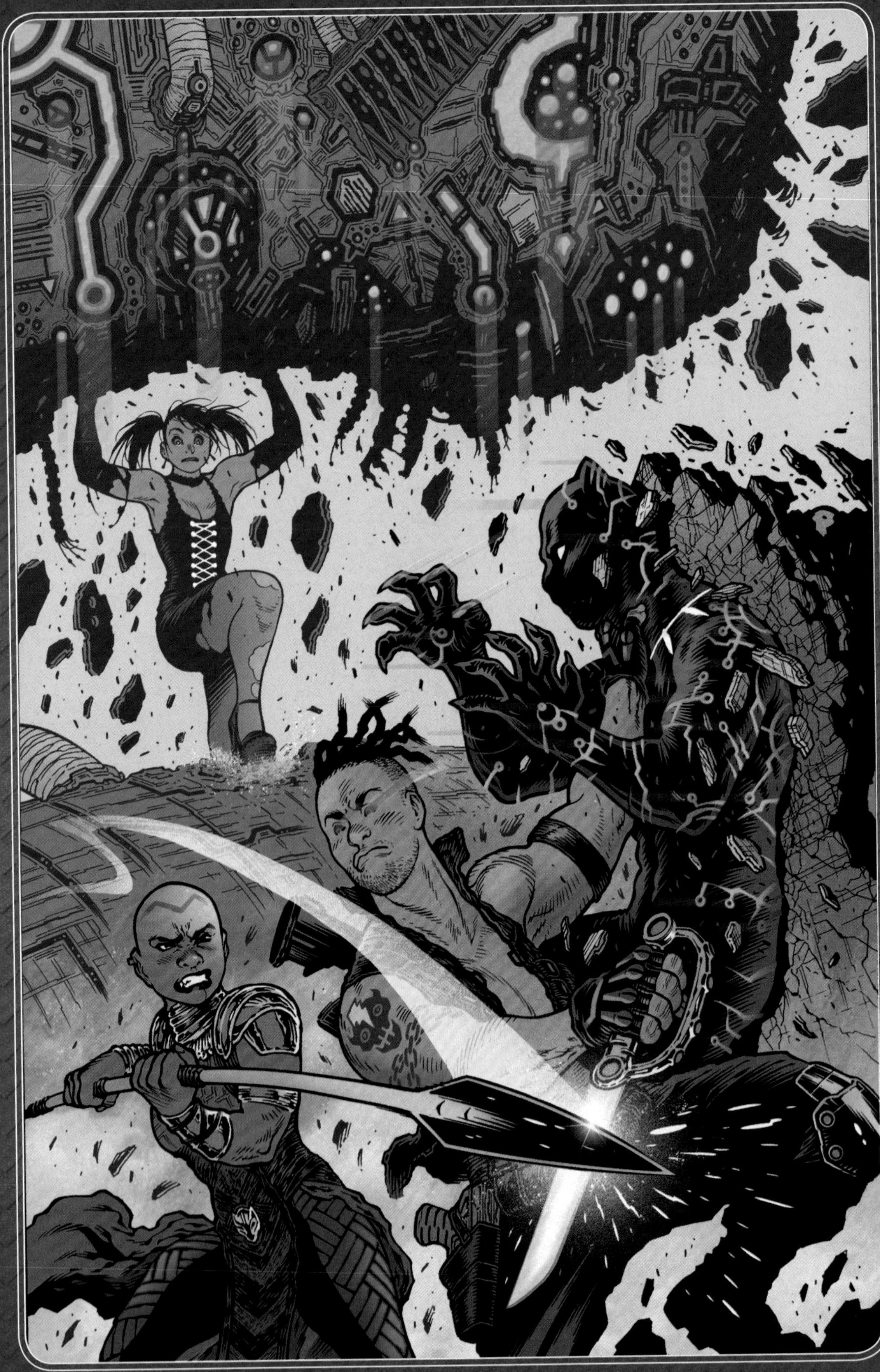

Adam Warren & Rico Renzi
5 VARIANT

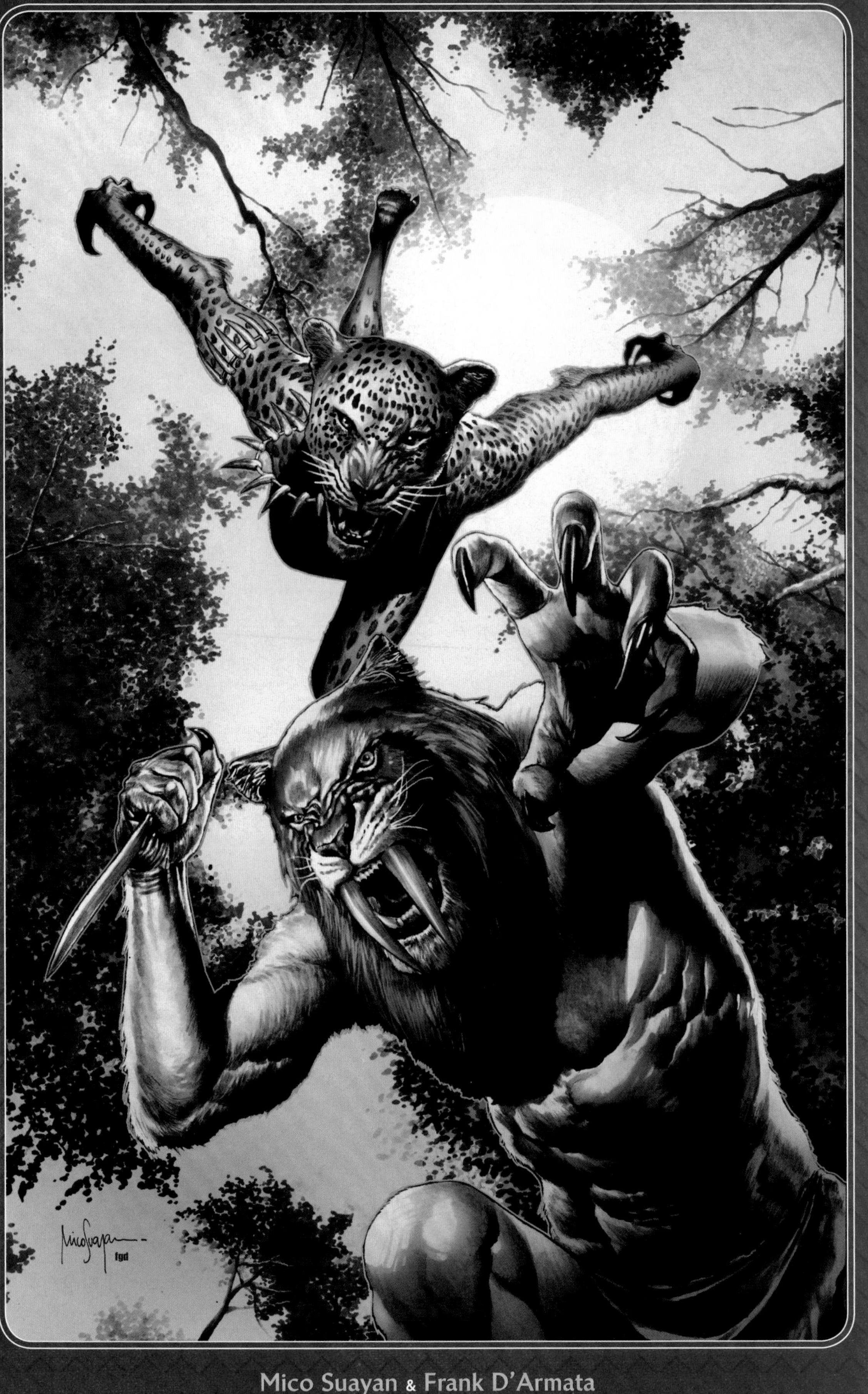

Mico Suayan & Frank D'Armata
5 MARVELS X VARIANT

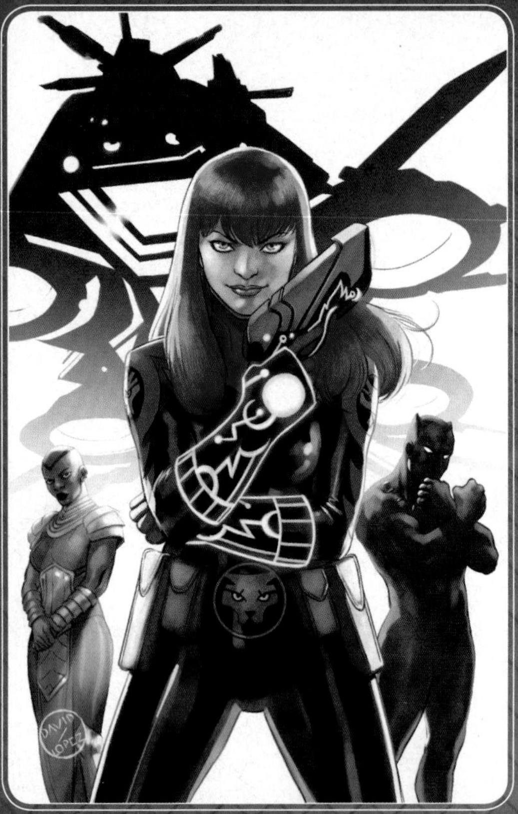

David Lopez
2 MARY JANE VARIANT

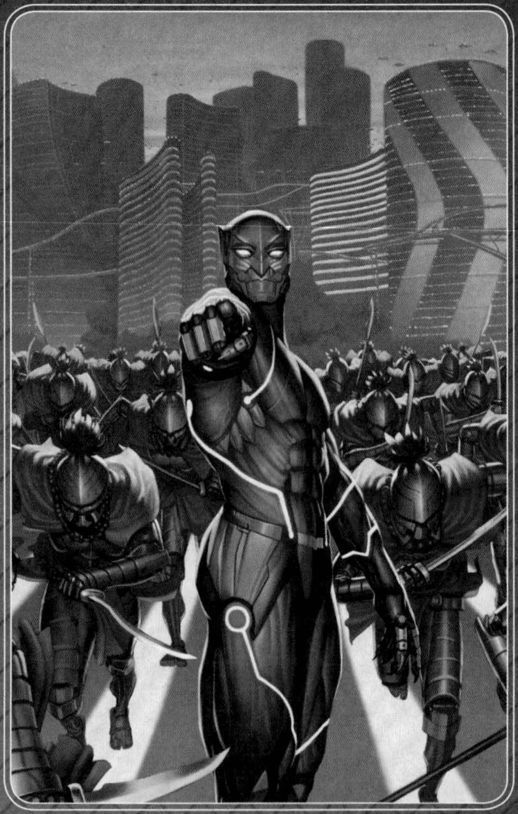

Rock-He Kim
3 2099 VARIANT

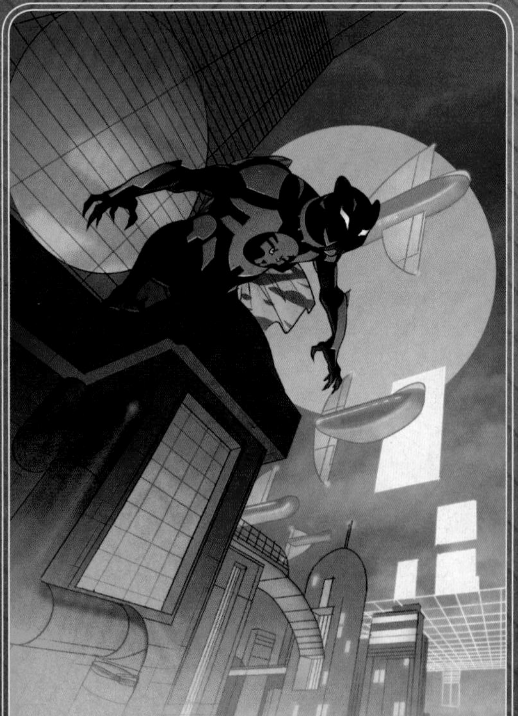

Pasqual Ferry & Chris Sotomayor
4 2020 VARIANT

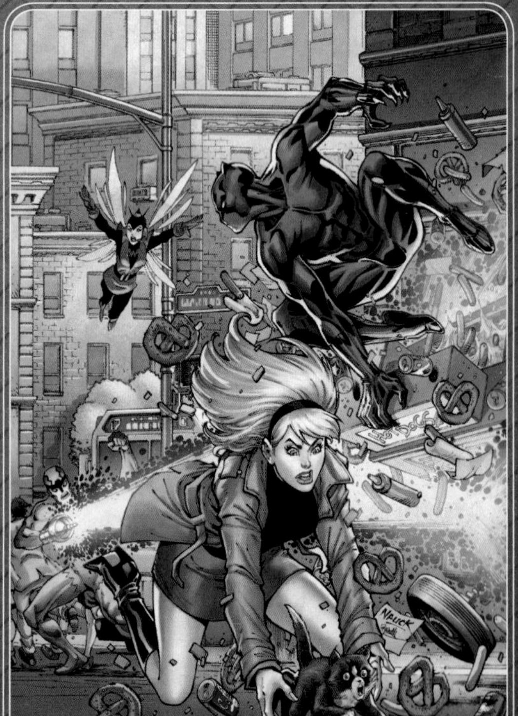

Todd Nauck & Rachelle Rosenberg
6 GWEN STACY VARIANT